A HISTORY OF FLAT RACING

A HISTORY OF FLAT RACING

EDITED BY MICHAEL SETH-SMITH

NEW ENGLISH LIBRARY
TIMES MIRROR

Introduction

People who love horseracing have a treasure trove of Turf history upon which to feast. Since the days when King James I became enchanted with the East Anglian village of Newmarket English Racing has become the absorbing entertainment for generation after generation of those who admire the courage, speed and stamina of noble Thoroughbreds. The importation of Arab stallions, the creation of Ascot racecourse at the command of Queen Anne, the establishment of the Jockey Club and the inaugural running of the Derby at Epsom in 1780 were highlights of the eighteenth century. During the next hundred years villainy and skull-duggery were stamped out through the efforts of Lord George Bentinck and Admiral Rous who were the undisputed dictators of the Turf. The century ended in a blaze of glory with the Derby triumphs of *Persimmon* and *Diamond Jubilee* in the colours of the Prince of Wales. As a nation Britain was at her zenith, the sun never set upon the distant outposts of her Empire, and in 1840 a renowned sporting historian wrote: 'it is not as an amusement only that the Turf puts in its claim to popularity. To the excellence of the British horse, originated and brought to perfection through the instrumentality of the sport, may be ascribed much of our superiority over other nations both in commerce and in war.' More significant were the words enviously spoken by Bismarck to Disraeli: 'You will never have a revolution in England whilst horseracing flourishes.'

In the past eighty years many changes have taken place and the modern technical services of starting-stalls, photo-finish, camera patrols and commentaries were unknown at the outset of the twentieth century. Yet the spectacular excitement has not altered, and champion horses and brilliant jockeys have thrilled racecrowds in every era. The cry 'Come on Steve', as beloved Steve Donoghue urged forward his Derby winners, changed to 'Gordon, Gordon' as the first 'Knight of the Pigskin' retained his position at the head of the Winning Jockeys List for twenty-five seasons. Now Sir Gordon Richards has been succeeded by Lester Piggott, perhaps the most skilful jockey of any era, and the crowds roar their approval as he wins Classic after Classic on short-priced favourites. Nothing gives these crowds greater pleasure than a success in the Royal colours, and in recent years the Classic victories of horses bred and owned by Her Majesty the Queen have been cheered with much more than loyal enthusiasm, for her patronage of Racing has been of inestimable benefit to the sport.

Today, Racing is international, with champions being bred in Europe, the United States of America, Canada and Australia. World competition is becoming keener and the Prix de L'Arc de Triomphe, run at Longchamp every autumn, is considered by owners, breeders and trainers to be the summit of fame and fortune. A Derby winner who also achieves an Arc triumph will be valued at many millions of pounds, and at stud can found a dynasty which may influence the breeding of bloodstock for decades.

In this book eminent authorities have contributed articles which, in my opinion, build up a comprehensive history of the evolution of Racing with its heroes and heroines, its excitement and glamour and above all the 'glorious uncertainty' which makes it such a fascinating sport.

Copy Editor: William J. Howell
Art Editor: Deborah Miles
Design: Nykola Stoakes
Picture Research: Susan Bluff, Elizabeth Walsh

This edition published in 1978 by
New English Library Limited,
Barnard's Inn,
Holborn,
London EC1N 2JR,
England

Set in 10/11 pt Times Roman by South Bucks Typesetters Limited
Printed by Fratelli Spada, Ciampino, Rome, Italy

450 03596 4

Contents

NAT FLATMAN: RIDER of LORD ZETLAND'S VOLTIGEUR IN
FAMOUS MATCH AT YORK AGAINST THE FLYING DUTCHMAN, 1851.

JEM ROBINSON.

CHARLES MARLOW: RIDER of FLYING DUTCHMAN IN MATCH
AGAINST LORD ZETLAND'S VOLTIGEUR AT YORK, 1851. Died 1852.

JOHN DAY, JUNR CRACK JOCKEY OF HIS DAY.

The Early
Years of Flat Racing

'Dungannon' leading 'Rockingham' approaching the winning post, Newmarket 1786. 'Dungannon' was owned by the infamous Colonel O'Kelly who bought 'Eclipse' by nefarious means and was never elected to the Jockey Club. THE JOCKEY CLUB

A LTHOUGH the enthusiasm of the Stuart monarchs had changed the unknown village of Newmarket into the headquarters of racing, it was not until the era of Tregonwell Frampton that any one individual dominated the sport.

Frampton, born in 1641, lived until the venerable age of eighty-six by which time he was acknowledged as 'The Father of the Turf'. Little is known of his youth save that he was a younger son of a Dorset squire, and that he showed unusual interest in the country pursuits of hawking, coursing and cock-fighting. As a young man he drifted eventually to Newmarket, and may have worked in the royal stables of King Charles II.

During the reign of William III he had made himself so indispensable that he was appointed Supervisor of the Royal Horses at Newmarket and given an official residence in the Royal Palace. For each horse under his care he was paid £100 a year out of which he had to pay for the maintenance of the stable-boys, their lodgings and the provision of hay, oats, bread and other necessities for the horses. Despite these costs there is little doubt that he pocketed a considerable sum each year.

He was known to dislike women, to be an eccentric, to have such little interest in clothes that he invariably wore the same costume, and to have complete familiarity with his superiors. Known to Queen Anne as 'Governor Frampton', he remained as Keeper of the Royal Horses during the reigns of four monarchs and was still actively matching horses from his Newmarket home, Heath House, at the time of his death in 1727.

He has been accused of vicious cruelty for having the stallion *Dragon* castrated in order to win a match for which only geldings were eligible – but the saga of this disgraceful action, although often quoted, is probably false.

There is no doubt, however, that he was totally unscrupulous where gambling was concerned, and would go to extreme lengths to win a match, whether it was at New-market or in Yorkshire. His knowledge of a horse's ability and merit was uncanny, and he amassed a fortune through astute betting against noblemen and squires. In the famous match when a horse of Frampton's was challenged by *Merlin*, owned by Yorkshire baronet Sir William Strickland, the gentlemen of the north were reputed to have claimed 'we shall bet them gold whilst gold we have, and then we might sell our land'. Frampton's horse won convincingly.

Accepted as the supreme arbiter on all matters appertaining to the Turf in the era prior to the advent of the Jockey Club (which was not founded until twenty years after his death), Tregonwell Frampton did much to establish racing firmly throughout the kingdom, and served his royal masters loyally. He was buried in All Saints' Church at Newmarket.

During the first years of the eighteenth century breeders were beginning to establish studs, and aristocrats such as the Dukes of Newcastle, Buckingham and Bolton were starting to take an interest in producing fast sleek Thoroughbreds. The Byerley Turk and the Darley Arabian were both in England before the time of Frampton's death, and the Godolphin Arabian was to arrive shortly afterwards.

Flying Childers, the first great racehorse in England, and a son of the Darley Arabian, was foaled in 1714. *Flying Childers* died in 1741, twenty-three years before the birth of *Eclipse* who became a legend in his lifetime. During this period in Turf history three other horses who were to have immense influence upon bloodstock breeding were foaled: *Matchem* in 1748, *Herod* in 1758, and *Highflyer* in 1774.

Whilst breeders were concentrating upon producing higher quality racehorses, the number of racemeetings was increasing. Encouraged by the success of meetings at Newmarket, Ascot, York, and Chester, local authorities frequently organised meetings to coincide with local fairs.

There was little sense of efficiency either in the creation of a course or in the production of a programme of events, and the meeting was invariably held in a haphazard fashion which was to the advantage of those to whom skullduggery was second nature. Even at the important courses where Royal Plates were competed for, many of the races were over an extreme distance of ground. Some of the matches were over six miles, with the horses ridden either by their owners or stable-grooms, for professional jockeys were unknown.

The first race for four-year-olds took place at Hambleton in Yorkshire in August 1727. Four years later races were instituted at York for three-year-olds, but such races did not acquire any popularity at Newmarket or the southern courses for another quarter of a century. Races for two-year-olds were not contemplated until the mid-1780s, and the July Stakes at Newmarket became the first race for young horses in the Calendar.

The first mention of jockeys' racing silks appeared in an order of the Jockey Club in 1762:

For the greater conveniency of distinguishing the horses in running, as also for the prevention of disputes arising from not knowing the Colours worn by each rider, the underwritten Gentlemen have come to the resolution and agreement of having Colours annexed to the following names worn by their respective riders.

Seventeen sets of colours were registered including the Duke of Devonshire's straw, the Duke of Cumberland's purple and the Duke of Grafton's sky blue. Only one of the registered silks was of more than a single colour.

Many of the races being held were detailed in racing calendars. As there was no

'Baronet' ridden by Sam Chifney Sen in the royal colours. Chifney was the first jockey to write his autobiography, 'Genius and Genuine'. Painting by George Stubbs. LORD IRWIN

law of copyright there was nothing to stop rival authors from producing similar volumes. One was published by John Pound, a Newmarket auctioneer, another by William Fawconer and a third by William Tutin. Eventually, at the invitation of Sir Charles Bunbury, a young Newcastle solicitor named James Weatherby came to Newmarket, published his first Racing Calendar in 1771, and was appointed Keeper of the Match Book and Secretary to the Jockey Club. His Calendar became the authentic record of the British Turf.

The important part played by members of the Weatherby family in the history of racing was supplemented in 1791 when James Weatherby's nephew produced the first General Stud Book.

Sir Charles Bunbury, who was responsible for bringing James Weatherby to Newmarket, was a leading figure in the Jockey Club and the breeder of *Highflyer*. At one time married to the beautiful Lady

10

Sarah Lennox, whose elopement with Lord William Gordon became a *cause célèbre*, Bunbury represented Suffolk as Member of Parliament. He was far ahead of his contemporaries in his consideration for his horses, and whereas many of them were brutal to their Thoroughbreds Bunbury never allowed his stable-lads or jockeys to touch his horses with a whip. He believed that such cruel treatment made horses vicious and restive, and even in matches was reluctant to allow his riders to wear spurs. He strongly disapproved of the fashion of sweating horses and was one of

those responsible for attempting to discourage races over long distances.

He was described by a contemporary as

a man of naturally benign, compassionate and friendly nature, and his plan for the treating of racehorses, without suffering them to be abused by whip or spur, which he laboured so long and so steadfastly, though unsuccessfully, to make general on the Turf, ought ever to be remembered to his honour.

After the death of Tregonwell Frampton,

Bunbury gradually became the accepted leader of the Turf in the latter half of the eighteenth century. He was closely involved in the *Escape* affair, which culminated in the Prince of Wales abandoning the Turf in 1791, and had the unpleasant task of informing the Prince that no gentleman would run his horses against him if he persisted in employing Sam Chifney as his jockey.

Chifney, born in Norfolk in 1753, was one of the first professional jockeys. He rode in an era when competition was lacking, but even so his genius would have

Top, left: Tregonwell Frampton, born in 1641, was acknowledged as the 'Father of the Turf'. He was Keeper of the Royal Horses during the reigns of four monarchs. THE JOCKEY CLUB

Top, centre: 'Diomed', winner of the inaugural Derby, was unsuccessful as a stallion in England, his fee at one time falling as low as two guineas. Transported to America in 1797, he gained a new lease of life and founded a dynasty. Some of the greatest horses in America are descended from him. THE JOCKEY CLUB

Top, right: 'Flying Childers', the first great racehorse in England. FORES LIMITED

Above: Soldier and playwright John Burgoyne who eloped with Lady Charlotte Stanley, daughter of the 11th Earl of Derby, and subsequently made his home at The Oaks, Epsom, before crossing the Atlantic to command English troops in the American War of Independence.

Right: 'Gimcrack', a grandson of the Godolphin Arabian, has his memory perpetuated by one of the Calendar's most important two-year-old races, the historic Gimrack Stakes run every August at York. THE JOCKEY CLUB

taken him to the forefront, no matter how great the competition. He claimed that his contemporaries disliked him and accused him of being a snob on the grounds that he was only prepared to discuss the merits of horses with their owners, and was unwilling to tolerate trainers and grooms. He was sufficiently conceited to believe that he knew more about horses than their trainers and had the intelligence to be able to put on paper his views on riding.

His advice on how a successful jockey should ride, although written more than 180 years ago, is still worth recalling:

The first fine part in riding a race is to command your horse to run light in his mouth; it keeps the better together, his legs are the more under him, his sinews less extended, less exertion, his wind less locked; the horse running thus to order, feeling light for his rider's wants, his parts are more at ease and ready, and can run considerably faster when called upon, to what he can when that he has been running in the fretting, sprawling attitudes, with part of his rider's weight in his mouth. And as your horse comes to his last extremity, finishing his race, he is better forced and kept straight with manner and fine touching to his mouth . . . this should be done as if you had a silken rein as fine as a hair, and that you were afraid of breaking it.

Sadly, Chifney was not always prepared to allow his mounts to run on their merit, and it was this dishonest habit when riding *Escape* for the Prince of Wales at Newmarket which finally led to his downfall. After his disgrace he fell into debt, was sent to the Fleet prison, and died penniless in 1807. There is a story that shortly before his death he was visited by a friend who proposed that the parish priest should come and see him. Chifney replied: 'I

am obliged to you and I have thought about it. I have made up my mind. I'll stand it all. I won't hedge.'

Sir Charles Bunbury's further claim to Turf immortality is that his colt *Diomed* won the first Epsom Derby in 1780.

The story of the Derby really began with the birth of Edward Stanley twenty-eight years earlier. Whilst he was a young undergraduate at Oxford his father died, and Edward Stanley found himself turning more and more towards his uncle by marriage, John Burgoyne, a gambler, wit, soldier and playwright. Burgoyne had eloped with Lady Charlotte Stanley in 1743. Her father, the eleventh Earl of Derby, was furious and swore he would never see his daughter again. Once the Seven Years War was over the young lovers were forgiven, largely due to the

distinction and bravery shown by Burgoyne in the campaigns.

He was elected Member of Parliament for Preston, and acquired an old inn near Epsom which had originally been the headquarters of local sportsmen. He built additions to the inn and in recognition of the fact that there were several oak trees in the garden named his home The Oaks.

His income was now considerable, but inadequate for his roistering spirit. He gambled, hunted, and raced on a lavish and foolhardy scale. Such high living appealed to the young Edward Stanley who longed to share his uncle's standard of living.

His opportunity came in 1773 when the Boston Tea Party and the war against the American colonists resulted in Burgoyne's recall to the Army. Stanley bought The Oaks, and commenced a life which would

have made Burgoyne almost green with envy. Rich and influential, he kept a pack of staghounds, bought countless racehorses, and entertained his friends and acquaintances with sumptuous hospitality. He matched his horses against those of Sir Charles Bunbury, the Duke of Grafton and Lord Foley and thought nothing of turning his drawing-room into a cockpit as he and his guests wagered on the result of the mains.

In 1776 the death of his grandfather made young Edward Stanley the twelfth Earl of Derby. In the same year General Anthony St Leger introduced a new race for three-year-olds at his home racecourse of Doncaster. The news that the Yorkshire race was a success was brought south and discussed in the London clubs.

Legend suggests that one evening at The Oaks when Lord Derby's guests included Sheridan, Charles James Fox and General Burgoyne, recently home after his surrender to the Americans at Saratoga, the conversation turned to the possibility of holding a race at Epsom for three-year-old fillies comparable to the St Leger. The possibility became reality and seventeen subscribed to the race which was given the title The Oaks as a compliment to Lord Derby. When the race was run in 1779 the winner, to everyone's delight, was Lord Derby's *Bridget* who had been bred at Knowsley and whose jockey wore the Derby colours of green and white stripes (these colours were not altered to black, white cap until 1788).

On the evening of the race, as celebrations were being held at The Oaks, it was agreed to have a similar race for colts and fillies the subsequent year. No one could decide if the race should be called The Derby or The Bunbury. A coin was tossed, and the most famous race in the world became known as The Derby.

The race took place on 4 May 1780, and

was run over a straight mile which started in the parish of Banstead. It was not considered of any great consequence either by the aristocrats who had attended a local ball the previous night, or by the spectators who were also interested in the bear-baiting, wrestling, the cock-fighting mains between the gentlemen of Surrey and the gentlemen of Middlesex, and the side-shows.

The winner, *Diomed*, was not a success at stud and eventually Sir Charles Bunbury sold him to America. Shipped across the Atlantic he seemed to gain a new lease of life and founded a dynasty from which many of the best horses in American history are descended.

Although by the end of the eighteenth century the three Classic races had been established, the authority of the Jockey Club proven, and the auctioneering business of Tattersalls founded, the Turf was still unco-ordinated. After the *Escape* affair the Prince of Wales withdrew his patronage, and the outbreak of the Napoleonic wars gave sporting Englishmen something else to think about. Consequently little progress was made with Turf reform in the first twenty years of the new century.

Villainy was rife on the Turf and in 1812 Daniel Dawson, a petty crook in the pay of others, was hanged at Cambridge for poisoning racehorses at Newmarket. His crime was to have put arsenic into drinking troughs used by trainers to water their horses after gallops on the Heath. Before his execution, which was witnessed by 12,000 people, he confessed that he had also poisoned horses at Doncaster.

Men such as Dawson and his confederates brought racing into disrepute – disrepute which lasted until the advent of Lord George Bentinck, who followed Sir Charles Bunbury as the outstanding racing personality of his time.

The Byerley Turk

THE MODERN Thoroughbred can be traced to the great triumvirate of the Byerley Turk, the Darley Arabian and the Godolphin Arabian.

During the campaigns against the Turkish invaders in Hungary – the last serious threat to the existence of Western Christendom – Captain Robert Byerley acquired a magnificent cavalry charger from a Turkish officer whom he had either captured or killed. There is little doubt that the charger had been stolen by the Turkish officer in some previous campaign, for he was a well-bred Arabian of beautiful proportions.

The intrepid Captain Byerley brought the horse back to England, and later rode him at the Battle of the Boyne in July 1690 when he commanded the 6th Dragoon Guards. The charger was much admired by other English cavalry commanders, for he was far swifter and sleeker than the heavy and cumbersome horses which comprised the cavalry of William of Orange. If the Byerley Turk had been killed at the Battle of the Boyne English bloodstock would have been the loser, for on his return to England he was sent to stud where he founded a dynasty.

At first he stood at Middridge Hall in County Durham and later at Goldsborough Hall, near York. It appears from the General Stud Book that he covered few well-bred mares but through his son *Jig* he became the great-great-grandsire of *Herod*, from whom twentieth-century stallions such as *The Tetrarch* and *Tourbillon* are descended.

Herod, sired in 1758, and bred by the Duke of Cumberland, was the great rival of *Eclipse* at stud. Through his two sons, *Woodpecker* and *Highflyer*, his blood has been passed on to such famous horses as Derby winners *Bay Middleton* and *The Flying Dutchman*. *Diomed*, winner of the inaugural Derby at Epsom, was one of his grandsons and subsequently founded a dynasty in the United States of America. The *Herod* line from the Byerley Turk, although flourishing in France, had become almost extinct in England by the end of the nineteenth century but was revived, and a direct male line can be traced from *Herod* to 1969 Derby winner *Blakeney*.

John Wootton (c 1678-1756), whose childhood and upbringing are veiled in obscurity, was befriended and patronised by the Duke of Beaufort. He painted many of the Arab horses imported into England, and although he tended to exaggerate the large oriental eye of the stallions, faithfully represented their elegance and perfect symmetry. At the height of his career he would charge a patron about twelve guineas for an equestrian painting.

Right: The Byerley Turk, from a painting by John Wootton. FORES LIMITED

3

The Darley Arabian

An Arabian Horse, belonging to JOHN. BREV

R DARLEY · ESQ^r of ALDBY.

THE DARLEY ARABIAN was bred by the Anazeh tribe who lived on the edge of the Syrian desert. Foaled in 1700, he was considered perfect, being faultless in symmetry with a curved neck and a long head on which was a large white blaze.

In 1704 Mr Thomas Darley, English Consul in Aleppo, bought the stallion from Sheik Mirza for three hundred sovereigns. No sooner was the deal completed and the money paid than the double-crossing Sheik announced that no one was to remove his prize stallion from the Royal stables upon pain of death. Not to be defeated by such treachery, Mr Darley arranged for sailors from a British man-o'-war to row ashore at dead of night, overpower the stable guards and return to their ship with the Darley Arabian. The Sheik wrote to Queen Anne complaining that 'my incomparable Arabian is worth more than a king's ransom and has been foully stolen from me by your subjects', but to no avail.

The Darley Arabian was treated with the greatest care on the voyage to England. Luckily the weather was set fair, and there was no buffeting in the notorious Bay of Biscay. When the stallion arrived he was critically examined by many English breeders. None could fault his conformation. He stood 14.2 hands and exemplified the perfection of the Arab horse, some of whose pedigree could be traced back for more than a thousand years. Many of these horses, according to renowned Turf historian T. A. Cook and others, had large, loose and pliant throats; shoulders which sloped a great deal, being deep and strong by the withers; heart room which appeared large when viewed from the front, and backs which were short with only just sufficient room for the saddle. The stride of these superb animals was long and flowing; their hocks were large, and their quarters both long and deep.

The Darley Arabian stood at the Darley family estate, Aldby Park in East Yorkshire. Before his death in 1730 he had immense influence as a sire. One of the mares he covered was *Betty Leedes*, herself an Arabian mare. The resulting colt foal was given the name *Flying Childers* and became the first really outstanding racehorse. Returned to the Darley Arabian, *Betty Leedes* produced *Bartlett's Childers*, the great-grandsire of *Eclipse*. The modern male lines of *St Simon*, *Gainsborough*, and *Blandford* can all be traced back to the Darley Arabian.

Blandford sired four Derby winners: *Trigo*, *Blenheim*, *Windsor Lad* and *Bahram*. In more recent years *Royal Palace*, 1967 Epsom Derby winner, is a descendant in direct male line from the Darley Arabian.

Left: The Darley Arabian, from a painting by John Wootton. FORES LIMITED

G. EDWARDS.

J. CARTWRIGHT.

F. BUCKLE, JNR. DUKE OF RICHMOND'S JOCKEY.

WILL SCOTT.

4

The Jockey Club

THE JOCKEY CLUB has been the hub around which English racing has revolved for the past two hundred years. The fact that other countries, where racing is staged on a significant scale, have virtually all chosen to base their own Jockey Clubs on similar lines is the best tribute to the efficacy of the Jockey Club, for in the words of the old adage 'imitation is the sincerest form of flattery'!

Basically the Jockey Club is responsible for maintaining the Rules of Racing that it introduced in the early days of its existence and which have been amended as necessary. The various departments deal with all facets of the racing industry, ranging from the licensing of trainers, jockeys, officials and racecourses to security matters including the regularly recurring problem of dope detection.

The current Senior Steward of the Jockey Club, of which there are more than a hundred members, is Lord Howard de Walden, and his deputies are Captain M. A. Gosling and R. N. Richmond-Watson. This trio is assisted by a working task force of six other Stewards.

Criticism of the Club is usually based on the grounds that it does not move rapidly enough to keep up with the times. Fair-minded men would agree, however, that reforms which would affect the large number of persons involved in the racing industry should be approached with caution and all likely ramifications explored before any irrevocable decision is reached. One has only to look at recent innovations such as the amalgamation of the Jockey Club and the National Hunt Committee for the purpose of simplifying racing's administration and cutting down costs, the introduction of starting-stalls, photo-finish cameras, the significant move toward graded racing and the acceptance of Women's Lib in the form of lady trainers and of ladies' races, to see that the Club is dedicated to achieving the best for English racing.

There is no exact record of the date at which the Jockey Club came into existence but it developed from a regular gathering of aristocrats and gentlemen interested in horse riding and racing, who used to enjoy passing the time of day in the company of others with similar inclinations.

The first reference to the club is found in the Sporting Calendar printed in 1752 by the Newmarket and Covent Garden auctioneer John Pound, which stated that 'a Contribution Free Plate will be run for at Newmarket on Wednesday 1 April, by horses the property of noblemen and gentlemen belonging to the Jockey Club at the Star and Garter in Pall Mall'.

Though mention was made of Newmarket in this proclamation, it is almost certain that at this stage of the proceedings the Club owned no land or property in the town with which its name and history were to be inextricably linked over the next two centuries. From the seventeenth century the Heath at Newmarket with its tremendous facilities for riding, hunting and hawking had attracted sportsmen. It was only natural that in due course the Jockey Club would gravitate in that direction.

Facing page: Famous 19th-century jockeys: G. Edwards, J. Cartwright, F. Buckle Jun, Will Scott.
THE JOCKEY CLUB AND TRYON GALLERY, LONDON

Below: A caricature of Jockey Club members in the 18th century by Thomas Rowlandson (1756-1827). THE JOCKEY CLUB

It is chronicled that in 1771 the Club leased a coffee-house in Newmarket for fifty years from one Richard Vernon, and once that lease expired they established a firm foothold in the town by acquiring the freehold of the property. A gradual process of buying more land and property in and around the town has been carried on since then and the Jockey Club's ownership of land at the present time stands in the region of 4,500 acres.

The reputation of the Club began to spread through the realm and before long it became the practice to refer disputes on racing matters to the Jockey Club. It was made quite clear from the outset that the Club was prepared to arbitrate only on races that were run under its own set of rules. A natural progression found more and more of the major racing courses in the country accepting its rules and it eventually held undisputed sway in such matters.

The members' integrity as gentlemen was generally respected and one of the Club's first leading lights, Sir Charles Bunbury, was greatly responsible for its reputation in the early days. By the time he died in 1821 the Jockey Club's star was very high and was given an unsolicited accolade in 1842, when Lord Abinger told a Court of Exchequer jury

neither you nor I are called upon to settle any controversy between members of the Jockey Club. They are gentlemen of high honour and in consequence of the law not making provision for the transactions in which they are engaged for their own amusement, have a law amongst themselves which they are competent, if they think fit, to decide upon.

Following on the heels of Sir Charles Bunbury came Lord George Bentinck (1802-48), whose innovations did much to bring about the pattern of racing that is known today. It was mainly due to his efforts that boards carrying the runners and racecards with their numbers came into existence, and he also decreed that all runners should be saddled in one place to prevent malpractice and that they should parade before each race.

Lord George Bentinck was closely involved in disclosing the 1844 Derby fraud, when a four-year-old, *Running Rein*, tackled his juniors and was first past the post. Persistent enquiries unearthed the plot to defraud and the perpetrator of the abortive coup, an unwholesome gambler called Goodman Levy, had to flee the country.

The formidable Admiral Rous took over where Bentinck left off and many of the changes he introduced have had a notable effect on racing's structure. Perhaps the most significant was his introduction of the weight-for-age scale by which younger horses are given a chance of competing against older, stronger rivals by skilfully calculated weight adjustments. It says much for Admiral Rous's understanding of horses that the weights he drew up have been virtually unaltered since they were framed last century. Not surprisingly he was acknowledged as one of the ·best handicappers of all time.

After Admiral Rous's death in 1877 there was a large influx of American trainers and jockeys, amongst whom came Tod Sloan with his 'acey-deucy' – one stirrup shorter than the other – style of riding, and with them came the spectre of doping. Fortunately one of the rules that was passed by the Jockey Club in 1879 laid down that jockeys were no longer legally entitled to own or have shares in a horse and they were also forbidden to bet – on the threat

of losing their licences to ride. This was the sanction applied against Sloan when he started mixing with bad company, for he was advised that it would not be worth his while applying for a licence in 1900 and he drifted back across the Atlantic.

A Jockey Club innovation at the turn of the century was the introduction of a starting-gate as opposed to the old method of starting a race by flag. This occasioned vigorous opposition in private circles as well as in the press, as did the introduction of starting-stalls over sixty years later, but in both instances the change has clearly proved beneficial to the sport.

Probably as a direct result of the rash of doping occasioned by the American invasion the Jockey Club brought in a new rule in 1903, which categorically stated 'if any person shall administer, or cause to be administered, for the purpose of affecting the speed of a horse, drugs or stimulants internally or by hypodermic or other method he shall be warned off the Turf'. Doping has always been one of the thorniest problems facing the Jockey Club, as it is very difficult to establish whether or not a trainer is liable to disqualification for negligence if he knew nothing about the doping.

There was a case in 1974 when the use of ordinary foodstuffs, that had become contaminated by traces of caffeine, produced a positive result in dope tests on horses conducted at the analytical laboratories that have been built for this purpose with Levy Board grants at Newmarket. In this instance the trainers were fined a nominal sum, but exonerated from any suggestion of malpractice. In 1964 Brigadier Henry Green was appointed the first Inspector of Security in a bid to keep racing's image as clean as possible and he and his staff have done a marvellous job. Identity cards for stable-lads and horses have been introduced and security at stables round the country has been tightened up to counter the would-be dopers.

On the administrative front the Jockey Club instituted Stewards' secretaries, more commonly known as 'stipes', in 1936, and their function was to offer local Stewards advice on whether or not the running of certain horses should be questioned. As could be easily imagined this did not go down at all well with a large number of racecourses, whose Stewards had been content with a policy of *laissez-faire* rather than face the harsh reality of hauling over the coals acquaintances whose horses had not appeared to be running on their true merits. When the local Stewards feel they are not in a position to take satisfactory action they refer their enquiry to the Stewards of the Jockey Club and the case is heard either at the Jockey Club's new main administrative offices at 42 Portman Square in London or at their premises at Newmarket during a racemeeting.

The Jockey Club's home at Newmarket has a gracious dignified neo-Georgian façade with its two wings in red brick con-

Facing page, above: Admiral Rous, the greatest handicapper in Turf history and a Steward of the Jockey Club for more than thirty years.
THE JOCKEY CLUB

Above: Lord George Bentinck, described by Disraeli as 'Lord Paramount of the Turf', by Lane. THE JOCKEY CLUB

Below: A scene outside the Subscription Rooms at Newmarket, 1825. THE JOCKEY CLUB

structed, as recently as 1933, on plans drawn up by the world-famous architect, the late Professor Albert Richardson. The facilities there can be used not only by the members of the Jockey Club but also by a further 250 members of the Jockey Club Rooms. The Rooms are busy during race weeks and sales, which are the only times they are open, when members can book one of the twenty-eight bedrooms at their disposal. At one stage there was even a royal suite for King Edward VII but this was eventually divided into several separate rooms. The original Coffee Room with its ten deep alcoves still survives with a few alterations and is built into the new structure.

The Jockey Club houses a collection of paintings that would be the envy of any connoisseur and includes canvases by George Stubbs and works by those masters of sporting painting, Sartorius, Wootton, Herring, Marshall, Lynwood Palmer, Emil Adam and Sir Alfred Munnings. These paintings adorn the walls of the sumptuous rooms with a George Stubbs of the great *Eclipse*, unbeaten in his twenty-six races, holding pride of place over the mantelpiece in the morning-room. In the same room another work by Stubbs immortalises *Gimcrack*, showing him both in action and also being groomed near one of the rubbing houses on Newmarket Heath.

In addition to the paintings there is a wealth of racing mementoes with great historical value. These include a lavish mounting of one of *Eclipse*'s hooves on a golden salver for use as a snuffbox, which was presented by William IV in 1838. In the Coffee Room hangs the Newmarket

The long hall inside the Jockey Club Rooms at Newmarket. By tradition, members of the Jockey Club who own a Derby winner present a painting of their horse to the Club. Many of these paintings by such artists as Lynwood Palmer and Sir Alfred Munnings hang in the long hall. THE JOCKEY CLUB

Whip, which is raced for annually by horses owned by members of the Jockey Club and Jockey Club Rooms and which contains golden hairs from the mane and tail of *Eclipse*. Another fascinating racing relic is a wheel from the first-ever horsebox that transported *Elis* from Goodwood to win the St Leger at Doncaster in 1836 and land a heavy gamble. The bookmakers had laid long odds against him in the belief he would never get to Doncaster in time, as horses had previously been walked to the racemeetings!

The capacious forty-feet-long dining-room was used to entertain the Queen when she lunched at the Jockey Club on the day she officially opened the new National Stud at Newmarket in 1967. On that occasion the only ornament on the table, which was decorated with banks of white and pink camelias, was the golden salver on which *Eclipse*'s hoof is mounted.

In the Committee Room hangs a superb portrait of Sir Winston Churchill, who was one of the few politicians to take an interest in the Turf in recent years. Churchill was so delighted with his election to the Jockey Club after the Second World War that he held a dinner for his fellow Club members at No 10 Downing Street in 1953 and the table-plan for that historic dinner is hung below his portrait.

No brief survey of the Jockey Club rooms would be complete without reference to the Stewards' Room, where offenders against the Rules of Racing have to plead their case. In the early days they had to defend themselves but a wise alteration to the rules now allows them the right of counsel. The defendant used to wait to be summoned in a side room, which has a collection of caricatures by 'The Tout' of 1920 Jockey Club members but, humorous though they are, it is unlikely that many trainers or jockeys waiting for judgement would really appreciate this levity! On entering the Stewards' Room the accused stands on a carpet facing the five Stewards conducting the enquiry and it is claimed that the expression 'on the mat' derives from this.

The right-hand wing of the Club building serves as a Newmarket *pied-à-terre* for the Weatherby family, which has been closely involved in the running of racing since Sir Charles Bunbury first persuaded James Weatherby to move down from Newcastle to set up as a solicitor in Newmarket in 1770. The Weatherbys are keepers of the Match Book and Stake Holders for all races that take place in this country, but their main offices are now at Wellingborough, Northamptonshire.

In the left-hand wing are found the offices of the Newmarket Estates and

Properties Company, and the Newmarket Racecourses Trust, which were formed a few years ago, when it was decided necessary as a matter of policy to separate the Jockey Club's dual functions as the ruling and legislative body controlling racing and as owner of the Newmarket racecourses, Heath, Jockey Club Rooms and land in Newmarket.

The control of the Heath is the responsibility of Robert Fellowes, who is the current Agent to the Jockey Club. His duties include maintaining the vast areas of training grounds on both the Bury and Racecourse sides of the town. To preserve the pre-eminence of the training facilities at Newmarket the gallops have to be husbanded and each day a board outside his offices shows which training grounds are open. Each gallop is moved a few feet a day to open new ground and ensure that the resilient turf is not damaged by overuse. During the last decade a watered gallop has been established alongside the Rowley Mile course and this enables the racecourse sprinkling system to be used for the benefit of owners of horses wanting good ground during long dry spells. They pay £3 for the privilege of working their horses on this gallop.

A further innovation to improve the town's unparalleled training facilities was the introduction in 1976 of an all-weather gallop. This is situated on Long Hill on the Bury side of the town and its seven furlongs enable trainers to work their horses when the rest of the Heath is rock-hard.

As long ago as 1819 the Jockey Club first introduced a Heath tax of £1 a horse and the proceeds went towards the cost of maintaining the workforce needed to keep the gallops in perfect trim. Nowadays an owner has to find more than £60 a year Heath tax and this figure is even greater for owners of jumpers utilising the schooling grounds and National Hunt gallops round the Links golf-course on the Cambridge side of the town. All in all, the payment of these levies enables horses to be worked on some twenty-eight miles of different gallops that are open at the busy stages of the season.

As can be seen from this brief survey of Jockey Club activities, racing's ruling body has a great deal on its plate, and it speaks volumes for the dedication of those at the helm that racing runs so smoothly in this country. There is little doubt that the Jockey Club will continue to look after the interests of racing for a long time to come, and whatever modifications to the original body may eventually be embarked upon, the name will always be synonymous with all that is best in English racing.

 **5**

The Godolphin Arabian

THE GODOLPHIN ARABIAN, born almost twenty-five years after the Darley Arabian, was foaled in the Yemen in 1724. Exported to Tunis, he was sent by the Bey as a gift to Louis XIV of France. There is some uncertainty as to the life he led in Paris, one report claiming that he pulled a dust-cart, but there is no doubt that in 1729 he was bought by Edward Coke of Longford Hall, Derbyshire.

When Coke died in 1733 he bequeathed to the Earl of Godolphin all his mares, foals and horses in training. His stallions were left to another beneficiary, but the Earl bought the Arabian stallion whom he sent to his stud, Gog Magog, near Newmarket. Legend claims that at first the Arabian was merely used as a 'teaser' and fought another stallion for the privilege of serving the mare *Roxana*.

In 1734 *Cade*, by the Godolphin Arabian out of *Roxana*, was born. Years later *Cade* was to sire *Matchem*, whose influence on

The Godolphin Arabian from the painting by George Stubbs. FORES LIMITED

bloodstock has lasted to the present day through *Hurry On* and *Precipitation*. Five years after *Cade* was born, the Godolphin Arabian sired *Regulus* who became the sire of *Spiletta*, dam of *Eclipse*.

When the Godolphin Arabian died in 1753, at the age of twenty-nine, people came from all over East Anglia to pay homage to the great stallion.

23

6

'Eclipse'

IN THE YEAR 1750 the Duke of Cumberland exchanged one of his chestnut Arabians for a brown yearling colt bred by John Hutton who lived in the village of Marske near Richmond in Yorkshire. The colt, named *Marske*, did not have a distinguished Turf career, although he won a Jockey Club Plate at Newmarket. Consequently, when he was retired to the Duke's stud at Cranbourne Chase in Windsor Great Park, he was only considered a suitable stallion for farmers' mares at a fee of half a guinea and half a crown for the groom. Later he was allowed to serve more valuable mares, including *Spiletta* who had been beaten in her only appearance on a racecourse, but had the merit of being a granddaughter of the Godolphin Arabian. On All Fools Day 1764 *Spiletta* gave birth to a small chestnut colt to whom the name *Eclipse* was given to commemorate the total eclipse of the sun which had taken place in the year of his birth. It was a perfect choice of name, for the colt was destined to eclipse all his rivals and become one of the greatest horses of all time.

In 1765 the Duke died, and the yearling *Eclipse* was sold to a Smithfield meat trader, William Wildman, for seventy-five guineas. He maintained a stud of racehorses at Mickleham, and sent them to be trained at neighbouring Epsom. Legend tells a curious story of Wildman's purchase of *Eclipse* whose ability had reached his ears. He arrived at the sale to discover that the colt had already been sold for seventy guineas. Determined to acquire *Eclipse* he came up with the ingenious demand that the auction should be reheld – on the grounds that the sale had taken place prior to the advertised time and was therefore unlawful. He persisted to such an extent that the sale was begun again, and his bid of seventy-five guineas successfully acquired the colt.

Horses were not seriously trained until they were four- or five-year-olds, but in his youth *Eclipse* proved so fiery-tempered that it was thought that he should be gelded. An alternative solution was found by loaning him to a local rough-rider who rode him both by day and by night: by day about his normal business and by night raiding the neighbouring farms – for he was the most renowned poacher in the district!

Such constant activity reformed *Eclipse* who made his racing début on 3 May 1769 in a Noblemen and Gentlemen's £50 Plate at Epsom, the race to be run in four heats. *Eclipse*'s form was not unknown to the touts whose information included news given them by an old woman who had unintentionally witnessed a secret trial on Banstead Downs. She told the touts that she had seen a horse with a white leg

running away at so monstrous a rate that he could never be caught if he ran to the world's end.

Eclipse won the first heat so easily that the notorious Irishman Captain Dennis O'Kelly offered to place the runners in the order in which they would finish in the second heat. Challenged to make good his boast he replied '*Eclipse* first – the rest nowhere', meaning that *Eclipse* would win by more than 240 yards. The result of the heat vindicated O'Kelly's judgement, for *Eclipse* won by a distance, in consequence of which none of his rivals was placed by the judge.

In the same year *Eclipse* won King's Plates at Winchester, Salisbury, Canterbury, Lewes and Lichfield, and Wildman sold a half-share in him to O'Kelly. At a later date the disreputable O'Kelly acquired

the other half for £1,000. This second sale was engineered in typical swashbuckling fashion by the incorrigible Irishman. He proposed to Wildman that the price should be £2,000 or £1,000 and, after showing three notes each of £1,000, proceeded to put two of them in one pocket of his coat and one in another pocket. Wildman was invited to choose whichever pocket he preferred. He chose wrongly!

The following season *Eclipse* won at Newmarket, York, Guildford, Nottingham and Lincoln. At one time his reputation was so high that Lord Grosvenor offered 11,000 guineas for the horse. The offer was instantly refused. On another occasion O'Kelly stated that he was prepared to sell *Eclipse* for £20,000, an annuity of £500 a year for life and three brood mares.

During *Eclipse*'s career it was claimed that he had great size, lowness and obliquity. His forequarters were short, his quarters ample and finely proportioned, and the muscles of his thighs greatly developed. Undoubtedly he was a big horse with a tremendous stride, and at a later date the Turf historian Theodore Cook wrote: 'he never had a whip flourished over him, or felt the rubbing of a spur, outfooting, outstriding and outlasting every horse that started against him'. He retired to O'Kelly's stud unbeaten, and initially stood at the princely fee of fifty guineas.

At the Clay Hill stud at Epsom he was an outstanding success. Three of the first five Derby winners were sired by him, and he also sired two influential horses in *King Fergus* and *Pot-8-os*. (This unusual

name was derived from the fact that an illiterate stable-boy was told to paint the name '*Potatoes*' over the stable door. He spelt the word Pot-oooooooo!).

Towards the end of his life *Eclipse* was moved to Cannons in Middlesex where he died on 26 February 1789. Death was caused, according to the veterinary surgeons who measured and dissected his body, by inflammation of the bowels. They weighed his heart and discovered to their amazement that it scaled 14lbs. At his burial mourners were given cakes and ale, as had also been offered at the burial of the Godolphin Arabian.

Below: 'Eclipse'. The famous painting of the great stallion by George Stubbs.

7

Flat Racing
in the Nineteenth Century

THE HISTORY of racing England in the first fifty years of the nineteenth century can be traced in outline through the lives of three men: Lord George Bentinck, John Gully and William Crockford.

Their backgrounds were very different, for Bentinck was a son of the Duke of Portland, and had been brought up amidst the grandeur of Welbeck Abbey where his father lived in opulent splendour. Gully's father was a west country publican and butcher who died when John was a stripling of thirteen, whilst Crockford's father died when William was a small boy, bequeathing to his wife and family a fish shop at Temple Bar.

Considering that the area of London in which Crockford lived swarmed with criminals, beggars and pickpockets, and that the majority who were born there amidst its filth and squalor never improved their lot, it is remarkable that Crockford should have amassed a fortune amounting to half a million pounds, and should have died at his home in Carlton House Terrace having 'won the whole of the ready money of the aristocracy and gentry of England'.

Crockford, born in 1776, was a rich man by the time that the Napoleonic wars ended. Determined that his gambling hells should bring him further gain, he used every means within his power to lure those of affluence into his clutches. He knew little of horses but realised that horses and gambling were the sole topics of conversation amongst his clientele. Willing to profit by this he employed every blackleg, tout, bookmaker and informer in the racing world.

He bought a house at Newmarket, bribed jockeys and trainers, offered ante-

Lord Eglington's 'Flying Dutchman', ridden by Charles Marlow, leading Lord Zetland's 'Voltigeur', ridden by Nat Flatman, at the end of their historic match at York in 1851. This race was considered one of the greatest ever witnessed. Painting by J. Herring Sen.
THE JOCKEY CLUB

post prices, and was invariably the first to know the result of supposedly secret gallops. In an age of skullduggery he reigned supreme. Totally unscrupulous, he was as unattractive in his appearance as he was in his dealings with others. A contemporary wrote of him: 'his cheeks appeared white and flabby through constant night work. His hands were entirely without knuckles, soft as raw veal and as white as paper . . .'

In 1819 Crockford's colt *Sultan* was beaten by a head in the Derby by *Tiresias*, owned by Lord George Bentinck's father. The Duke, who was an active member of the Jockey Club and owned part of Newmarket Heath, abhorred the villainy of men such as Crockford, and did his utmost to prevent his children from gambling. He did not always succeed and in 1826 after the Doncaster St Leger meeting he was compelled to come to the aid of his son, who had lost more than £30,000 when the

of whom were delighted on the occasions that he outwitted Crockford. When *Sultan* broke down in his preparation for the St Leger Gully learned the news long before Crockford. Thinking that his colt was an assured winner Crockford backed it heavily with Gully – and failed to get a run for his money. He swore vengeance but had to wait almost ten years for it.

Soon after the Derby of 1827 Lord Jersey sold the winner, *Mameluke*, to John Gully for 4,000 guineas – a huge price by

During the next thirty years Gully was to have considerable success on the Turf. In 1832 *St Giles*, which he owned in partnership with Robert Ridsdale, won the Derby, but there was the gravest suspicion that the colt was a four-year-old. In the same year his colt *Margrave* won the St Leger and Gully won a fortune. Years later an old stable lad, in reminiscent mood, said 'When John Gully was a-carrying all before him, I can mind when pails of champagne wine were stood by the winners

favourite was defeated. The following year the St Leger again saw the favourite beaten, with huge sums of money being won by Crockford at the expense of his archenemy John Gully.

John Gully, ten years younger than Crockford, had been Champion Prizefighter of England before acquiring the Plough Inn in Carey Street, Lincoln's Inn Fields. A popular landlord with the owners, jockeys and gamblers who frequented the inn, Gully soon realised that the taking of bets was far more profitable than running a public house. From that moment he and Crockford were on a collision course.

The two men loathed each other. Crockford, ugly and obscene, was feared by those who worked for him and was virtually friendless. Gully, strong and handsome, had countless admirers, many

the standards of the day. The conditions of the sale included the proviso that the news should not be announced until after Royal Ascot, in order that Gully could get the best possible price for the St Leger! He backed *Mameluke* to win £40,000 believing the colt to be a certainty. He overlooked Crockford's interest.

On the day of the race several badly trained, kicking horses were sent to the post with the express purpose of frustrating the highly strung *Mameluke*. Jockeys were bribed, and the starter, who was subsequently dismissed, was responsible for seven false starts, all of them designed to upset Gully's horse. When the race eventually started, *Mameluke* was left almost a hundred yards. Despite this misfortune he finished second, but his failure enabled Crockford to feel that his score with Gully was at least even.

'Cyllene' after winning the Newmarket Stakes on the Rowley Mile course in 1898. Subsequently 'Cyllene', owned by Mr C. D. Rose, became the sire of 'Minoru'. Painting by Isaac Cullin.
BY KIND PERMISSION OF DAVID D'AMBRUMENIL ESQ

and stable lads turned up their noses at it. Gentlemen would think nothing of giving me a sovereign for a-holding their hacks for ten minutes.'

However Gully, who won the Derby again in 1854, did not always have his own way, and on one occasion the Rules of Racing were altered to prevent him running a horse in the Ascot Gold Cup. Whereas Crockford was an out-and-out villain, Gully had some sense of honour; he was MP for Pontefract for five years (1823-37) and ended his life as a country gentleman. Yet both men were anathema to Lord George Bentinck.

Bentinck, who died a bachelor in 1848, made up his mind after suffering serious financial losses on the Turf that he would devote his life to ridding racing of the nefarious corruption which was bringing it into disrepute. Arrogant and unrelenting, he hated being thwarted, and his code of honour was not always consistent. His cousin, Charles Greville, once accused him of 'thundering away against poor low rogues for the villainies they have committed whilst he has been doing things which high-minded men like his father would think nearly if not quite as discreditable and reprehensible'.

One of his most successful coups which confounded the bookmakers concerned the 1836 St Leger. Everyone knew that there was only one method of horse transportation, and that was on foot. Consequently horses seldom raced far from their training quarters. Derby candidates from Newmarket would be walked to Epsom weeks before the Derby, and although the exceptional mare *Cyprian*, trained at Malton in Yorkshire, was walked almost five hundred miles within a month to come south to win the Oaks, it was seldom that horses were successful after exhausting journeys with the ensuing leg weariness, and change of stables, feed and water.

Lord George Bentinck decided to overcome such complications. In secret he had a van built by Mr Herring of Long Acre which was capable of holding two horses. The inside of the van was padded and a mattress provided in case the horses fell to their knees as the cumbersome van, drawn by six post horses, travelled from Goodwood to Doncaster. The journey took less than a week, and Bentinck won a fortune from the astounded bookmakers whose touts had told them that his St Leger candidate, *Elis*, was in Sussex and could not possibly reach Yorkshire for the race.

Eight years later Bentinck was responsible for bringing to light one of the greatest frauds in Turf history when he revealed the true facts concerning the Derby winner *Running Rein*, who was proved to be a four-year-old. Crockford, old and tired, was fully aware of the plot which included such ingredients as the substitution of horses, the bribing of jockeys, and the deliberate 'pulling' of the more favoured horses, including *Ratan* which he owned. The strain proved too much for him and he died two days later.

Bentinck was the hero of the hour, but less than five years later he too was dead, his body being found in a water meadow near Welbeck Abbey. In his diary Greville wrote: '. . . the world will never know anything of those serious blemishes which could not fail to dim the lustre of his character. He will long be remembered and regretted as a very remarkable man . . .' Certainly he had brought racing from the abyss of nefarious corruption to a state of integrity which appealed to mid-Victorian England.

The year after Bentinck's death a curious challenge was received from the Pasha of Egypt who wished to test the relative merits of the Arab and the English Thoroughbred. The Pasha proposed a race to be run in Egypt over a distance of ten miles, without limitation to age or weight, for £10,000 a side. The Stewards of the Jockey Club would not countenance the proposals, especially as the ten-mile course was known to be both sandy and full of stones. In consequence the match never took place.

One of those intrigued by the proposed match was Admiral Rous, who was to dominate English racing for the next twenty-five years. The younger son of the Earl of Stradbroke, Henry John Rous was born in 1795 and was therefore seven years older than Bentinck. However he and his racing contemporaries were overshadowed by Bentinck, and it was not until after Bentinck's death that he began to blossom as a Turf administrator.

During his naval career he had spent many months in Australia where he had encouraged the growth of horseracing in New South Wales. On his return to England and his retirement from the Royal Navy he became a member of the Jockey Club, a Steward for the first time in 1838, and racing adviser to the Duke of Bedford.

He had a genius for the making of matches, which reached its zenith when he was entrusted with the handicapping of Lord Zetland's *Voltigeur*, winner of the Derby and St Leger of 1850, against the Earl of Eglinton's *The Flying Dutchman*, successful in the 1849 Derby and St Leger, in their famous two-mile match on York racecourse. Rous set *The Flying Dutchman* to carry 8st 8½lbs and *Voltigeur* 8st. After a tremendous struggle *The Flying Dutchman* won by the curious distance of a 'short length'. Many years later when he had made an important handicap the Admiral turned to a friend and remarked with relish: 'that handicap is so good that none of the horses can win!'

In 1850 he published his book *On the Laws and Practice of Horse Racing* in which he traced the history and development of the Thoroughbred and racing, and wrote sections on the Rules of Racing, the duties of officials, racing cases, betting, handicapping and the standard weights for age. This weight-for-age scale was so brilliantly conceived that it is still the accepted basis for all handicaps.

Five years after the publication of his book Rous was appointed honorary handicapper to the Jockey Club, a post he retained for the next twenty-two years. As a handicapper he was a pioneer, for until his appointment handicaps were made by local Stewards whose honesty and integrity were not always above suspicion.

Every morning throughout the racing season Rous could be seen on his hack on Newmarket Heath watching the trainers' strings through his telescope. Nothing seemed to escape his notice. On race days he would review the horses in the paddock, and determine the state of the odds in the ring, before cantering down to the bushes from where he watched the race. On his return he made meticulous notes in his handicap book to which he constantly referred. His greatest handicapping triumph came in the 1857 Cesarewitch when *Prioress*, *Queen Bess* and *El Hakim* ran a triple dead heat.

Rous was convinced that the English Thoroughbred of the mid-nineteenth century was infinitely superior to its Arab ancestors, and believed that over any distance up to ten miles a first-class English racehorse could give as much as six stone to the best Arabian. He also thought that during the past hundred years the Thoroughbred had improved to such an extent that *Flying Childers* might not be capable of winning a modest Plate.

He hated gambling, although he appreciated the necessity for betting, and deplored the financial ruin caused by excessive wagering, especially when the gamblers were those he considered to be his social equals. Such incidents as Francis Villiers, younger brother of Lord Jersey, fleeing the country in 1855 owing his creditors more than £100,000 whilst a Steward of the Jockey Club, filled him with horror and indignation. He also intensely disliked the fact that at times stupendous sums of money were won by gambling, and did not hesitate to fire impulsive broadsides in the form of letters to *The Times*.

The Admiral died in June 1877, respected by all racing England. A month before he died Fred Archer had won his first Derby in the colours of Lord Falmouth, a great patron of racing, whose black jacket, white sleeves, red cap were seen on racecourses from 1857 until 1884. During his halcyon days he owned two Derby winners, three winners of the Two Thousand Guineas, the Oaks and the St Leger, and four winners of the One Thousand Guineas.

In 1863 his filly, *Queen Bertha*, trained at Malton by John Scott, won the Oaks. The filly had wintered so badly that Lord Falmouth wished to scratch her from all engagements. This decision caused consternation, and Scott's wife exclaimed 'I'll bet your Lordship sixpence that she wins the Oaks'. The wager was accepted and after the race Lord Falmouth had a brandnew sixpence set with diamonds and made into a brooch which he gave to the trainer's wife.

After Scott's retirement Lord Falmouth sent his horses to Matthew Dawson at Newmarket with the best of results. Eighteen-seventy-nine proved a vintage year, and one morning as Lord Falmouth witnessed his horses in a trial gallop Dawson turned to him and said 'There's a sight, my Lord, the like of which you may never see again' for those taking part in the trial included a Derby winner and younger horses who subsequently were to win three Classics and a Jockey Club Cup.

Lord Falmouth typified the affluent, utterly honourable owner who patronised the Turf in the later years of the century. Others were the Duke of Westminster, the Duke of Portland, Lord Rosebery and the Rothschilds. With jockeys such as Archer, Fordham, Cannon and Loates, and trainers of the skill of Dawson, Porter and Marsh it was a golden era. The advent of the Prince of Wales as an owner set the seal upon the sport which, due to the reforms of Bentinck and Rous, had fully recovered from the disrepute caused by the villainy of Crockford and his confederates.

Flat Racing, 1880~1914

'Minoru' winning the 1909 Derby at Epsom by a short head from 'Louviers'; painted by F. Beer. THE JOCKEY CLUB

THE PERIOD from 1880 until the outbreak of the First World War has been described as the golden age of the English Turf. The sport, during the last twenty years of the nineteenth century, had become more reputable, with meetings better organised, discipline more firmly applied, and the turbulence and villainy that had disfigured mid-Victorian racing for the most part eliminated.

There was no lack of owners who raced solely for sport, whilst control of racing, through the Jockey Club, lay firmly in the grasp of the aristocracy, who still wielded immense power through wealth and political influence.

It was nevertheless an era during which profound changes occurred. At the turn of the century came the 'American Invasion', which was brought about by legislation in the United States hostile to racing and betting. This legislation caused a massive migration to Europe of trainers, jockeys, horses, gamblers and hangers-on. In certain respects the invasion proved beneficial, in others the reverse.

One of the evils was an alarming increase in the practice of doping horses. Some of the American trainers were extremely skilful in the application of dope, notably Wishard, who in 1900 landed huge gambles with the seven-year-old *Royal Flush* in the Royal Hunt Cup at Ascot and the Stewards' Cup at Goodwood.

By 1903 doping, not prohibited under the Rules of Racing, had reached scandalous proportions and threatened not only to ruin racing but to inflict immense danger on bloodstock breeding. The Hon George Lambton, the eminent trainer, warned a Steward of the Jockey Club how dangerous the situation was, but his words fell on ears that were wilfully deaf. It was only after Lambton, having warned the Stewards of his intended action, doped five bad and unreliable horses, of which four won and the fifth came second, that the authorities began to take serious notice. A rule was then introduced to the effect that 'If any person shall administer, or cause to be administered, for the purpose of affecting the speed of a horse, drugs or stimulants internally, by hypodermic or other method, he shall be warned off the Turf.'

Some of the American gamblers who took up residence in England were totally devoid of moral scruples and many eventually departed owing large sums of money to the bookmakers. One American trainer was asked by an English friend if there were many villains in American racing. 'None at present,' he replied, 'they are all over here.'

The most important result of the 'invasion' was that it revolutionised English jockeyship. In previous eras English jockeys had ridden with long leathers and great length of rein, and there was little difference between their racing seat and that of a man out hunting or hacking. For the most part races were run at a modest pace and long-distance events tended to be a dawdle followed by a sprint. Races run in that

29

fashion were less exacting for a horse than one run at a true gallop which may explain, partially at least, why horses were liable to run twice, or even three times, at Royal Ascot and Goodwood. On the other hand jockeys were hard on their horses in a finish, wearing sharp spurs, which they did not scruple to use, and wielding long whips which could really hurt their mounts.

The American style, as employed to perfection by Tod Sloan, was to crouch low with short stirrup leathers and short rein. Although this more streamlined method was soon shown to possess considerable advantages, Sloan was at first ridiculed as a mere monkey on a stick. A superb judge of pace, he frequently shocked conservative English opinion by setting off in front and making every yard of the running. Before long his astonishingly high percentage of successes had convinced all but a few unrelenting diehards that his methods were more effective than the traditional English ones. English jockeys were compelled to shorten their leathers or drop out of racing for ever.

It was unfortunate that Sloan, a genius with an uncanny understanding of horses, was surrounded by some of the most repellent scoundrels on the Turf. His conduct became an intolerable scandal and at the close of the 1900 season he was informed that it would be pointless for him to apply for a licence again.

During the years 1900 to 1914 the standard among English jockeys was not as high as between 1919 and 1939. In consequence American riders were greatly in demand. The best of them was Danny Maher, a wonderful judge of pace with beautiful hands. He was a man of great charm, but unable to resist burning the candle at both ends. He won the Derby on *Rock Sand* (1903), *Cicero* (1905) and *Spearmint* (1906).

Other Americans to win the Derby were Lester Reiff on *Volodyovski* (1901), 'Skeets' Martin on *Ard Patrick* (1902), Johnny Reiff on *Orby* (1907) and *Tagalie* (1912), and Matt MacGee on *Durbar II* (1914). The Reiff brothers were brought over to England by Wishard. Lester, tall and much troubled by weight problems, worked hand in glove with some of the more notorious American gamblers. Johnny first appeared on English racecourses as an angel-faced little boy in knickerbockers and an Eton collar. He was, however, a good deal less innocent than he looked.

As the French jockey George Stern won the 1911 Derby on *Sunstar*, the only English jockeys in this period to ride a Derby winner were Herbert Jones on *Diamond Jubilee* (1900) and *Minoru* (1909), Kempton Cannon on *St Amant* (1904), William Bullock on *Signorinetta* (1908), Bernard Dillon on *Lemberg* (1910) and E. Piper on *Aboyeur* (1913).

The flood of horses from America, and to a lesser degree from Australia, was a source of worry to those determined at all costs to preserve the purity of the English

Right: 'Persimmon', bred by the Prince of Wales at Sandringham and winner of the 1896 Derby, with his trainer Richard Marsh, painted by Emil Adam. THE JOCKEY CLUB

Persimmon

'Pretty Polly', heroine of the 1904 One Thousand Guineas, Oaks and St Leger, painted by A. C. Harell. FORES LIMITED

Thoroughbred as in many cases the pedigree of these imported horses could not be proved beyond a certain point. Accordingly in May 1901 the following notice appeared in Volume XIX of the General Stud Book:

The increased importation of horses and mares bred in the USA and Australia, which, as stated in the last volume, though accepted in the stud books of their own country, cannot be traced back in all cases to the Thoroughbred stock exported from England, from which, more or less, they all claim to be descended, induced the Publishers to refer the question of the admission of such animals into the Stud Book to the Stewards of the Jockey Club as the highest authority on all matters connected with the Turf. The Stewards, after kindly consulting most of the principal breeders, came to the conclusion that any animal claiming admission should be able to prove satisfactorily some eight or nine crosses of pure blood,

to trace back for at least a century, and to show such performances of its immediate family on the Turf as to warrant the belief in the purity of its blood. Therefore, all the imported horses and mares which are included in this volume have been submitted to this test.

This ruling proved to be one of the greatest importance. For example, among those who thus secured admission were *Rhoda B*, dam of the Derby winner *Orby* who sired the Derby winner *Grand Parade*; *Americus Girl*, whose many distinguished descendants include *Mumtaz Mahal*, *Mahmoud*, *Masrullah*, *Royal Charger*, *Fair Trial*, *Tudor Minstrel* and *Petite Etoile*; and the One Thousand Guineas winner *Sibola*, great-granddam of the magnificent racehorse and most influential sire *Nearco*. Without the relaxation afforded by the 1901 ruling, not one of the descendants of *Rhoda B*, *Americus Girl* and *Sibola* would have been entitled to the description Thoroughbred.

In 1909 further legislation in the United States brought racing in America virtually to a standstill for a number of years. The authorities in England, nervous of another

flood of American horses into this country, rescinded the 1901 ruling. However the rescinding of that ruling was not rendered retrospective and horses admitted between 1901 and 1908 remained in the Stud Book and their descendants were judged eligible for admission.

For some this new barrier was insufficient. At a meeting of the Jockey Club in 1913 Lord Jersey, who had been Senior Steward the previous year, put the following proposal before the Stewards: 'in the interests of the English Stud Book no horse or mare can, after this date, be considered as eligible for admission unless it can be traced, without flaw on both sire's and dam's side of its pedigree, to horses and mares already accepted in the earlier volumes of the book.'

The Hon F.W. Lambton, Senior Steward, replied that the Stewards had already considered Lord Jersey's question and were prepared to adopt the suggestion it contained if it was the wish of the Club generally. On a show of hands the members signified approval. Thus came into existence what in due course was known as the 'Jersey Act'.

The Americans were furious and not surprisingly so as the Jockey Club had placed the stamp of 'half-bred' on American horses, after American breeders had spent fortunes on importing English horses. Naturally the export to all parts of the world of American sires and mares, now classified as 'half-breds', dwindled to negligible proportions. American opinion was not in the least impressed by the English claim that the 'Jersey Act' was passed to preserve the purity of the Stud Book; on the contrary, it was firmly believed that the primary object had been to protect the export trade in English horses. The entire business was judged typical of English selfishness and hypocrisy, and considerable satisfaction was shown in America when the 1914 Derby was won by *Durbar II*, a French-bred colt ineligible for the Stud Book on account of his American-bred dam.

Before leaving the question of the American influence on English racing in the early years of the century, it must be said that the Americans taught many useful lessons in stable management, particularly in respect of light, ventilation and fresh air, while their method of plating was a long way in advance of that of English blacksmiths.

The two outstanding horses during this period were the mares *Sceptre* and *Pretty Polly*. *Sceptre* was bred by the Duke of Westminster, one of the great owner-breeders of the latter half of the nineteenth century. The Duke died in 1899, the year his colt *Flying Fox* gained the Triple Crown; and *Sceptre*, by *Persimmon* out of *Ornament*, a full sister to the Duke's first Triple Crown winner, *Ormonde*, came up for sale as a yearling in 1900. It was *Sceptre*'s ill-fortune that Mr Robert Sievier, a bold, unscrupulous gambler, was in funds at the time – a fairly rare occurrence – and went up to Newmarket with £20,000 in ready money, determined to buy her. He bought her for 10,000 guineas, easily a record price at that time for a yearling sold by auction.

For her first season, during which she won two of her three races, *Sceptre* was trained by the very able Charles Morton, but at the end of the year Morton became private trainer to Mr J.B. Joel. As a three-year-old *Sceptre* was trained at Shrewton by Sievier himself. Disregarding the fact that she was not at her best, Sievier went for a big win with her in the Lincolnshire Handicap, in which she was slowly away, indifferently ridden and narrowly beaten. This was a weird start to the season for a filly with classic potentialities but it clearly did her little harm as she won the Two Thousand Guineas, the One Thousand Guineas, the Oaks and the St Leger. She had been stopped in her work by a bruised foot shortly before the Derby, in which she was fourth to *Ard Patrick*, but redeemed her reputation by an easy victory in the Oaks two days later.

Sievier was merciless in the demands he made of *Sceptre*. Immediately after the Epsom meeting she was packed off to Paris for the Grand Prix, in which her rider elected to cover the entire journey on the extreme outside, so that *Sceptre* travelled almost a furlong further than the winner.

Immediately after her return to England *Sceptre* went to Royal Ascot where she was beaten in the Coronation Stakes and won the St James's Palace Stakes. At Goodwood she won one of her two races, the Nassau Stakes. After the St Leger, which she won in a canter, Sievier could not resist running her two days later in the Park Hill Stakes; she was beaten, exhausted by the unfair demands of her owner.

The following season Sievier again went for a large win in the Lincoln, but *Sceptre* could only finish fifth. By then Sievier was hard up and he sold her for 25,000 guineas to Mr (later Sir) William Bass, a young officer in the 10th Hussars. Bass sent her to Alec Taylor at Manton where she arrived in exceedingly poor condition. She won the Hardwicke Stakes at Royal Ascot, but Taylor still had not got her quite to his liking when, in a memorable race for the Eclipse Stakes, she lost by a neck to *Ard Patrick* with *Rock Sand*, winner of the 1903 Triple Crown, a long way behind them. In the autumn *Sceptre* was at the peak of her form, winning the Jockey Club Stakes, the Duke of York Stakes, the Champion Stakes and the Limekiln Stakes. She remained in training at five, but she was past her best and failed to win. All told she had won thirteen races worth £38,283.

It is interesting to speculate on what *Sceptre*'s career would have been if the Duke had not died and she had been trained throughout by the great John Porter of Kingsclere.

Pretty Polly was bred and owned by Major Eustace Loder and trained by Peter Gilpin. A big chestnut she was by *Gallinule*, who was both a 'bleeder' and a 'roarer', out of *Admiration*, whose racing career was dim in the extreme and who once took part in a military steeplechase at Punchestown. As a two-year-old *Pretty Polly* was brilliant, winning all her nine races including the National Breeders Produce Stakes, the Champagne Stakes, the Cheveley Park Plate and the Middle Park Plate. At three she won successively the One Thousand Guineas, the Oaks, the Coronation Stakes, the Nassau Stakes, the St Leger and the Park Hill Stakes. She was the idol of the racing public and it came as a painful shock when she was beaten by *Presto* in the Prix du Conseil Municipal at Longchamp. On returning to England she won the Free Handicap, giving the Derby winner *St Amant* 3lb.

The following season she ran four times, winning the Coronation Cup, the Champion Stakes, the Jockey Club Cup and the Limekiln Stakes. Her target at five was the Ascot Gold Cup and it was regarded almost as a national disaster when she was narrowly beaten by *Bachelor's Button*. Before that defeat she had won the March Stakes and the Coronation Cup. At the time of her retirement she had won twenty-two races worth £37,297.

Other notable winners during the era included *Diamond Jubilee*, *The Tetrarch*, *Bayardo* and *Prince Palatine*. *Diamond Jubilee*, a brother to *Persimmon*, was a brilliant but ill-tempered horse and carried off the Triple Crown for the Prince of Wales in 1900, the year the Prince also won the Grand National with *Ambush II*.

The royal colours were also successful in the Derby in 1909 with *Minoru* who, in addition, won the Two Thousand Guineas. *Minoru* was leased for racing from Colonel W. Hall-Walker (later Lord Wavertree). Exported to Russia, *Minoru* disappeared during the Revolution. *Diamond Jubilee* was exported to Argentina.

The Tetrarch was something of an equine freak. A big grey with curious white spots, he was sired by the French-bred plodder *Roi Herode*. Owned by Mr Dermot McCalmont of the 7th Hussars and trained by Atty Persse, he was probably the fastest horse ever seen on the English Turf. His two-year-old performances in 1911 were phenomenal; some of his trials at home even more so. Unfortunately he could not be raced as a three-year-old. Whether a horse with his remarkable speed would ever have stayed the distance of the Derby is a matter of conjecture. The fact is that in an all-too-brief stud career he sired three St Leger winners in five years.

Bayardo, a half-brother by *Bay Ronald* to the Derby winner *Lemberg*, was bred by his owner, the eccentric Mr A.W. Cox, who had made a fortune in Australia. The best horse Alec Taylor ever trained at Manton, he was unbeaten as a two-year-old. In the course of his career he won twenty-two races worth over £44,000, including the St Leger, the Eclipse Stakes, the Champion Stakes and the Ascot Gold Cup. He could not be prepared in time to do justice to himself in the Two Thousand Guineas and the Derby. He was only once subsequently beaten and that was when the over-confident Danny Maher let *Magic* steal a lead of a furlong in the Goodwood Cup and *Bayardo* failed to get up by a neck. *Bayardo* was proving a highly successful sire when he died aged eleven. He got two Triple Crown winners in *Gay Crusader* and *Gainsborough*.

Prince Palatine, by *Persimmon*, bred by Lord Wavertree and owned by Mr T. Pilkington, was a great stayer who won the St Leger, the Coronation Cup, the Gold Cup twice and the Doncaster Cup. He also had the speed to win the Eclipse Stakes. He was not successful as a sire, but from him is descended *Princequillo*, who brilliantly revived the *St Simon* line in America.

The most sensational race during the era was the 1913 Derby, in which a suffragette brought down King George V's horse at Tattenham Corner. Considerable ill-feeling existed among certain jockeys taking part and in consequence the race would have been exceptionally rough and ugly even without this incident. Mr C. Bower Ismay's *Craganour*, the favourite, won by a head from *Aboyeur*, who finished a neck ahead of *Louvois* and *Great Sport*. There was no objection by the connections of the 100 to 1 *Aboyeur* but the Stewards themselves lodged an objection to the winner on the grounds that he had jostled the runner-up.

After a long enquiry in which the evidence of the Judge, Mr C.E. Robinson, may have been decisive, the Stewards disqualified *Craganour* and awarded the race to *Aboyeur*. It was the first time in the history of the Derby that the winner had been disqualified.

'St Simon'

COUNT BATTHYANY, a Hungarian who spent most of his life in England, was elected to the Jockey Club in 1859. Sixteen years later his colt *Galopin* won the Derby.

At stud *Galopin* was not outstandingly successful until 1880 when the fifteen-year-old mare *St Angela* was sent to him. Although her sire, *King Tom*, had been second in the 1854 Derby, *St Angela*'s record was little short of abysmal. Her racing record was moderate and she had produced nothing of merit in her years at stud. The resulting colt foal, named *St Simon*, was destined to become the greatest horse of the nineteenth century, and one of the most influential sires in Turf history.

Through a curious quirk of fate *St Simon* never ran in any of the important two-year-old races, did not run in any of the Classics, and did not win a prestige race until he triumphed in the Ascot Gold Cup as a three-year-old. Yet he competed in nine races, was never beaten, and in his first season at stud sired *Memoir*, who won the Oaks and the St Leger, and *Semolina* who won the One Thousand Guineas.

On the day of the 1883 Two Thousand Guineas Count Batthyany had a heart attack outside the Jockey Club luncheon room at Newmarket, and died within moments. Half an hour later Lord Falmouth's *Galliard*, a son of *Galopin*, won the first Classic of the season. In July the Count's bloodstock was sold. *Galopin* was bought by Mr Henry Chaplin for £8,000 and the unraced two-year-old *St Simon* by the young Duke of Portland for a mere 1,600 guineas. His purchase was to prove the bargain of the century, though the Duke's immense affluence precluded any necessity for such financial considerations.

At the time of the sale *St Simon* was big and backward, but the Duke felt confident that he had made a wise purchase when he was offered a substantial profit on the transaction by a friend whose judgement he respected. Under the care of the renowned trainer Mat Dawson, *St Simon* improved rapidly, was given five races before the end of the season and won them all in effortless style. Dawson, never prone to lavish praise, emphatically remarked: '*St Simon* is the best horse I have ever trained – he will possibly make the best racehorse who ever ran on the Turf'; and this comment came from a man who had already trained three Derby winners!

The crux of the problem with regard to *St Simon*'s future career was the Jockey Club rule that all nominations became void on the death of an owner. Consequently *St Simon*'s entry for the Two Thousand Guineas was invalidated. Count Batthyany had not entered his colt for either the Derby or the St Leger, presumably on the grounds that he did not think it worth the expense to enter a horse whose dam's record was so indifferent. Thus *St Simon* was not eligible for any of the Classics. Dawson advised the Duke of Portland not to submit *St Simon* to an arduous season, and suggested that his main objective should be the Ascot Gold Cup. The advice was accepted.

Early in the season Fred Archer was riding *St Simon* at exercise on the Heath, and on Dawson's recommendation touched the colt with his spurs. *St Simon* took off as though jet-propelled, and Archer had almost reached Newmarket before he regained control. Later in the morning he told Dawson 'as long as I live I will never touch that animal with the spur, he's not a horse, he's a blooming steam engine'.

After receiving a walk-over for the Epsom Gold Cup, *St Simon* won the Ascot Gold Cup by twenty lengths. An insight into the magnitude of that victory was that the runner-up, *Tristan*, was saddled for the Hardwicke Stakes the following afternoon, and thrashed the Derby dead-heater *Harvester*. Later in the year *St Simon* won the Newcastle Gold Cup and the Goodwood Gold Cup, in which he beat the previous year's St Leger winner by twenty lengths. He was then retired to stud, although, again heeding Dawson's advice, the Duke of Portland rested him for a year before his first mares were sent to him.

For almost his entire stud career *St Simon* stood at his owner's Nottinghamshire estate, Welbeck Abbey. Initially his fee was fifty guineas, but by the end of his life it had increased tenfold to 500 guineas. In the 1886 season he served twenty mares, and served more than forty for each of the next ten years. The majority of his offspring were highly strung, inheriting this characteristic from him, but from the outset his success was phenomenal. Third in the list of champion sires his first season, he was champion sire from 1890 to 1897 and again in 1900 and 1901. His sons and daughters, *Persimmon*, *Diamond Jubilee*, *St Frusquin*, *La Flèche*, *Memoir*, *Amiable*, *La Roche*, *Mrs Butterwick*, *Semolina* and *Winifreda*, won seventeen Classics between them. To add to his brilliant record during this period his sons sired twelve Classic winners, including *Sceptre* and *Ard Patrick*, whilst one of his daughters was the dam of *Rock Sand*, Triple Crown winner of 1903.

Such was his influence that one learned Turf historian wrote that *St Simon* and his progeny set the standard by which trainers judged horses. His statement was

Right: 'St Simon', from the painting by Lynwood Palmer who was born at Market Rasen, Lincolnshire in 1868 and began his career in the USA before returning to England at the end of the 19th century. He died in 1941. THE JOCKEY CLUB

justified for *Persimmon* became leading sire four times, *St Frusquin* twice, and another of his offspring, *Desmond*, once in the years prior to the outbreak of the First World War. In more modern times, *Hyperion*, *Nearco* and *Ribot* were all inbred to *St Simon*.

St Simon died at Welbeck at the age of twenty-seven, dropping dead one morning whilst returning from exercise. The Duke presented his skeleton to the Natural History Museum in South Kensington, whilst preserving his skin at Welbeck. In 1973 two of *St Simon*'s hooves, mounted in gold, were given to the Racing Museum at York.

The Princess of Wales' Stakes, Newmarket

AT THE END of the nineteenth century fashionable Society would flock to the summer race meetings held on the July course at Newmarket. The Prince of Wales would drive over from Sandringham, watch his horses trained by Richard Marsh at Egerton House at morning exercise, and attend the race-meetings in the afternoon. On 29 July 1899 he saw the Duke of Westminster's brilliant colt *Flying Fox* win the valuable Princess of Wales' Stakes, only two months after the colt's scintillating victory in the Derby. The scene, as *Flying Fox* was saddled prior to the race, has been graphically depicted by Isaac Cullin in his painting on pages 38-9.

In the centre of the painting the Prince of Wales can be clearly seen, immaculately attired in grey summer suit and grey homburg. Also in the centre of the picture is Princess Alexandra, talking to the Duke and Duchess of Westminster. Amongst the other personalities whom the artist has included are the Duke of Devonshire; Viscount Falmouth; Lord Marcus Beresford, racing manager to the Prince of Wales; his brother, Lord William Beresford

VC and Lily, Duchess of Marlborough, whom he married a fortnight later; Lord Rothschild; and Captain Henry Greer, who years later became manager of the National Stud and subsequently introduced the Aga Khan into British racing.

Six years earlier the Duke of Westminster had asked his trainer, John Porter, to buy him a mare. For 1,000 guineas Porter bought *Vampire*, whose temper soon after she arrived at the Duke's stud at Eaton left much to be desired. She mauled a stud groom, and killed his first foal. Her future seemed uncertain. However, her second foal was *Batt*, second to the outsider *Jeddah* in the 1898 Derby, and her third foal *Flying Fox*.

Flying Fox, described as a spare wiry bay with a beautiful action, won at Royal Ascot as a two-year-old, but was defeated in the Middle Park Stakes at Newmarket in the autumn. At the start of the Two Thousand Guineas he behaved abominably, and the official starter had to exert

Below: The 1st Duke of Westminster, 1825-99.
ILLUSTRATED SPORTING AND DRAMATIC NEWS, 10 JUNE 1899

limitless patience before *Flying Fox* would condescend to line up. Once the race started he won with consummate ease – but his victory was to some extent overshadowed by the astonishment of racegoers in the members' enclosure who heard the Duke of Westminster, usually the most

dignified of aristocrats, let out a high-pitched and almost deafening 'View Halloa' as his favourite passed the winning post.

Flying Fox won the Derby, the Princess of Wales' Stakes, the Eclipse and the St Leger, and it seemed that he would stand at his owner's stud at the end of his racing career. However, in 1900 the Duke of Westwinster died, and his colt was sold to M Edmond Blanc for 37,500 guineas – a price thought to be astronomically high and totally uneconomic at the time. In fact he proved a bargain and his influence as a stallion through his progeny dominated bloodstock in France, Italy and the USA for decades.

Flying Fox's jockey, Mornington Cannon, seen in the painting to be taking off his overcoat, had been born in 1873. He was the son of the famous rider, Tom

Cannon, who had won the 1873 Derby on the Duke of Westminster's gallant filly, *Shotover*. A superb horseman, he was at the peak of his riding career in the last years of the nineteenth century before the 'American invasion' revolutionised the style of jockeyship. The Cannon tradition of greatness in the saddle continues to the present day, for Mornington Cannon's sister married Ernest Piggott, grandfather of Lester Piggott.

In Isaac Cullin's painting two other horses besides *Flying Fox* can be clearly seen. In the white silks with the tartan sleeves and red cap is *Birkenhead*, owned by Captain Greer and ridden by Tod Sloan. Sloan, who was known as 'the monkey on a stick', spearheaded the 'American invasion'. In the 1899 Derby he was riding the French challenger, *Holocaust*, who shatter-

ed a fetlock two furlongs from the winning post and had to be destroyed.

In the chocolate colours with the yellow sleeves is Lord Allington's *Royal Emblem*. Lord Allington, like the Duke of Westminster, had his horses trained by John Porter at Kingsclere and had won the Derby in 1883 and 1891 with *St Blaise* and *Common*, whom he owned in partnership with Sir Frederick Johnstone.

Below: 'Flying Fox' from a painting by Emil Adam who was brought to England to paint the horses of the Duke of Westminster. THE JOCKEY CLUB

Overleaf: The 1899 Triple Crown winner 'Flying Fox', owned by the Duke of Westminster, about to be mounted before leaving the paddock on the July course, Newmarket. From the painting by Isaac Cullin. SEASCOPE LIMITED

'Diamond Jubilee'

WHEN THE PRINCE OF WALES (later Edward VII) decided to establish a stud at Sandringham he was advised by the famous Kingsclere trainer, John Porter, to purchase *Perdita II* as one of the foundation brood mares.

The price was £900 and as Sir Dighton Probyn was handing over the cheque on the Prince's behalf he gloomily commented 'You will ruin the Prince if you go on buying these Thoroughbreds'. In reality *Perdita II* proved a gold mine, for amongst her progeny were *Florizel II*, who won the St James's Palace Stakes at Royal Ascot and the Jockey Club Cup; *Persimmon*, who won the 1896 Derby and St Leger and the Ascot Gold Cup and the Eclipse Stakes the following year, and *Diamond Jubilee*, a full brother to *Persimmon*, who won the Triple Crown in 1900.

It was obvious that the Prince's racing advisors had the highest hopes for *Diamond Jubilee*. Alas, those hopes were sadly dashed when *Diamond Jubilee* arrived at Egerton House, Newmarket, to be trained by Richard Marsh.

Described by Marsh as 'a rather spoilt young gentleman who had cultivated a taste for succulent carrots and other tit-bits', he was impossible to fault on conformation. He stood 15.3½ hands when he was sent from Sandringham to Newmarket, and in colour was a bright bay with dark legs and a dark line down the middle of his back to the root of his tail. He had a very intelligent head and a perfect back and loins. He seemed almost too good to be true – and proved it once his racing career began.

His two-year-old début was in the Coventry Stakes at Royal Ascot, for which he started a red-hot favourite. To his trainer's consternation he gave a disgraceful exhibition at the start, rearing up on his hind legs and refusing to come into line with his rivals. As was to be expected after such a display he was beaten, and his jockey, J. Watts, claimed that the colt had tried to bite him.

For the remainder of the season *Diamond Jubilee* was a sad disappointment. Watts did not appear to get on with him, and he went hardly any better for Mornington Cannon who rode him at Goodwood and Newmarket. In trial gallops at Egerton House he was invariably ridden by Herbert Jones, a young stable-boy of eighteen whose father had trained steeplechasers for the Prince of Wales at Epsom. The fact that Jones and *Diamond Jubilee* had formed the happiest of relationships was completely overlooked until the spring of 1900.

One morning Cannon came to ride the colt in a trial gallop. No sooner had Cannon dismounted than *Diamond Jubilee* attempted to savage him. Rescuers came to his aid and the jockey was unhurt, but he made it clear that he had no intention of ever riding *Diamond Jubilee* again.

This decision put Richard Marsh in a quandary. However, as he cogitated over *Diamond Jubilee*'s future it dawned on him that the horse seemed to behave perfectly when ridden by young Jones. With some trepidation he approached the Prince's racing manager, Lord Marcus Beresford, and suggested that Jones should ride *Diamond Jubilee* in the Classics.

His suggestion was accepted, with the happiest of results. *Diamond Jubilee* won the Two Thousand Guineas convincingly, and the Derby by half a length. Patriotism was at its height in the summer of 1900, for after many setbacks in South Africa it seemed that the tide was turning, and news was received on the morning of the Derby that Lord Roberts was within a few miles of Johannesburg.

Diamond Jubilee's Derby victory set off a demonstration of loyalty. There were memorable scenes on Epsom Downs as the Prince led his colt into the winner's enclosure and the National Anthem was sung with fervour by the tens of thousands who packed the grandstands and the enclosures.

Diamond Jubilee duly won the St Leger, although the Prince was unable to witness his success because of Court mourning for the Duke of Edinburgh. As a four-year-old, *Diamond Jubilee* was unsuccessful and failed to win a race before being retired to stud at Sandringham. Five years later he was sold to a South American breeder.

Below: The finish of the 1900 Derby. 'Diamond Jubilee', who behaved perfectly when ridden by his young stable-boy Herbert Jones, winning by half a length from 'Simondale' and 'Disguise II', ILLUSTRATED LONDON NEWS, 9 JUNE 1900

Overleaf: 'Diamond Jubilee' painted by Emil Adam. Adam's painting of 'Diamond Jubilee's' full brother 'Persimmon' is to be seen on pages 30-31. THE JOCKEY CLUB ROOMS AND TRYON GALLERY, LONDON

Opposite page: Fred Archer, the greatest jockey of the 19th century.

12

Flat Racing, 1914 ~ 1930

RACING NEVER CEASED completely, even during the most grim phases of the First World War, and the Jockey Club emerged with increased prestige due to the tactful manner in which it had maintained the sport without embarrassing the conduct of the war.

For a few years after the Armistice there was a tremendous boom in racing. Money was plentiful and, following a long period of austerity, a natural desire to spend it existed. The price of bloodstock soared and racecourse attendances were enormous.

Not all the people who swarmed into racecourse enclosures could be described as an asset to the sport and for a time welshing and pocket-picking thrived in a manner reminiscent of the mid-Victorian era. Worse still, there was an unpleasant eruption of gang warfare, chiefly conducted between thugs from London and Birmingham.

A protection racket was imposed on bookmakers, who found themselves day after day compelled to pay exorbitant prices for sponges and chalk. There was corruption, too, over bookmakers' pitches. Those who were bold enough to defy the gangs were liable to be subjected to extreme physical violence.

The gangs became so powerful and so disdainful of authority that they set about their victims in broad daylight and in public view, sometimes on the racecourse, sometimes on railway platforms crowded with racegoers waiting for a train.

Another post-war nuisance was a series of frauds perpetrated by individuals who ran three-year-olds masquerading as two-year-olds in races restricted to two-year-olds. In 1920 investigations revealed that *Coat of Mail*, winner of the 1919 Faceby Plate at Stockton for two-year-olds, was in reality a three-year-old called *Jazz*. The same confederacy of criminals had also won a two-year-old race at Chester with a three-year-old and had operated a number of ringers with success under National Hunt Rules. When the facts were known the Jockey Club instituted proceedings in the Criminal Court and several men were sentenced to terms of imprisonment.

A minor worry was provided by a group of owners who combined ownership with the sale of racing tips. In 1923 a rule was formulated whereby any owner of horses offering to give information about his own or other horses for money was liable to be declared a disqualified person.

Such disqualification was considered justifiable by the authorities, who were beginning to turn their attention to the future of betting. In the early 1920s there was no totalisator in Britain and the bookmakers, firmly entrenched within the English racing system, were taking fortunes out of the sport whilst under no compulsion to make contributions to its benefit.

Lord Hamilton of Dalzell, His Majesty's

Representative at Ascot, was an extremely active, able and progressive racing administrator who believed that betting ought to be made to contribute to racing. He became the prime mover and instigator in the introduction of the totalisator, and stood at the right hand of Sir Ralph Glyn MP who introduced the Totalisator Bill into the House of Commons in 1928. To his chagrin the Bill was mauled out of recognition in the Committee stages.

If the Bill had been passed in its original form, the totalisator would have been controlled by the Jockey Club instead of operating as a statutory body under the cold and cautious hand of the Home Office, and no doubt it would have had a very different history. It was at Newmarket in July 1929 that the totalisator first went into action. Nowadays when there is talk of the possibility of a tote monopoly, bookmakers speak piously of the right of punters to freedom of choice. By the violence of their opposition they showed they were not greatly concerned about 'freedom of choice' in the early days of the tote.

The totalisator soon ran into financial difficulties. In the first place it was undercapitalised and has remained in that uncomfortable position ever since. Secondly, costly mistakes were made by the original Racecourse Betting Control Board, chiefly through too-ready acceptance of advice from tote operators overseas where conditions were invariably entirely different from those existing here.

At the outset the bookmakers were nervous of the inroads the tote might make on their business and as a defence they offered, for a brief period, extravagant prices about outsiders. Thus on the first day the tote operated, Lord Rosebery's colt *The Bastard*, later a leading sire in Australia under the more refined name of *The Buzzard*, was returned at 100 to 1.

The 1920s were hardly noted for striking reforms or innovations on the Turf, but in 1923 the Jockey Club instituted an insurance scheme for the benefit of jockeys or apprentices killed or injured when following their profession. It was ordered that at all race meetings held in Great Britain the owner of every horse running should pay a shilling, and that a shilling should be deducted from the fee paid to the jockey, by way of contribution to the fund. In the case of death or permanent injury resulting from an accident while riding in a race, a maximum sum of £2,000 was henceforth payable to a jockey or his dependents, and weekly allowances were to be paid in cases of temporary disablement. The fund was to be administered by the Jockey Club at its discretion.

This period was not notable for great horses. Historically the result of the 1924 Derby was significant, for *Sansovino* be-

came the first horse for 137 years to win the Derby in the famous black, white cap of the Earls of Derby. Mr H.E. Morriss's *Manna*, who also won the Two Thousand Guineas in 1925, was one of the best of the Derby winners. Lord Woolavington's *Captain Cuttle*, winner of the Derby in 1922, was another good horse, though never an easy one to train. He was sold for export to Italy. His owner also won the Derby and the St Leger in 1926 with the hard-pulling, flaxen-tailed *Coronach* who, like *Captain Cuttle*, was by *Hurry On*. *Coronach* went wrong in his wind, apart from which he was inclined to lack resolution if matters did not go his own way. He ended his days in New Zealand.

Lord Astor, unlucky never to win a Derby although his colts finished second five times in seven years, won the Oaks with *Pogrom* (1922), *Saucy Sue* (1925), *Short Story* (1926) and *Pennycomequick* (1929). *Saucy Sue* also won the One Thousand Guineas. In 1928 King George V enjoyed his sole classic success when *Scuttle*, by *Captain Cuttle*, won the One Thousand Guineas. Racing meant less to the King than it had done to his father, but he was the better judge of a horse.

The outstanding St Leger winners were Sir John Rutherford's *Solario* (1925) and Lord Derby's *Fairway* (1928). *Solario* won the Coronation Cup and the Ascot Gold Cup the following year and later proved a highly successful sire. *Fairway*, who did even better as a sire than *Solario*, and who

Right, above: 'Unsaddling', a cartoon by The Tout depicting celebrities outside the weighing room at Newmarket. THE JOCKEY CLUB

Right, below: 'They're Off', another cartoon of distinguished members of the Jockey Club by The Tout. On the right is HRH the Prince of Wales. THE JOCKEY CLUB

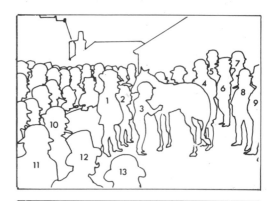

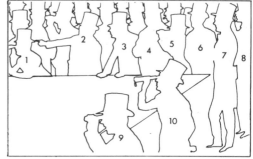

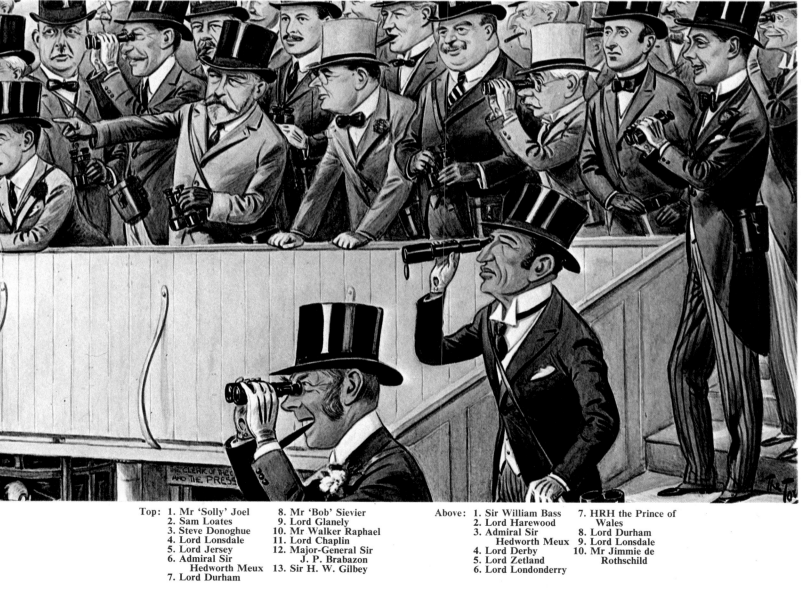

Top: 1. Mr 'Solly' Joel   8. Mr 'Bob' Sievier   Above: 1. Sir William Bass   7. HRH the Prince of
      2. Sam Loates   9. Lord Glanely   2. Lord Harewood   Wales
      3. Steve Donoghue   10. Mr Walker Raphael   3. Admiral Sir   8. Lord Durham
      4. Lord Lonsdale   11. Lord Chaplin   Hedworth Meux   9. Lord Lonsdale
      5. Lord Jersey   12. Major-General Sir   4. Lord Derby   10. Mr Jimmie de
      6. Admiral Sir   J. P. Brabazon   5. Lord Zetland   Rothschild
            Hedworth Meux   13. Sir H. W. Gilbey   6. Lord Londonderry
      7. Lord Durham

won the Eclipse Stakes at three, was the best of his age in 1928, and would probably have won the Derby but for the fact that the crowd at Epsom got out of control and mobbed him on the way to the start. He had lost the race before it began and the Derby was won by Sir Hugo Cunliffe-Owen's 33 to 1 outsider *Felstead*, most intelligently ridden by Harry Wragg. *Felstead*, who never ran again, sired a very fine filly in *Rockfel*, winner of the One Thousand Guineas and the Oaks in 1938. She started her career in a selling race at Sandown, thus illustrating the 'glorious uncertainties of the Turf'.

Jockeyship stood at a high level between the wars. For the first six years of the 1920s Steve Donoghue was at his peak and rode *Humorist*, *Captain Cuttle*, *Papyrus* and *Manna* to victory in the Derby. First champion in 1914, he remained so until 1923, in which year he shared the honours with Charles Elliott, then an apprentice. Elliott, intelligent and articulate, rode *Call Boy* to victory in the 1927 Derby. Twenty-two years later he won on *Nimbus* in a thrilling finish with *Amour Drake* and *Swallow Tail*.

Donoghue was one of the nation's sporting idols and the cry of 'come on Steve' was familiar throughout the British Isles. Quite fearless, he loved and understood horses and was blessed with beautiful hands. He was also generous to the point of folly, unpunctual, unreliable and a mere child over matters connected with finance. Women found it hard to resist him and his charm enabled him to get away with lapses and weaknesses that would not have been readily forgiven in others. Though the brilliance of his star faded with the years, he retained his popularity to the day of his death in 1945.

It was in the twenties that Gordon Richards established his reputation. He was champion in 1925 and again in 1927, 1928 and 1929. A genius with a style not easily copied by others, he combined the highest professional skill with an unblemished reputation for integrity. No jockey has lost fewer races that he ought to have won and punters have never had a more thoroughly trustworthy friend.

The beetle-browed and occasionally irascible Joe Childs, who was proud to ride for the King, was a specialist in waiting tactics. His strength of finish was equalled by that of the saturnine Bernard Carslake, who excelled in sprint races and whose career entailed an endless battle with his weight. The light-hearted Tommy Weston had come up the hard way. Brilliant on his day, he rode many winners for Lord Derby. Harry Wragg was more thoughtful than most, an intelligent horseman who planned his tactics in advance with the utmost care. Fred Fox was thoroughly sound, and Michael Beary, though not consistent, a master on 'difficult' horses.

Apart from these there were the stylish Frank Bullock, the self-assured Charlie Smirke who reached his zenith only after a period of misfortune, Victor Smyth, Jack Leach who became the wittiest of racing correspondents, Bobby Jones, the Beasley brothers Harry and Rufus, Dick Perryman, Henri Jelliss and George Archibald. It is arguable that a champion in those times faced considerably fiercer opposition than does Lester Piggott today.

Of the trainers who were well established before the First World War, Charles Morton retired soon after the tragedy of *Humorist*'s death, which had affected him deeply. Alec Taylor, a frugal bachelor who looked like a country banker and left over half a million pounds, remained at Manton until succeeded in 1928 by Joe Lawson. The Hon George Lambton, charming, beautifully dressed, a great lover of animals, continued to train for Lord Derby and, though replaced for a short period by Frank Butters, soon returned again to Stanley House. His reminiscences, *Men and Horses I Have Known*, is generally rated the best book ever written on racing.

Atty Persse never lost his knack of inducing fast two-year-olds to win first time out, usually at nice odds, since discipline in the Chattis Hill stable was extremely strict and leakages of information were rare. Richard Dawson, a most untypical Irishman, became the Aga Khan's first trainer and a close friend till a bitter quarrel separated them in 1931. At one time Dawson parted with Sir Edward

Hulton because he thought fifty shillings a week was inadequate weekly reward for training his horses!

Fred Darling became established as the Master of Beckhampton, and in striving for perfection was apt to become a peppery martinet. He trained seven winners of the Derby, three of them, *Captain Cuttle*, *Manna* and *Coronach*, in the 'twenties. However, the best horse he ever trained was *Hurry On*, whose career was restricted by the war. Captain Cecil (later Sir Cecil) Boyd-Rochfort was making a name for himself, fortunate in the patronage of a number of rich American owners.

Jack (later Sir Jack) Jarvis made his name with *Golden Myth* who won the 1922 Ascot Gold Cup and shortly afterwards the Eclipse. He followed Frank Hartigan as trainer to the fifth Earl of Rosebery and subsequently trained for the sixth Earl, with whom he formed an outstandingly happy and successful racing partnership that lasted until Jarvis's death in 1968. Frank Butters did not really achieve the peak of his success till he succeeded Dawson as trainer to the Aga Khan. Stanley Wootton won a great many races, mostly of small significance, but his true value to racing lay in his skill as a trainer of jockeys.

Of the leading owners in this period Lord Derby, Lord Rosebery, Lord Woolavington (as Mr James Buchanan), Lord Astor, Mr J.B. Joel and his brother Mr 'Solly' Joel, Sir Edward Hulton, Sir Abe Bailey, Major D. McCalmont and Mr Washington Singer were all to a greater or lesser degree familiar to the racing public at the time the war ended. The most important newcomer was an Indian prince, HH the Aga Khan, who had originally been inspired to take up racing on a large scale by Lord Wavertree and Lord Glanely.

The 1919 Derby was won by *Grand Parade* owned by Lord Glanely, a shipping magnate, who had been born William James Tatem at Appledore in Devonshire. His original interest in horses lay with hunters and hackneys. He had his first racing winner in 1909 but it was only after the war that he really became a leading figure on the Turf. In 1919 Glanely had seven winners at Royal Ascot, all trained for him by Frank Barling, originally a veterinary surgeon in Wales. Barling's health was poor, and he did not remain Glanely's trainer for long.

The Aga Khan wanted the Hon George Lambton to be his trainer but Lambton was unable to accept, although he agreed in 1921 to buy some yearlings on the Aga Khan's behalf. Among those he purchased were *Cos* and *Teresina*, both destined to make names for themselves on the racecourse and at stud. The following year he bought not only the amazing *Mumtaz Mahal*, but also *Diophon*, who won the Two Thousand Guineas, and *Salmon Trout* who won the St Leger. The Aga Khan was well and truly launched on one of the most spectacular and successful careers in the history of English racing.

Left: Lord Woolavington's 'Captain Cuttle', winner of the 1922 Derby, with Steve Donoghue up. THE JOCKEY CLUB

Flat Racing, 1930~1939

Above: HH the Aga Khan's Triple Crown winner 'Bahram' with his trainer Frank Butters and jockey F. Fox, painted by A. G. Haigh.
THE JOCKEY CLUB

ALTHOUGH aristocrats such as Lord Derby, Lord Rosebery, Lord Astor and Lord Woolavington patronised the Sport of Kings by racing superbly bred horses reared at their own stud farms, it was HH the Aga Khan who dominated British racing throughout the 1930s.

He had been initiated into racing when he visited Colonel Hall Walker's stud farm at Tully in 1904, but another twenty years elapsed before he decided to lavish his wealth upon the Turf. He explained: 'Between 1904 and 1921 I was very busy with political work. I wanted to do the thing thoroughly or not at all. The idea of having a small stud did not appeal to me, so I waited until I could do it as I had planned.'

He had considerable success in the late 1920s, but not until 1930 did he win his first Derby at Epsom, when *Blenheim* carried his chocolate and green hoops to victory.

He was never averse to running more than one of his horses in the same race, and in the 1930 Derby his other runner, *Rustom Pasha*, was much more fancied than *Blenheim*. On the eve of the race he made it clear that he thought *Rustom Pasha* would win, but tempered his remarks by adding '. . . but who can tell. What course in the world is like the Derby course at Epsom.' His words were proved prophetic within twenty-four hours.

From his seat in the Epsom Grandstand it seemed to the Aga that his life's ambition of owning a Derby winner that he had bred was about to come true as *Rustom Pasha* took up the running once the foot of Tattenham Corner was reached. Suddenly the colt's stamina gave out, and he dropped back a beaten horse. The Aga put down his glasses in misery and despair. As he was doing so *Blenheim*, brilliantly ridden by Harry Wragg, started to make headway on the outside, cut down the leaders and stormed home to win by a length before the flabbergasted Aga had time to recover!

Blenheim, who had been bought from Lord Carnavon at the July Newmarket sales for 4,100 guineas, never raced again. In early July he jarred a tendon, left R.C. Dawson's Whatcombe stables and was taken to his owner's stud at Marly-la-Ville near Paris which was presided over by Madame Vuillier. In 1902 her husband had formed his theory of breeding, in which he traced the pedigree of horses to the twelfth generation (4,096 ancestors). From these tables he propounded a system of dosages which were desirable in the sire and dam of a potentially top-class racehorse. The Aga Khan believed implicitly in the Colonel and made him responsible for the matings of all his horses.

Blenheim's Derby victory virtually opened a floodgate for the Aga, whose triumphs throughout the next decade enabled him to head the Leading Owners List in 1930, 1932, 1934, 1935 and 1937.

In 1931, with Great Britain in a parlous economic state, and the Labour Government resigning in favour of a Coalition under Ramsey MacDonald, the bloodstock industry inevitably suffered, and the price of yearlings dropped alarmingly. Curiously, however, the news of the formation of the Coalition brought back a feeling of confidence and more than 250 of the lots in the Newmarket December sales were withdrawn, as their owners felt it was worth while keeping them after all.

In the previous two years two incidents important to the future of racing had occurred. One concerned a horse named *Don Pat* who won an insignificant race at Kempton. After the race the winner was examined by the Jockey Club veterinary surgeons who took samples of his sweat and saliva to be tested. The tests proved positive and showed that a dose of caffeine had been administered. The Jockey Club disqualified *Don Pat* on the grounds that the horse had been doped and warned the trainer off Newmarket Heath. When the Jockey Club published their decision it was inadvertently worded in a manner which implied that the trainer had been

47

guilty of the misdemeanour. A law case ensued which vindicated the trainer's character although it in no way altered the fact that *Don Pat* had been doped. From this moment the problem of doping, which appeared to have been extinguished after the expulsion of the American dopers at the beginning of the century, began once more to cause anxiety.

The other incident also concerned a law case. In 1929 the famous detective writer Edgar Wallace, always a staunch supporter of racing, became largely responsible for the alteration of the Jockey Club rule whereby the death of an owner resulted in all entries for his horses becoming null and void on the grounds that the Club was unable to recover fees and forfeits by legal process. With the willing and friendly co-operation of the Jockey Club Edgar Wallace refused to pay two small forfeits that he owed, and invited it to sue him for their recovery. Eventually in the Court of Appeal the case went in favour of the Jockey Club who paid all Wallace's costs.

The result of the case was that when Lord Dewar died in April 1930 the nomination for his colt *Cameronian* for the 1931 Derby did not become void. As *Cameronian* flashed past the post to win at Epsom, Edgar Wallace was entitled to feel that he had contributed to Turf history. For a time in his career he had been a racing journalist, an owner and a breeder of racehorses. Sadly, however, he personified the 'mug punter' and lost far more than he won by gambling.

At the end of the 1931 season the Aga Khan quarrelled with his trainer R.C. Dawson and sent his horses to Frank Butters at Fitzroy House, Newmarket. Butters, an absolute perfectionist, had trained from 1926 to 1930 for Lord Derby, but at the end of the 1920s economic conditions and the state of the nation caused Lord Derby to reduce his racing commitments, and he did not renew Butters' contract. For the first time in his life fifty-two-year-old Butters, who had been born in Vienna and had trained privately in Austria and Italy before coming to England, became a public trainer.

His success for the Aga Khan throughout the 1930s was such that his patron once wrote:

... Mr Butters, one of the most delightful human beings one could ever hope to meet, with a nature as clean and clear as a diamond without its harshness ... trained for me a succession of magnificent horses. Even more wonderful than his success with great horses was his way with the quite moderate ones. He had a knack of getting out of any horse the very best the horse could do. He never needed races as preparation for his horses. If his two-year-olds were capable of winning, they won the first time they were out. No nonsense about needing two or three eye-openers.

Due to Butters the Aga's success in 1932 was immense. *Dastur* finished second in the Two Thousand Guineas and the Derby, *Udaipur* won the Oaks, and in the St Leger

his trainer saddled four horses and they finished first, second, fourth and fifth! This was a unique feat although the Middleham trainer Croft had saddled the first four for different owners in 1822.

The Rules of Betting in England differed from those of many other countries in that horses in the same ownership running in the same race were not treated as one unit. As the Aga seldom resorted to private trials, preferring to see his horses tested on the racecourse, his supposed 'second string' frequently won, causing unjust and unfair criticism from disgruntled punters who had supported the apparently more fancied runner.

The Aga was always adamant that the most important ingredient in a Thoroughbred was *speed*, and believed that many breeders did not attach sufficient emphasis to it. Years later in a letter to *The Times* he wrote: '... to those on the lookout for ways and means to keep up the prestige of the English Thoroughbred I have only one piece of advice to offer – be careful when you throw out the water from the tub. Do not let the baby fall as well – and that baby is speed.'

In 1933 the Aga Khan's horses were overshadowed by the exploits of Lord Derby's *Hyperion*, who was to prove the most influential horse bred in Britain during the 1930s. As a result of *Hyperion* having four white feet many so-called experts never gave him his just deserts during his racing career, and liked to quote:

One white foot – ride him for your life
Two white feet – give him to your wife
Three white feet – give him to your man
Four white feet – sell him if you can.

Throughout the 1930s the standard of jockeyship was supremely high, and in the opinion of many it was a vintage era *par excellence*. The incomparable Steve Donoghue, his great rival Joe Childs, Michael Beary, Freddie Fox and 'Brownie' Carslake were veterans – but a younger generation abounding in talent were appearing to replace them: E.C. Elliott, Tommy Weston, Harry Wragg, Eph Smith and, above all others, Gordon Richards.

Born in Shropshire in 1904, Richards rode his first Classic winner in 1930 – *Rose of England* in the Oaks and *Singapore* in the St Leger, both horses being owned by Lord Glanely. Three years later he equalled Fred Archer's record of 246 winners in one season and on a memorable November day at Liverpool rode his 247th winner. The jubilation was immense, for the newspapers had been full of his achievements for weeks, and had continually compared his feats in the saddle with those of the 'Tinman'. The comparison was of interest – and in some respects in Archer's favour. In the last years of his career Archer could not go to scale weighing less than 8st 7lbs while Gordon Richards could go to scale at 7st 8lbs. In 1885 Archer rode 246 winners from 667 mounts. In 1933 Richards rode 247 winners from 667 mounts. As against this the number of runners in each race in 1933 was far more than in the years when Archer rode – so it was infinitely harder for Richards to ride a winner.

One racing journalist, commenting on Gordon Richards' artistry in the saddle, wrote:

Richards invariably waits until his mount is balanced and travelling smoothly before calling upon him for his challenging effort. Many, who have not watched him so closely as I, give his whip a lot of the credit. I attribute his success to the looseness of rein and perfect balance. How, with a loose rein, he keeps his horses so straight is marvellous. Seldom does a horse swerve with him.

In nature Gordon Richards was totally unlike Steve Donoghue, whose crown he inherited. Sadly, Steve, for all his charm and genius, suffered from a lack of integrity towards those owners and trainers who were his employers. By the end of the 1920s his star was in the descendant, and only his association with the lovable *Brown Jack*, who won six consecutive Queen Alexandra Stakes at Royal Ascot, and his own irrepressible character kept him in the public eye. The cry 'Come on Steve' gave pride of place to shouts of 'Gordon, Gordon'.

Yet six weeks before Gordon Richards broke Archer's record disaster nearly overtook him. After the final race at Doncaster of the St Leger meeting, trainers Fred Darling and Herbert Blagrave, Mrs Martin Hartigan and jockeys F. Lane, A. Burns and Gordon chartered a plane to fly them to London. The plane crashed as it took off, killing the pilot. Luckily none of the passengers was seriously hurt, and Gordon rode a winner the next afternoon.

The following season Steve Donoghue, in his fiftieth year, was a central figure in a momentous Derby in which Lord Glanely's *Colombo*, ridden by Australian jockey Rae Johnstone, started a screaming favourite. Johnstone rode an injudicious race, and many believed that Steve had deliberately misled him by suggesting wrong race tactics which cost him the race.

The winner was *Windsor Lad*, owned not by the Aga Khan but by another Indian Prince, the Maharajah of Rajpipla. *Windsor Lad* was a very high-class colt who, before his St Leger victory, had been sold to Mr Martin Benson for the enormous sum of £50,000. The reason for the sale was that the Maharajah did not possess a stud farm where he could stand his Derby winner. Generously he sold his Derby champion under the condition that the colt should remain in England so that his blood and breeding capabilities could be retained for the benefit of English racing. Benson sent *Windsor Lad* to his Beech House stud at Newmarket.

Tragically *Windsor Lad* died in 1943 but five years earlier his stud career came virtually to an end, and Benson bought the Italian champion *Nearco* to replace him.

The reason behind Benson's purchase of *Windsor Lad* illustrates the grip, tantamount to a stranglehold, that a select group of immensely wealthy owners and breeders had upon English racing in the 1930s. Benson had bought Beech House in 1930, and acquired expensive brood mares.

He then found himself faced with a stumbling block, for he was compelled to accept the fact that it was almost impossible for him to obtain nominations to the most fashionable stallions. These nominations were strictly reserved for the owners of the stallions, their friends and the established and accepted breeders. Benson realised that there was but one course open to him – to buy a stallion of his own, and one whose racecourse performances were second to none. Hence his purchase of *Windsor Lad*.

Windsor Lad's sire was *Blandford*, undoubtably the greatest stallion of the era. *Windsor Lad* was his third Derby winner in five years, the others being *Trigo* and *Blenheim*. In April 1935 *Blandford* died of pneumonia at R.C. Dawson's stud at Whatcombe. His death at the comparatively young age of sixteen was a tragedy for the bloodstock industry. He had been transferred from his owner's Cloghran stud in Ireland in 1933 because English breeders wished to patronise him – and under Irish law as long as he stood in Ireland a forty per cent *ad valorem* duty was levied on any of his progeny coming into England from the Irish Free State. Five weeks after his death his son *Bahram* added lustre to

his glory by winning the Derby and subsequently being hailed as a Triple Crown winner in the colours of the Aga Khan.

The following year the Aga Khan's star was still in the ascendant for he owned both the winner, *Mahmoud*, and the runner-up, *Taj Akbar*, in the Derby. *Mahmoud* was only the second grey to score in the history of the race, and was sired by *Blenheim* whose sale to an American syndicate for £45,000 was announced a month after the Derby. A week later *Blenheim* sailed aboard the *Berengaria* en route for Arthur Hancock's Claiborne Stud in Kentucky. The sale caused a furore and many breeders only begrudgingly accepted the Aga Khan's explanation: 'I have had him at my stud for six years, and now have a great deal of his blood, notably his son *Mahmoud*. Then there are his yearlings and foals, and there will be more foals next year.'

Many English breeders who had booked nominations to him for 1937 and 1938 were deeply concerned at the sale, the negotiations for which resulted in a court case over *Blenheim*'s agreed value and the Aga's liability to pay commission on the sale which had begun prior to *Mahmoud*'s victory and was not concluded until after he had won at Epsom. *Blenheim* was the

fourteenth English Derby winner to be sold to the United States and the first to be sent across the Atlantic after one of his sons had won the Epsom Classic.

The final three years of the decade did not bring such success to the Aga, and in 1940 *Bahram* and *Mahmoud* were also sold to the United States. Before being exported *Bahram* had sired two top-class horses in *Big Game* and *Persian Gulf*, but at stud in America the Triple Crown winner was a comparative failure. He died in the Argentine in 1956. *Mahmoud*, however, proved an influential sire and headed the Leading Sire List.

The Aga's decision to sell these two horses did not meet with approval although his reasons were justifiable. He was not in the best of health, was living in France, and was worried about the ultimate outcome of the war. His worry caused him to consider the possibility of selling his vast racing empire lock, stock and barrel, but nothing ever materialised.

During the decade such outstanding Turf personalities as 'Solly' Joel, Lord Wavertree, Lord Woolavington and Richard Marsh, trainer to King Edward VII and King George V, died. So too did great horses including *Blandford*, *Pharos*, *The Tetrarch* and *Pretty Polly*. It was as though a curtain was drawn down upon an era when the outbreak of the Second World War brought racing England to a standstill. A few days before the St Leger meeting in September 1939 all racing was abandoned until further notice. This upheaval was a serious blow to breeders, many of whom were left with valuable yearlings upon whose sale their livelihood depended. There was an exodus of horses in training to Ireland and some racing stables closed down.

Although racing was restarted in October, it was not possible to stage the St Leger which had promised to be one of the crucial races of the decade. Lord Rosebery's *Blue Peter* had won both the Two Thousand Guineas and the Derby and in the opinion of his trainer, Jack Jarvis, was an exceptional colt who was unbeatable. On the other side of the English Channel was another colt considered unbeatable – M Marcel Boussac's Grand Prix winner *Pharis II*.

The match between the two champion colts in the St Leger would have gone a long way towards deciding the supremacy of English or French racing. *Pharis II* had actually arrived at Folkestone *en route* for Doncaster before English racing was cancelled. Lord Rosebery announced that *Blue Peter* was to be sent to stud forthwith.

The argument over the rival performances of the two colts was a topic of conversation in racing circles for many months, but for the next six years the sport only survived in a very low key. There was no doubt, however, that in the immediate post-war years English Classic races were dominated by French-trained Thoroughbreds.

Left: Steve Donoghue in the colours of Lady Torrington, from the picture by Sir Alfred Munnings.

14

'Hyperion'

HYPERION, bred by Lord Derby, was born at Newmarket on Good Friday 1930. At the time of his birth he was so small that one of the stud grooms complained that he looked more like a golden retriever than a racehorse.

Despite his size his trainer, the Hon George Lambton, never lost confidence in him for he remembered that *Hyperion*'s grandsire, *Chaucer*, was also small, and that his dam, *Selene*, was a great race-mare who won fifteen races. She did not run in any of the Classics, but as a three-year-old won over distances from ten furlongs to fourteen furlongs.

Hyperion was her sixth foal, and of her first five progeny, *Sickle* was to become a leading sire in the USA, *Pharamond* was also a successful sire in America and *Hunter's Moon* became the leading sire in the Argentine. *Hyperion*'s sire, *Gainsborough*, had won the 1918 Derby for Lady James Douglas, and at stud had already sired two St Leger winners in *Solario* and *Singapore*. As *Gainsborough* was by the great horse *Bayardo* out of the Oaks winner *Rosedrop* it was obvious that *Hyperion* was superlatively bred, and that the sky was the limit for his future . . .

In the spring of 1932 Lambton reported to Lord Derby that *Hyperion* seemed backward. It was decided, however, that the colt should be given an outing at the Doncaster May meeting, more with the intention of allowing him experience of the hustle and bustle of a racecourse than with any hope of victory. On the Newmarket gallops he had shown himself to be a bit of a character, but his work was uninspiring and consequently stable jockey Tommy Weston was not optimistic as he walked towards the Doncaster paddock on an afternoon which was dull and overcast.

His first surprise came when he saw *Hyperion* walking around the paddock obviously relishing the noise and excitement of the racecourse. His second surprise came moments later as he rode the colt to the start. Gone was the indolence shown at Newmarket. In its place was a *joie de vivre* which nearly lifted him from the saddle.

Obeying the trainer's instructions not to touch *Hyperion* with the whip, Weston finished a respectable fourth of nineteen. He had no doubt that if the race was re-run he would have won by at least two lengths. His judgement was vindicated at Royal Ascot three weeks later when *Hyperion* won the New Stakes by three lengths, slamming his rivals in faster time than that recorded by any other two-year-old at the meeting. He ran on three other occasions before the end of the season, ending up in a blaze of glory by beating the Middle Park winner, *Felicitation*, in the Dewhurst Stakes at Newmarket.

During the winter *Hyperion*'s lethargy on the gallops developed to such an extent that his work riders considered him far inferior to his stable companions *Scarlet Tiger*, *Highlander* and *Thrapston*. Six months later *Hyperion* had won the Chester Vase; the Derby in record time, beating his rivals pointlessly with *Scarlet Tiger* trailing in fourth; and the Prince of Wales' Stakes at Royal Ascot. He scored a convincing victory in the St Leger, and enabled one knowledgeable racegoer who was also a literary expert to point out that *Hyperion* was the first-ever Classic winner to be named after a god.

Sadly, *Hyperion*'s career as a four-year-old was a tragic fiasco. The Hon George Lambton had retired at the end of 1933 and was succeeded by Colledge Leader who did not appear to appreciate the amount of work that a horse of *Hyperion*'s character and laziness required. After winning two unimportant races at Newmarket he finished an ignominious third in the Ascot Gold Cup before being beaten by a short head in a farcical two-horse race on the July course at Newmarket. After such a defeat Lord Derby decided to retire *Hyperion* to stud at his Woodland Stud, Newmarket, where *Chaucer*, *Swynford* and *Pharos* had stood. Fully booked at a fee of 400 guineas, *Hyperion* joined *Bosworth* and *Fairway*. The stud career of a horse who was to prove one of the greatest stallions in Turf history had begun.

Hyperion started his stud career in brilliant fashion. From his first crop he produced *Admiral's Walk*, *Heliopolis* and *Casanova*. As three-year-olds they proved the best colts in the country with the exception of *Blue Peter*, and enabled *Hyperion* to be leading sire of the 1939 Royal Ascot meeting. In 1940 he was leading sire for the first time, and achieved his first Classic victories as a sire when *Godiva* won the One Thousand Guineas and the Oaks. He was again leading sire the following year due to the wartime Derby triumph of *Owen Tudor* and the St Leger success of *Sun Castle*. Before the end of the war *Sun Chariot*, *Hycilla*, *Sun Stream* and *Hypericum* had brought further renown and Classic victories. In the postwar years the influence of *Hyperion* reached out to every corner of the globe, for he remained at stud for twenty-five seasons. In 1950 he sired *Aureole* whose great victories as a four-year-old enabled him once again to stand at the head of the winning sires table.

Hyperion was painlessly destroyed at the age of thirty in December 1960, six months after his grandson *St Paddy* had won the Epsom Derby. He had been in failing

Right: 'Hyperion', one of the most influential stallions in modern Turf history. Painting by Sir Alfred Munnings.

health for some time, and bitterly resented any efforts to maintain his health by the doctoring of his food and drink with medicine. He seemed listless and paralysis of his near hind leg was causing him pain. The end of his sufferings at the hands of the veterinary surgeon who had looked after him for the past ten years was the sensible but heart-breaking solution.

In the year after his death Lord Derby commissioned John Skeaping to sculpt a life-size statue of *Hyperion* which now stands at the entrance to the Woodland Stud, as a memorial to one of the most influential horses in the history of the British Turf.

15

'Nearco'

NEARCO was bred by Signor Federico Tesio, the Italian genius who is entitled to be considered one of the greatest breeders of bloodstock in Turf history. His career had begun as an officer in the Italian cavalry, but whilst still a young man he decided to devote his life to the improvement of Italian bloodstock.

He toured the world visiting stud farms and examining breeding methods which he discussed with acknowledged experts. At heart a romantic, Tesio claimed that whilst in Patagonia he studied the way to listen to the stars and speak to horses after spending days amongst the herds who roamed the desolate country from the Andes to Cape Horn.

In 1898 Tesio established his stud at Dormello on the shores of Lake Maggiore. Eleven years later he achieved his first victory in an Italian Classic. During the next decade horses bred at Dormello monopolised Italian racing, but it was not until the mid-1920s that Tesio was successful in France and Italy. These triumphs proved to him that horses bred south of the Alps could be victorious when competing against top-class English and French Thoroughbreds.

Tesio was satisfied but his ambitions were still unfulfilled, for he was determined to breed a horse who would be hailed as the Champion of Europe. This ambition became a reality with *Nearco*, although even in his wildest dreams it is doubtful if Tesio imagined that the Dormello-bred colt would become one of the most influential stallions in the world.

Tesio bought *Nearco*'s granddam, *Catnip*, at the 1915 December sales at Newmarket for a mere seventy-five guineas. She appealed to him for she was classically bred, being by the Derby winner *Spearmint* out of *Sibola*, winner of the 1899 One Thousand Guineas. Even though the war news was causing prices to be low, Tesio's purchase was a bargain by any standards. In fact *Catnip* proved a gold mine, for her offspring won more than thirty races.

The best of her progeny was *Nogara*, who won the Italian Two Thousand Guineas and the Italian One Thousand Guineas. At stud *Nogara* produced a colt who won thirteen modest races before being sent to Lord Derby's great stallion *Pharos*, who was standing at the Haras d'Ouilly in Normandy. On 24 January 1935 *Nogara* gave birth to a colt foal to whom Tesio gave the name *Nearco*.

Unbeaten as a two-year-old, *Nearco* won the Italian Two Thousand Guineas and Derby in the early summer of 1938. At the end of June Tesio sent him to contest the Grand Prix de Paris at Longchamp.

His seventeen rivals included the winner of the English Derby, the winner of the French One Thousand Guineas and Oaks, and the winner and runner-up in the French Derby. It was one of the most high-class fields ever seen at Longchamp, and even Tesio was apprehensive that his beloved *Nearco* might not be equal to the occasion. He need not have feared, for *Nearco* won decisively, pulverised his opposition and was acclaimed as the Champion of Europe.

A week later Tesio sold *Nearco* to Mr Martin Benson for £60,000 – a prodigous sum for a Thoroughbred. Before the sale was allowed Tesio had to receive permission from Mussolini, as the colt was con-

sidered a valuable asset to Italian bloodstock. As recompense Tesio was made to promise that he would sell his next future champion to the Italian Government for £10,000 less than he would ask on the open market.

On 3 July *Nearco* arrived at his new owner's Newmarket stud, Beech House. Soon after his arrival a knowledgeable breeding expert wrote:

> There is no surer test of goodness than that a horse should look smaller than he really is. It is certain proof of correct balance and symmetry. He is more of a bay than a brown, lighter in colour than his sire *Pharos* who was a strong horse with very powerful quarters. I can see in *Nearco* many of *Pharos*'s finest attributes. He has not the same width of hip, but he has his sire's grand iron-like limbs and tendons. He is more like his progenitor in front than behind the saddle. He is higher at the withers, hence his deceptiveness in height. His withers run so far back that there is little behind him when he is saddled up. *Nearco*'s head cannot be faulted.

Nearco remained at Beech House Stud for the next nineteen years. At the age of twenty-three he developed cancer of the hip and pelvic bone and did not have sufficient strength to stand on his hind legs. He was painlessly destroyed at the Equine Research Station, Balaton Lodge, in June 1957.

As a sire *Nearco* had proved a brilliant success. For fifteen consecutive years he was in the leading ten in the sires list, was leading sire in 1947 and 1948, and second in 1949 and 1951. His Classic winners included *Dante*, *Nimbus*, *Sayajirao*, *Masaka* and *Neasham Belle*. His daughters bred two Derby winners, *Tulyar* and *Arctic Prince*.

Curiously, three of *Nearco*'s most influential offspring were not amongst his highest stakes winners during their racing careers. *Nasrullah*, bred by HH the Aga Khan, was a temperamental colt but at stud sired *Never Say Die*, *Nearula*, *Musidora* and *Grey Sovereign* before being exported to the United States of America where he sired *Nashua* and *Bold Ruler*. *Mossborough*, another of *Nearco*'s greatest progeny, sired *Ballymoss* whilst *Royal Charger* sired Classic winners before, like *Nasrullah*, being exported to the USA where he added to *Nearco*'s reputation by siring *Turn To*.

At the time of *Nearco*'s death there were more than eighty of his offspring standing at stud throughout the world. Signor Tesio had died three years earlier, but had lived long enough to bask in the glory brought to him and the Dormello stud by *Nearco*.

History is made up of 'ifs' but an interesting sidelight on *Nearco*'s influence on world bloodstock is the fact that when he was en route for Paris the train transporting him passed through the Modane Tunnel only a few hours before a landslide caused the tunnel's collapse. How very different the history of bloodstock might have been if his train had been involved in the disaster.

Left: The great Italian champion 'Nearco' painted by M. Lucas.
BY KIND PERMISSION OF E. BENSON ESQ

16

Flat Racing, 1939-1977

IN MANY RESPECTS racing has undergone more changes in the past thirty-plus years than in all the years prior to the Second World War, for starting-stalls, the Levy Board, evening racing, races for women, sponsorship and even the photo finish – all of which are now accepted as part of the normal turn of events – have been introduced since 1945.

At the end of the war racing, in common with every other spectator sport, enjoyed a tremendous boom. Many people had never been able to see any of the limited, zoned racing during the war, and for once in their lives they had money to spend. Racing was just one of the sports which reaped the benefit of this situation.

Crowds at the important races in those days were of quite remarkable proportions; photographs show hardly a visible blade of grass, apart from on the racecourse itself, and it is easy to wonder how the spectators were able to see anything of the racing.

With the dubious benefit of hindsight this boom may not in the long run have been a good thing for racing, any more than for such other sports as football,

cricket, boxing and speedway, which reaped the temporary harvest of the post-war spending spree. In all fairness racing authorities at the time cannot really be blamed for rubbing their hands and counting the cash, but arguably they should have done more than that.

In the early 1960s there came the establishment of the Horserace Betting Levy Board, following an investigation into the feasibility of such a scheme by a commission under the chairmanship of Sir Kenneth Peppiatt. This levy was imposed on bookmakers and the Totalisator, as it was believed that those who ran credit offices, without ever going onto a racecourse, were wholly dependent on racing for their considerable profits and yet failed to contribute towards the sport's well-being.

The levy was originally based on a firm's profits but later, when the Board was chaired by Lord Wigg, this was changed to the firm's turnover. The yield from the levy began around the £2 million mark in the early 1960s. The expected yield for 1975-6 was in the vicinity of £8 million.

Above: 'Nonoalco', winner of the 1974 Two Thousand Guineas at Newmarket.
E. G. BYRNE

Facing page: Leaving the paddock, Ebor meeting York 1966. BRITISH TOURIST AUTHORITY

The amounts brought in from the levy are not spent only on prize-money, but are also used for improvement to racecourse amenities.

Inevitably there have been arguments among interested parties as to how the levy's income should best be spent but in general terms the system has worked well in its dozen or so years of existence and it has not gone unnoticed that many other sports do not enjoy the benefits of a similar scheme.

Coincidentally with the advent of the Levy Board, whose first chairman was Field-Marshal Lord Harding of Petherton, the Betting and Gaming Act allowed the establishment of betting shops. For years there had been a permanent illegal trade in betting off the course, with bookmakers accepting bets via their runners on street corners and representatives in factories. All this was against the law and it was planned by the new Act that the arrival of betting shops, where those without credit accounts could bet in cash during the day, would eliminate illegal street betting.

To a very considerable extent it did so, and the fact that all office owners had to receive a permit from their local magistrates in order to run a betting shop meant that they and their office were down on official record. Thus their transactions were easily verified for imposing both the levy and, later on, the betting tax.

The betting tax was introduced by the Labour Government in 1966 when it was considered likely to raise £11 million a year. Various amendments, including a differential between on- and off-course bets, were introduced but the Government's take went up every year and is now around £100 million, ten times its original estimate.

The Levy Board's intention to raise prize-money has undoubtedly been successful in many cases. Their boosts to the added money of the Classics, for example, mean that the Derby, worth £35,000 for *Relko* in 1963, had soared to £74,000 three years later and to £89,000 in 1974.

Ordinary prize-money has advanced by nothing like such strides, so that with the inevitable effects of inflation run of the mill races are not worth much more than they were when the levy's proceeds were first directed towards prize-money. On the other hand training costs have gone up considerably, and it is now quite unrealistic to expect the cost of keeping a horse in training for a year, including entrance and jockey fees, to be less than £2,500.

Yet for many years the number of horses in training seemed to be going for ever upwards. The direct consequence was that many of the horses proved unable to win a race of any sort, for even the most modest of maiden events was almost always strongly contested. It was only in the autumn of 1974 that there was a general decline in the number of yearlings being bought to go into training.

At the highest level of competition, the Classics, there has been an interesting change of emphasis in the post-war years. In the period up to the mid-1960s the Classic and other big races went regularly to challengers from France, who carried off Britain's top prizes with a regularity which bordered on monotony. It was suggested that our bloodstock was defunct, that our training methods were obsolete, that our jockeys could not ride and that everything else was wrong too.

Then in the mid-1960s, when the success emphasis switched towards horses bred and bought in the United States, the same diagnosis was offered as the reason why every Classic and important race was not won by a horse with exclusively British connections. In fact the increasing number of American-breds racing and winning in England is far more the result of the international influence of racing throughout the world, which can be illustrated by the victories of Australian horses in the United States.

In the immediate post-war years the French winners of English Classics included *Pearl Diver*, *Galcador* and *My Love*, with the last two belonging to two of the most influential owners of all time in Anglo-French racing. *Galcador* carried the orange and grey colours of M Marcel Boussac, who retired only at the end of 1974 as the supremo of French racing, while *My Love* was owned by the Aga Khan, whose widespread resources were divided between England and France in the post-war years.

My Love was just one of the Aga's English Classic winners since 1945, for *Tulyar* also won the Derby and the St Leger, *Palestine* the Two Thousand Guineas, *Rose Royale* the One Thousand Guineas and *Masaka* the Oaks.

Nor was *Galcador* the only jewel in M Boussac's crown. He won the Oaks with *Asmena* and two St Legers in successive years with *Scratch* and *Talma*, the latter putting up one of the most remarkable performances ever witnessed in a Classic race. But whereas the Aga's success went on until his death and was followed by that of his son, Prince Aly Khan, and is still being enjoyed by the present Aga, M Boussac's English Classic fortunes have slumped since their halcyon days of the 1950s.

The Aga and M Boussac were by no means the only owners to whom Classic success came almost as a matter of course. The late Sir Victor Sassoon won four Derbys in eight years with *Pinza*, *Crepello*, *Hard Ridden* and *St Paddy*, to which *Crepello* added the Two Thousand Guineas and *St Paddy* the St Leger. Sir Victor's success was not confined to his colts, for he also won the One Thousand Guineas with *Honeylight*.

Pinza's success was one of the most popular results that British racing has ever known, and not only because he was one of two co-favourites. The reason for the tremendous acclaim he received was that he was ridden by Gordon Richards, beyond doubt one of the best jockeys ever seen, certainly one of the most popular, and at long last riding the winner of the Derby.

For nearly thirty years Richards had dominated the jockeys' championship. He invariably had ridden well-fancied horses in the Derby and yet success had always eluded him until now. A short while before the Epsom summer meeting he had been created a knight, the first and only jockey so far to receive such an honour. *Pinza*'s four lengths defeat of Her Majesty the Queen's colt *Aureole* was the signal for cheering, conspicuous by both its length and its sincerity.

Only just over a year later, however, Richards was forced to retire after he fractured his pelvis when thrown by a two-year-old filly owned by the Queen as they left the Sandown parade ring. Thus ended a career which set record after record with 21,384 mounts and 4,870 winners, 269 of them in one season. Such winning figures are the best ever achieved in this country.

British racing has always somehow needed to have a jockey hero to represent it. Before Gordon Richards it was Steve Donoghue, and in the years since his retirement it has been Lester Piggott.

Piggott, who comes from a long line of successful riders, was already a well-known name when Sir Gordon retired in 1954. He had won the previous year's Derby at the age of eighteen, on *Never Say Die*, and thus became the youngest jockey to win the race with the solitary exception of John Parsons, successful on *Caractacus* in 1862. In his early days Lester's conspicuous determination to win often led him into trouble with the authorities but this same quality has in many ways been responsible for his success. He rides all over the world, often on a schedule of amazing severity, and can reduce a natural bodily weight of 10st or more down to as little as 8st 4lbs (with a barely visible saddle) for a greatly fancied mount in the height of the summer.

He won the jockeys' championship in 1960, taking over from Douglas Smith, who had won in five of the six seasons since Sir Gordon Richards' retirement, lost it to the Australian Scobie Breasley a year later, but regained it in 1964 and retained it for the next seven consecutive years.

He has inevitably been associated with some of the very best horses to race in this country and his partnership with New-market trainer Noel Murless was one of the features of the post-war era. Hardly a season went by without them winning a classic. *Crepello*, in Piggott's opinion one of the five best horses he ever rode, the filly *Petite Etoile* and *St Paddy* were three of the most outstanding of their Classic successes.

Piggott's rivalry with Breasley was one of the interesting battles of the era. Breasley was one of the vanguard – and was certainly one of the most artistic jockeys – who came over to the British Isles from Australia in the years following the Second World War.

Some of these Australians were top class. Breasley and Bill Williamson undoubtedly came into this category. Others were up to the standard of their English rivals, but a number were distinctly mediocre and seemed to arrive simply to cash in on the temporary vogue adopted by a number of owners and trainers, that any jockey from Australia had *per se* to be better than his counterpart here.

Eventually the exposure of some of these jockeys for their real worth enabled the home team to assert themselves once more and nowadays the older school, including Joe Mercer, Edward Hide, Geoff Lewis and, inevitably, Piggott, fight out the championship with the younger element headed by Willie Carson and Pat Eddery, both of whom have been champions in the last three seasons. Breasley and Williamson have retired and Ron Hutchinson is virtually the only man from Australia who gets into competition now.

Noel Murless, whose long full-time association with Piggott ended in 1966 when the jockey opted to ride *Valoris* for Vincent O'Brien's stable in the Oaks, rather than Murless's *Varinia*, has been one of the absolutely top trainers in this period. O'Brien has likewise enjoyed outstanding success and the vast majority of his prestige race-runners in Europe have been ridden by Piggott.

Murless, who retired at the end of 1976 and was knighted in 1977, first headed the trainers' list in 1948 and has done so seven times since. O'Brien has headed his rivals in only one year, while others who have shown training ability of the highest quality have included Dick Hern, Peter Walwyn, Ian Balding, Sir Cecil Boyd-Rochfort and the late Sir Jack Jarvis (both of them of pre-war vintage) and O'Brien's counterpart Paddy Prendergast. Inevitably they all trained some of the best horses of the era at a time in which the standard of Classic winners varied from the truly great to the undeniably ordinary.

The most famous horse trained by O'Brien was *Nijinsky*, who in 1970 became the first winner of the Triple Crown since *Bahram* thirty-five years earlier. He was representative of one of the new trends in British racing, being owned by an American and bred in that country. There have been American horses on the scene for many

Above: **Lester Piggott on the scales under the watchful eye of his valet.**
GERRY CRANHAM, TRANSWORLD FEATURES

Right: **'Scobie' Breasley, one of the greatest Australian jockeys to ride in England.**
GERRY CRANHAM, TRANSWORLD FEATURES

years – *Iroquois* in 1881 had been the first American winner of the Derby – but in the 1960s they arrived in unprecedented numbers.

For all that, there can be no doubt that British racing was immeasurably the richer for the support it received from Paul Mellon, Charles Engelhard, John Hay Whitney and many other Americans. Mr Mellon, owner of the incomparable *Mill Reef*, and Mr Whitney had had horses in training here for some years but Mr Engelhard did not really appear on the scene until the 1960s.

In no time the combination of him, Vincent O'Brien and Lester Piggott met with victory after victory, headed by *Nijinsky*'s Triple Crown, and they were ably supported by *Ribocco* and *Ribero*, who were trained for Mr Engelhard by Fulke Johnson Houghton.

France and Italy also produced their own champions to grace British racing in the years after the war. The many good horses who came from France have included none superior to *Sea Bird II*, who won the 1965 Derby and later took the Prix de l'Arc de Triomphe in a style which can only be described as majestic. Italy's star was *Ribot*, dual winner of the Arc and later a brilliant stallion.

Sea Bird later went to stand at stud in Kentucky, where he sired *Allez France*, a filly of outstanding merit who climaxed her career by winning the Prix de l'Arc de Triomphe in 1974. English racegoers saw very little of this filly – she was surprisingly beaten in the 1973 and 1975 Champion – but we saw plenty of her great rival filly *Dahlia*.

In many ways *Dahlia* illustrated the international aspect that racing has now adopted. Bred in the United States, she was by a British-bred stallion out of an American mare and raced for a Texas oil millionaire. She was trained in France by a man of Hungarian-Turkish descent who originally began his profession in Egypt and she raced across the world.

Whatever the truth may be, racing has always been acquainted with those who are prepared to claim that it is one long chronicle of villainy from start to finish, and certainly it would be impossible to deny that there are skeletons in its cupboard. One of the problems which reared a very ugly head was that of doping, and there have been instances when the appearance of a horse – and its racecourse performance – have caused suspicion that its pre-race diet had included some effective stimulant.

Most serious, however, was doping to lose. The idea behind this practice was to administer a modest depressant to a horse that ought to be well fancied, not so much to prevent its running, but to prevent it from showing its best form. Armed with such knowledge the villains would then be able either to lay this horse at longer odds than it might have been, or alternatively to back its chief rival with increased confidence.

There was a time when neither the police nor the Jockey Club seemed to be making much headway in this sphere, and when doping was extended to cause steeplechasers to lose the crime took on even more serious proportions. However, in due course a number of villains were caught, the post-race dope testing procedure was greatly increased and the incidence of such crime subsided markedly. It is impossible to say it has gone for good, as the essence of any successful crime is for it to remain undetected, not just for its perpetrators to avoid detection; but, for all that, the integrity of racing has never been higher.

The system of dope testing – usually one or two winners and losing favourites, or some of each, chosen at random at each fixture – is financed by the Levy Board. It is they also who are responsible for the cost of the patrol camera film, the photo-finish and starting-stalls, and the racecourse commentaries.

All these are post-war innovations and none was received with greater opposition than starting-stalls. These, described as 'sardine tins' among the more printable expressions of their detractors, had long been in use in the United States, France and Australia before the Chesterfield Stakes, at Newmarket on 8 July 1965, earned itself a place in the record books by being the first British race started from stalls.

One of the arguments against them was the possibility of injury to a horse while entering or leaving the stalls. More strongly in their favour were the facts that even the best-schooled horse can lose his chance at the barrier if an ill-tutored rival gets in his way, and that if the end of races is to be decided by inches, with the help of the photo-finish, then the start should be as level as possible. Gradually the opposition to stalls faded away, their use steadily increased and, by the 1975 Flat season, they were in use for almost every programme.

The Epsom Derby

THE DERBY at Epsom, first run in the year 1780, is the most famous horserace in the world. For nearly two hundred years the history of the race has been packed with drama, for favourites have been nobbled, fortunes lost, winners disqualified and 100 to 1 outsiders successful. A modern Derby winner can command huge fees when he is retired to stud, and it is the ambition of every owner, breeder, trainer and jockey to win the 'Blue Riband of the Turf' – a phrase coined by Disraeli in the library of the House of Commons a few days after the 1848 Derby.

The first Derby, on Thursday, 4 May 1780, was run over a mile, and not until 1784 was the distance of the race changed to a mile and a half and the course altered so that it included the descent to Tattenham Corner. This course was unsatisfactory as the start and the first few furlongs were

by hordes of thoughtless admirers who even pulled hairs from his tail as souvenirs.

In 1801 a filly, *Eleanor*, made racing history by winning the Derby and the following day easily defeating her own sex in the Oaks. Since then five fillies have won the Derby: *Blink Bonny* (1857), *Shotover* (1882), *Signorinetta* (1908), *Tagalie* (1912) and *Fifinella* (1916).

Eleanor was owned by Sir Charles Bunbury whose colt *Diomed* had won the first Derby. A few days before *Eleanor*'s triumphs at Epsom her trainer, a man named Cox, was dangerously ill and not expected to recover. A priest was called to the dying man who was frantically trying to speak. The priest imagined it was a final confession which was to be uttered. To his surprise Cox struggled up in his bed, gasping: 'Depend upon it, *Eleanor* is a damned fine mare!' Within moments the

The Committee beg to inform the Nobility and Gentry frequenting Epsom Races that this elegant new Grandstand will be ready for the reception of company at the ensuing meeting. The Committee have provided a room for the members of the Jockey Club and the New Rooms at Newmarket, and for the Stewards of the Races ... The Magistrates for the County of Surrey are respectfully informed that they will be admitted free.

One of the most historic Derbys was that of 1837 – the first year of Queen Victoria's reign. It was the last Derby to be run on a Thursday, the first to be started by flag, and has been vividly described by Disraeli in his novel *Sybil*.

A few days before the race the eccentric elderly bachelor Lord Berners discovered

Above: Mrs N. Philips' 'Snow Knight', ridden by B. Taylor, winning the 1974 Derby.
E. G. BYRNE

out of sight of the spectators in the grandstand and consequently in 1848 the start was repositioned in Langley Bottom. This gave an uninterrupted view of the start, and also resulted in a stiff uphill climb in the first half-mile.

The unique characteristics of the course brutally expose the limitations of those three-year-olds devoid of stamina or lacking in speed, and many home reputations have been shattered within minutes at Epsom.

A Derby winner must show the ability to overcome the undulating twists and turns without becoming unbalanced, and also be able to cope with the hubbub and excitement caused by the enormous Derby Day crowds. At least one Derby favourite (*Fairway* in 1928) lost his chance before the start was reached due to being swamped

trainer was dead, but his final words proved true!

In those early years of the race the Prince of Wales often patronised Epsom, especially after his colt *Sir Thomas* had won the Derby in 1788. A contemporary commentator described the scene as the Prince, in his green jacket, white hat and tight-fitting nankeen pantaloons, watched the races from his wooden grandstand surrounded by his cronies, who included the Dukes of Bedford and Dorset, Lord Jersey and the dandy Beau Brummell.

When the young bucks became bored by the races they wagered on cock-fighting. When even this wearied them they made such bets as 'We the undersigned agree that the last person remaining unmarried shall receive one hundred guineas from each of the other three'.

The original grandstands were inadequate, and in 1830 an announcement appeared on the front page of the *Morning Chronicle*:

that his entry *Phosphorus* was lame. Although he had backed his colt to win £30,000 he wrote a letter to Weatherbys scratching the horse from the race. The letter was given to a servant to deliver. The servant had also backed *Phosphorus*, wagering far more than he could afford to lose. Guessing the contents of the letter he succumbed to temptation and tore it up! The story had a happy ending for *Phosphorus* recovered, won the Derby by the proverbial whisker, and Lord Berners, delighted to have won a fortune, forgave his servant.

The following year the Derby was won by the Epsom-trained outsider *Amato*, owned by Sir Gilbert Heathcote. It was the first year that Londoners were carried to the course by railway, but the company officials hopelessly underestimated the size of the crowds and by mid-day, although they had used every train at their disposal, many thousands of angry racegoers were still stranded at Nine Elms station, Battersea.

Amato's victory was popular, for Sir Gilbert Heathcote owned the land upon which the Derby paddock and parade ring were situated and lived at The Durdans, an estate which adjoined the course. Years

Above: Runners parading in front of the grandstand. BRITISH TOURIST AUTHORITY

Below: Racing at Epsom on Derby Day.
GERRY CRANHAM, TRANSWORLD FEATURES

later The Durdans was sold to the Earl of Rosebery.

Amato had never run before his Derby triumph, and broke down soon afterwards so that he never raced again. He was buried beneath a magnificent monument at The Durdans, and had his renown perpetuated by an Epsom inn named in his honour. Traditionally the name of the supposed Derby winner is chalked up every year at the *Amato* Well at the side of the inn.

In 1839 the Derby was run in a snowstorm. Such appalling conditions did not prevail in 1840 when Queen Victoria paid her first – and last – visit to the Derby. It was a great occasion for never before had a reigning monarch been to Epsom on Derby Day. The Epsom executive spent £200 preparing for the Queen's visit, the main problem being the creation of a new paddock for saddling the horses since the usual paddock had been turned into a promenade for the Queen.

The Queen and the Prince Consort attended the races on a glorious sunny afternoon, but their visit seemed less popular with the crowds than with the executive. The Derby winner, *Little Wonder*, was almost certainly a four-year-old, and his jockey, MacDonald, one of the

youngest stable-lads ever to ride in the race. Later in the afternoon the boy was presented to the Queen who, seeing his diminutive size, asked him his weight. To her surprise he answered 'Please, Ma'am, my master won't allow me to tell anyone my weight.'

The second occasion that the Derby was run in a snowstorm was 1867. Again the race was full of drama. It was won by *Hermit* who was owned by twenty-five-year-old Mr Henry Chaplin, an enormously wealthy Lincolnshire landowner and a friend of the Prince of Wales.

Three years earlier Chaplin had been engaged to Lady Florence Paget who eloped with the reckless and utterly improvident Marquis of Hastings. The marriage was a failure and Hastings, fawned upon by hordes of touts and hangers-on, gradually sank into the abyss of financial ruin. His gambles came unstuck, his estates were mortgaged and it was only a question of time before he would be unable to meet his commitments. Chaplin never appeared vindictive, although his fiancée's elopement, a *cause célèbre* of the social scene, caused him great unhappiness.

The Marquis of Hastings was convinced that *Hermit* could not win the Derby and wagered accordingly. *Hermit*'s victory cost Hastings more than £100,000, and he died soon afterwards, a broken man ashamed at the dishonour he had brought upon his family and true friends. At the date of his death, hounded by his creditors, he was only twenty-six years old.

Two years earlier *Gladiateur* became the second horse to win the Triple Crown (the Two Thousand Guineas, Derby and St Leger) and became known as 'The Avenger of Waterloo'. *Gladiateur*'s owner, Count de Lagrange, was the son of one of Napoleon's Marshals. His bloodstock in England was trained by Tom Jennings at Newmarket who sent out *Gladiateur* for his Triple Crown victories.

On the night of the Derby the Count was entertained to dinner at Marlborough House by the Prince of Wales. Amongst the other guests was Lord Derby, after whose ancestor the Epsom Classic had been named. *Gladiateur* was a brilliant colt, but his French breeding caused Admiral Rous to clamour that English breeders should look to their laurels. French breeders and racegoers were delighted at *Gladiateur*'s success and on Count de Lagrange's return to Paris he was lionised. When he took his seat in the Senate he was cheered to the echo.

West Australian (1853) was the first Triple Crown winner, *Gladiateur* the

second, *Lord Lyon* (1866) the third and *Ormonde* (1886) the fourth, and possibly the greatest horse ever to win at Epsom, bearing in mind that neither *Eclipse* nor *St Simon* competed in the Derby.

Ormonde, owned by the Duke of Westminster and ridden by Fred Archer who was to commit suicide in a fit of depression five months later, stood sixteen hands, and has been described as having good bone, perfect shoulders, a slightly short neck, and as being the most powerful Thoroughbred ever to look through a bridle.

On one occasion the Duke elected to ride *Ormonde* in a· gallop at Kingsclere, where the brilliant colt was trained by John Porter. Later the Duke said he felt that at every moment he was going to be shot over *Ormonde*'s head, so terrific was the colt's propelling power.

After his great victories *Ormonde* was guest of honour at a reception held at Grosvenor House. As he made his way from Waterloo Station all traffic was stopped on his behalf, and at Grosvenor House he was fed orchids and sugar by debutantes, before serenely returning to Kingsclere.

Such is the glorious uncertainty of racing that *Ormonde* was a failure at stud. He sired *Orme*, who would almost certainly have won the Derby had he not been doped, and *Orme* subsequently sired *Flying Fox*, Triple Crown winner in 1899, and *Orby*, the 1907 Derby winner, but otherwise *Ormonde* produced nothing of any account. He was sold to the Argentine, resold to a Californian breeder, and died in 1904. His skeleton was presented to the Natural History Museum in South Kensington.

The year after *Orby*'s Derby victory the 100 to 1 outsider, *Signorinetta*, won the Derby. Her breeding is both romantic and unorthodox for a Classic winner, as her dam *Signorina* was barren for her first ten years at stud. Then she produced *Signoro*, who finished third to *Cicero* in the 1905 Derby.

Encouraged by this success her owner, the Italian Chevalier Ginistrelli, acquired a nomination to the fashionable sire *Cyllene*, but at the last moment the nomination was withdrawn. The Chevalier had noticed that whenever a stallion named *Chaleureux*, whose principal victory had been the 1898 Cesarewitch, was led past *Signorina*'s paddock she whinnied softly and insistently. The stallion always answered. Exclaiming 'They love each other, they shall be married', the romantic Chevalier arranged the mating. The result of the love match was *Signorinetta*, who won not only the Derby but also the Oaks.

In 1913, the last Epsom Derby before the European catastrophe, another 100 to 1 outsider, *Aboyeur*, was successful in the Derby. The favourite *Craganour* had been first past the post, but following a Stewards' enquiry he was disqualified. The entire proceedings were involved, and even today there are factors which have never been satisfactorily explained concerning the outcome of the race.

Moments earlier a suffragette had rushed out onto the course as the Derby runners descended to Tattenham Corner and brought down the King's horse *Anmer*. The reason for this incident has never been made clear, but the inescapable truth is that to deliberately bring down one pre-determined horse is virtually impossible.

After the suffragette's death it was suggested that she had brought down King George V's horse as a protest, but this theory does not seem valid. Neither, however, does the theory that she thought the race to be over and was merely walking across the course to the railway station to return to London.

Falls in the Derby have caused accidents and at times results which have not truly represented the merits of some of the contenders.

In 1899 the American jockey Tod Sloan had been introduced to the owner of the brilliant French colt *Holocauste* at the Savoy Hotel and had been engaged to ride the colt. *Holocauste* was second favourite to the great horse *Flying Fox*, who had already won the Two Thousand Guineas. There seemed little chance of beating the Duke of Westminster's champion, but on Derby Day there were five false starts and on each occasion *Flying Fox* raced nearly a quarter of a mile before he was pulled up. Meanwhile *Holocauste* stood quietly at the start with Sloan's confidence steadily increasing.

Years later in his autobiography Sloan wrote:

At last at the sixth attempt we were off.

We went up the hill to the top and raced down to Tattenham Corner. I was a neck in front of *Flying Fox*, and to my delight saw that Morny had got his whip out on the favourite. Before that I had not the remotest idea of actually beating him, and anyhow, I should have had no pretensions to do so if it had not been for these false starts. We crossed the tan road and had only about a furlong and a half to go, with *Flying Fox* well beaten by this time and *Holocauste* not having been called upon for any effort at all. Suddenly something happened – I thought I had been cut into. There was a shock, and it was as much as I could do to keep in the saddle. The poor beggar rolled from side to side but he did not come down as many have asserted that he did. He was a horrible sight with his leg broken off short. I was never more certain then or now that I had another horse beaten than I was that day about *Flying Fox* . . .

Ten years later the American favourite, *Sir Martin*, was brought down, interfering with *Bayardo*. Few gave more than scant attention to this for *Minoru* was catching the leaders with every stride and as the winning post was reached was a short head to the good. As *Minoru* was owned by King Edward VII the scenes on Epsom Downs were more jubilant than ever known in living memory.

Steve Donoghue was peerless at Epsom, winning the Derby four times in five years on *Humorist*, *Captain Cuttle*, *Papyrus* and *Manna*. But he had a narrow escape from disaster in the 1920 Derby when his mount *Abbots Trace* fell a furlong from home after the tiring *Sarchedon* swerved towards him. Steve was given a crashing fall which looked appalling from the packed grandstands, for the oncoming horses did not appear to be able to avoid him. Steve, to the horror of the crowd, lay motionless for several moments before rising unsteadily to his feet. Miraculously no bones were broken, and to everyone's amazement he rode the winner of the fifth race.

Four years later as *Sansovino*, ridden by Tommy Weston, was winning in the colours of Lord Derby, one of the horses at the

rear of the field slipped up giving his young jockey a nasty tumble. The jockey trudged disconsolately back to the weighing room through the pouring rain, his face, racing silks and breeches plastered with mud and sodden grass. Outside the weighing room he was stopped by an official who mistook him for a racecourse tipster. As he pulled off his soaking wet riding kit the jockey thought that the miserable afternoon would be the most eventful Derby Day of his life. The jockey was Charlie Smirke, who years later was to win the Derby on *Windsor Lad*, *Mahmoud* and *Tulyar*.

Since the end of the Second World War other falls have marred the Derby. In 1958 the French favourite was brought to his knees at the top of the hill, and the following year *Shantung*, also favourite, was thought by his experienced jockey to have broken a leg and was virtually pulled up. In 1960 the French favourite *Angers* broke a fetlock six furlongs from home, whilst in 1962 occurred the worst collision in the history of the race when seven horses were brought down in the wake of *Romulus*. Luckily only Harry Carr, riding the favourite *Hethersett*, received serious injuries in a mêlée which might have been catastrophic.

For almost two centuries Derby Day has been a traditional part of English life. Attended by Royalty, by the aristocracy, by gypsies and by costermongers, and, as one spectator in the 1920s noted, 'by fat women in purple satin with ostrich feathers in their bonnets, and babies galore in traps with their fathers blowing cornets and drinking stout,' the afternoon has become a national institution. The remarks of one foreign visitor sum up the drama of the occasion:

The roar of a great crowd is a wonderful noise, it seems to have as many distinct sounds in it as Niagara. If you can hear the sea in it you can also hear the Carillon of Bruges and the hooting of steamships on the Banks. But I believe that no crowd, not even a New York baseball crowd at a great baseball match, roars so long and so loud as the Derby Day thousands roar.

18
Royal Ascot

QUEEN ANNE'S chief amusements were dancing, playing cards and hunting in Windsor Forest. She enjoyed the sport of horseracing, maintained a stable of Thoroughbreds at Newmarket and paid one thousand guineas for a horse which she presented to her Consort. In the summer of 1711 she commanded that a racemeeting should be organised on Ascot Heath and announced that she intended to give 'Her Majesty's Plate of one hundred guineas' to the winner.

Originally it had been decreed that the race should take place on 7 August, but the date was postponed, and not until four days later did the Queen drive from Windsor Castle to watch the afternoon's sport, attended by her courtiers and her maids of honour (who included the leading beauty of the era, mounted on a palfrey and wearing a long white riding coat and a cocked hat bound with gold lace). The Queen was pleased that the meeting was a success, and ordered the Master of the Buckhounds to arrange a similar entertainment in a month's time. Under her royal patronage Ascot races flourished.

Today, Ascot is acknowledged as one of the world's premier racecourses, and upon its lush green turf world champion Thoroughbreds compete for some of racing's richest prestige prizes. Every June, Classic winners try to add to their laurels and overseas challengers attempt to enhance their reputation by a Royal Ascot victory. Yet Royal Ascot is much more than a racemeeting *par excellence*, for it represents a part of England's heritage.

During the four glorious days women bedeck themselves in their most extravagant summer finery, men look their sartorially elegant best, and the world's fashion writers and society columnists swoon and croon over the scene. More prominence is given to the eating of strawberries and cream and the drinking of champagne than to world economic news, and the dress of a glamorous débutante photographed at Royal Ascot may be given more newspaper coverage than the exploits of a political leader.

Above all else, however, the Ascot meeting is *royal*, and the royal procession is the highlight. As the five open landaus, bringing members of the royal family and their guests from Windsor Castle, drive up the course each afternoon the spectacle is unsurpassable for pageantry and splendour. Outriders in scarlet coats and gold-laced top hats precede the first carriage in which are the Sovereign and the Master of the Horse, and each landau is drawn by four horses whose bewigged postillions are magnificently attired in purple, gold and scarlet livery. Each year, on the Saturday prior to Royal Ascot, the Hanoverian Cleveland Bay and Oldenburgh mares and geldings who comprise the horses used in

Queen Anne (1665-1714), founder of Ascot racecourse. ILLUSTRATED LONDON NEWS

the procession leave the Royal Mews at Buckingham Palace for Windsor. Every morning during Royal Ascot week the horses are inspected at noon by the Crown Equerry and the Master of the Horse before departing for Duke's Lane in Windsor Great Park to await the arrival of the Queen, members of the royal family and her guests who are to make the two and a half mile drive to Ascot racecourse.

After the death of Queen Anne Ascot races fell into a decline which lasted until the time when William Augustus, Duke of Cumberland, was appointed Ranger of Windsor Great Park and went to live at Ranger's Lodge. During the winter months he hunted the red deer in the Park and the surrounding country where 'the broom and the gorse and here and there impassable bogs and sheets of water dirty and deep' made hunting difficult for both horses and hounds. The Hunt servants, in their gold and scarlet livery, would single out from the herd the day's quarry. Those who wished to run their horses for the King's Guineas at Ascot races had to apply to the huntsmen for tickets by being present when the deer was pulled down by the hounds.

Nine years before the end of the eighteenth century Ascot staged the richest race held in the kingdom. The 1971 Epsom Derby was worth a little more than one thousand pounds to the winner, but The Oatlands at Ascot was a sweepstake for which there were forty-one subscribers at one hundred guineas each. Racing England

became madly excited at the prospect of the race, and as the great day approached all roads led to Ascot.

An enormous crowd, estimated at 50,000, watched *Baronet*, owned by the Prince of Wales, and ridden by Sam Chifney, win by half a length. The betting was fast and furious, the Prince won nearly twenty thousand pounds and more than half a million pounds changed hands on the result. After the race King George III congratulated his son and commented: 'Your Baronets are more productive than mine. I made fourteen last week, but I get nothing by them. Your single *Baronet* is worth all mine put together.'

There was no grandstand from which the royal party could watch the race, but an elaborate marquee had been erected for their use. Noblemen drew up their carriages and cabriolets to line the sides of the course, whilst scattered over the Heath were hundreds of tents in which the race crowds could gamble, drink or watch prize fights. Pickpockets, thieves and footpads were much in evidence and many of the afternoon's winners returned home in misery having been relieved of their purses and wallets.

The Prince of Wales forsook racing in 1793 and did not rekindle his interest for nearly thirty years, by which time he was King George IV. As King he made the first processional drive from Windsor Castle to Ascot races, arriving in a coach and four escorted by his Master of the Horse and outriders.

The institution of the royal procession caused an editorial in *The Sporting Magazine* to state:

It is owing to the presence of Royalty alone that Ascot undoubtedly ranks first amongst all our provincial meetings, and now that His Majesty has again taken to the Turf, the public seem more anxious than ever, by their attendance at the meeting, to evince their entire approval of his noble conduct in so spiritedly coming forward to support this our grandest and most beneficial of all British sports.

In 1829 the King saw one of the most memorable races ever held at Ascot: the Gold Cup, for which the runners included two Derby winners, a winner of the St Leger, a winner of the Oaks and the 1828 Gold Cup winner. A contemporary describing the scene wrote:

Thursday was considered by all as the grandest day ever seen at Ascot, both as to number of people, elegance of dress, and rank in life, and what they came to see was never equalled in the memory of the oldest man, nor recorded in history, apt as old men are to fancy what wonderful things were done in their younger days . . .

Sadly, the Gold Cup fell in prestige within two years due to the rule that horses belonging to anyone not a member of White's, Brooks's or the Jockey Club were not allowed to compete. Such a rule resulted in only two runners facing the starter in 1831.

After the death of George IV, his brother, King William IV, though not a great racing enthusiast, became patron of Ascot, and in 1836 at the annual dinner that he gave to members of the Jockey Club in St James's Palace insisted that the future of Ascot be discussed. Five Dukes and eight Earls were present at the dinner, at which it was agreed that a new grandstand should be built and that during race week the Master of the Buckhounds should be assisted by members of the Jockey Club in organising the details of the meeting.

Modern Ascot owes much to the kindly King William, who might easily have taken a dislike to the meeting after an old man dressed as a sailor threw a stone at him there. The stone hit the King's hat, causing no harm, and when it was realised that he was unhurt 'a great cheer of loyalty burst forth' from the grandstand.

Throughout the history of Royal Ascot the Masters of the Buckhounds, an ancient office created by Edward III, have played an important role. Sir William Wyndham was Master at the time Queen Anne ordered the first meeting to be organised, and it was his duty to supervise the preparations. In 1836 the Master was the Earl of Erroll, who had married a daughter of William IV. Under his guidance the plans for the new grandstand were drawn up,

and the foundation stone was laid in 1839. To finance the cost of the construction a company was formed with a capital of £10,000. At the same time another stand was built for the Master of the Buckhounds, beneath which were the weighing room, a jockeys' dressing-room and a room for the judge.

During the latter half of the nineteenth century other distinguished Masters of the Buckhounds were the Earl of Bessborough, the Earl of Hardwicke and the Earl of Coventry. Each of them is commemorated by races at the Royal Ascot meeting.

The Buckhounds were abolished during the reign of Edward VII and subsequently the Ascot Authority Act was passed in 1913, by which the Sovereign was empowered to appoint a representative and other trustees at Ascot 'to promote the success, welfare and prosperity of Ascot Races', subject only to the wishes of the Sovereign.

During the past hundred years many of the greatest horses in Turf history have triumphed at Royal Ascot. The Coventry Stakes for two-year-olds was won in 1902 by *Rock Sand*, in 1903 by *St Amant* and in 1904 by *Cicero*. What a record – for each of these champions went on as a three-year-old to win the Epsom Derby. In more recent times the Coventry has been won by such brilliant horses as *Fairway*, *Tudor Minstrel* and *Mill Reef*.

The Ascot Gold Cup, instituted in 1807, is today shorn of some of its prestige owing to the fact that breeders are reluctant to patronise stallions who are out-and-out stayers. But its list of victors includes *Touchstone*, *Isonomy*, *St Simon*, *Bayardo*, *Solario* and *Precipitation*, all of whom have greatly influenced bloodstock breeding.

In 1844 the Emperor of Russia visited Royal Ascot as the guest of Queen Victoria. He insisted on presenting annually a piece of plate valued at £500 to be raced for in lieu of the Gold Cup, and the race was renamed The Emperor's Plate. It might still bear that name if it had not been for the Crimean War.

Perhaps the greatest drama of all in the history of the Ascot Gold Cup occurred in 1907. As the race was being run, the actual Cup, supposedly guarded whilst on display at the back of the grandstand, was *stolen* and has never been recovered!

The Royal Hunt Cup has always been regarded as one of the biggest gambling races of the meeting. The first Royal Hunt Cup had been won by *Knight of the Whistle*, owned by the Earl of Chesterfield who had been Master of the Buckhounds. The Earl hunted the Buckhounds for three seasons with complete disregard for expense, and with equal disregard for the fact that the opulence in which he lived was ruining him.

One of the most outstanding handicappers to win the Royal Hunt Cup was *Irish Elegance*, who carried the record weight of 9st 11lb to victory in 1919. Owned by theatrical impresario and financier Jimmy White, *Irish Elegance* was almost scratched at the last moment because White learned a few days before the Royal Ascot meeting that he had been refused admission to the Royal Enclosure. In a fury he threatened to withdraw the horse, who was a public idol, but he was calmed down by his trainer, Harry Cottrill, who stood to win a small fortune if *Irish Elegance* was successful. With the typical brash confidence which had made him a millionaire, White turned to a friend just before the off and told him that if *Irish Elegance* did not win, he could have the horse for a fiver. After *Irish Elegance*'s victory Jimmy White gave his jockey a hundred shares in one of his property companies. The shares rapidly increased in value in the post-war boom and the jockey sold them at a very considerable profit.

No mention of Royal Ascot would be complete without reference to the record of the gallant *Brown Jack*, who won the Queen Alexandra Stakes – the longest Flat race in England – for six consecutive years. In an age devoid of television he was hero-worshipped for his indomitable courage from Land's End to John o' Groats. Owned by Sir Harold Wernher and invariably ridden by Steve Donoghue, he became the idol of Royal Ascot. Some years he made

Left: The finish of the Emperor's Cup, June 1845. FORES SPORTING GALLERY

Above: The winner's enclosure at Royal Ascot.
DAVID HASTINGS

two appearances at the meeting, but the final day, Queen Alexandra Stakes day, was *his* day.

He was an old gentleman of ten when he won for the last time in 1934 and was already a legend. After his triumph the scenes of jubilation were the greatest ever witnessed at Royal Ascot, with police having to make a lane through the vast admiring crowd before *Brown Jack* and Donoghue could reach the unsaddling enclosure.

Perhaps the most happy consideration is that *Brown Jack*, one of the most intelligent of horses, knew exactly what was happening and was loving it. He adored the homage of his admirers and was perfectly content to allow them to pat him from head to tail and to grab handfuls of his tail as souvenirs. It was his day and he knew it.

One of the last men to be Master of the Buckhounds before they were abolished was Lord Ribblesdale. He came to the conclusion that the grandstands and the racecourse were not sited in relation to each other to give spectators the best possible view of the races. After lengthy deliberations it was agreed that ultimately the solution would be to alter the layout of the course.

Years later Lord Hamilton of Dalziel, His Majesty's Representative at Ascot, and the Duke of Norfolk, who was appointed His Majesty's Representative in 1945, came to the same conclusions as Lord Ribblesdale. In 1946 King George VI approved plans for the reconstruction of the course which included moving the straight mile from the Golden Gates. Fifteen years later the Queen Elizabeth II Grandstand was built, and in 1964 the new Royal Enclosure Stand completed.

During the past twenty-five years, Her Majesty the Queen has seen her colours victorious on fourteen occasions at Royal Ascot, whilst her horses have also been placed on twenty-four other occasions. The triumphs of *Choir Boy*, *Landau*, *Almeria*, *Hopeful Venture*, *Pall Mall*, *Aureole* and *Above Suspicion* have been acclaimed, for there is no racecourse in Britain upon which a royal success is more popular than at Royal Ascot.

No one would deny that the prestige races at Royal Ascot have a great influence upon the remainder of the season. The winners of the two-year-old races often stay unbeaten throughout their juvenile careers, whilst to win the St James's Palace Stakes over a mile, or the Hardwicke Stakes over a mile and a half, can set the seal on a horse's renown and add considerably to his value when he is retired to stud.

Except as media for gambling the handicaps are not of real significance. But they do add spice to the proceedings, and not so many years ago a punter remarked after a disastrous Royal Ascot, when none of the handicap favourites won, 'I lost £15,000. Thank heavens it wasn't £1,500, I could have paid that.'

Certainly there have been black Ascots, and the June weather has not always been as hot and sunny as anticipated. In 1930 a bookmaker sheltering under an umbrella was killed by lightning during a torrential storm, and as recently as 1964 heavy rain caused the abandonment of the final two days. Such a disaster showed the British attitude towards adversity, for a Scotsman remarked 'Wonderful day, really. Went to Royal Ascot on Gold Cup Day and didn't lose a bob,' whilst an elderly aristocrat was overheard telling a friend 'Damned glad I was there. Expect that they will be talking about this at the Club for as long as there is a Royal Ascot.'

If Royal Ascot was not a part of Britain's heritage such remarks could not have been made, for they imply a far greater regard for the occasion than would be awarded merely to a racemeeting. For more than two hundred and fifty years Royal Ascot has retained a unique importance in Turf history, and as a racecourse has no equal for splendour, quality and tradition.

Lester Piggott

LESTER PIGGOTT must be considered the greatest genius ever to have ridden under Jockey Club Rules. His achievements make him a legend in his lifetime, and his eight Derby victories at Epsom constitute a record which will never be equalled. Fred Archer, Steve Donoghue and Sir Gordon Richards were champions, but even their triumphs must take second place to those of Piggott.

He was born on Guy Fawkes day – 5 November 1935 – with racing in his blood. His father, Keith Piggott, had been a successful National Hunt jockey before becoming a trainer and sending out *Ayala* to win the 1963 Grand National, whilst his grandfather, Ernie Piggott, rode two Grand National winners, *Poethlyn* and *Jerry M.*, and married a sister of the famous jockeys, Mornington and Kempton Cannon. Lester's mother was a Rickaby, another renowned racing family.

Lester, precocious, self-confident and dedicated, rode his first winner at the age of twelve when he steered *The Chase* to victory at Haydock Park on 18 August 1948. Long before he rode *Mystery IX* to a brilliant victory in the Eclipse stakes at Sandown Park in 1951 he had captured the imagination of the press and the general public who christened him the 'Boy Wonder'. Hailed as an infant prodigy, he became the youngest jockey of the twentieth century to ride an Epsom Derby winner when he succeeded on *Never Say Die* in 1954. Two years earlier, at the tender age of sixteen, he had ridden the Derby runner-up, *Gay Time*, who finished second to *Tulyar*. On that occasion Lester wished to object to the winner on the grounds that C. Smirke and *Tulyar* had leant on him inside the final furlong, but he was persuaded not to do so by *Gay Time*'s owner, Mrs J. V. Rank, and trainer Noel Cannon. A month after *Never Say Die*'s Epsom triumph Lester was suspended for the remainder of the season after the Stewards had found him guilty of reckless riding on *Never Say Die* in the King Edward VII Stakes at Royal Ascot. He missed riding *Never Say Die* to victory in the St Leger and spent the next few months as a stable-boy with Jack Jarvis. At the end of September the Stewards lifted their ban, cutting short the sentence by almost two months, and Lester celebrated by winning at Newmarket on *Cardington King* on the first day of his return to the saddle.

Sir Gordon Richards retired from his distinguished career as a jockey at the end of 1954, leaving Noel Murless with the decision of selecting a new jockey for his powerful Warren Place stable. His selection of young Lester Piggott was an inspired choice, for the partnership of Murless and Piggott was to achieve brilliant success throughout the next decade, and reach its zenith at Epsom in June 1957 when Murless

sent out *Crepello* to win the Derby for Sir Victor Sassoon, and *Carrozza* to win the Oaks in the colours of Her Majesty the Queen. With Piggott riding with incomparable artistry and skill Murless-trained horses won virtually every prestige race in the Calendar, but inevitably the partnership foundered. Piggott was inundated with requests to ride horses for other stables in Classic races, and understandably wished to have *carte blanche* where the choice of his rides was concerned. Murless, equally understandably, could not contemplate an

Above: The 'Maestro', whose international reputation acknowledges his supremacy as the most accomplished jockey in modern Turf history. WALLIS PHOTOGRAPHERS

arrangement whereby his retained stable jockey wished to ride for other owners and trainers. The break occurred at the end of the 1966 season.

For the past twenty years Lester Piggott has ridden with a consummate genius which has deservedly made him an International sporting star. His record includes eight Epsom Derbies on *Never*

Say Die, Crepello, St Paddy, Sir Ivor, Nijinsky, Roberto, Empery and *The Minstrel*; four victories in the Oaks; seven in the St Leger; three in the Two Thousand Guineas; five in the King George VI and Queen Elizabeth Stakes; the Prix de l'Arc de Triomphe, the German Derby and the Washington DC International. Such a prodigious record highlights the fact that Lester, more than any other jockey, has the ability to rise to the big occasion. It also highlights his expertise as the supreme student of form, for he invariably selects the correct horse when offered a choice of mounts. In 1977 Vincent O'Brien had practically no intention of running *The Minstrel* in the Epsom Derby until Lester informed him that he would accept the ride and that Robert Sangster's colt would win. Such confidence after *The Minstrel*'s failures in the Two Thousand Guineas at Newmarket and the Irish Two Thousand at The Curragh! After these disappointments only a genius or a prophet, or both in the guise of Piggott, could have foreseen his Epsom triumph.

Lester Piggott is reputed to have made and retained a fortune, and to have worldwide interests in bloodstock. At times he is accused of being taciturn to the point of rudeness, but his accusers forget his deafness. Known as 'The Long Feller' and 'Pokerface', he is married to Susan, daughter of trainer Sam Armstrong, and has two teenage daughters, Maureen and Tracy. They live at Florizel, an unpretentious house at Newmarket where Lester loves nothing better than to relax from the trials and tribulations of a hectic racing week which may find him flying to Ireland and France in addition to riding all over England. Unlike Sir Gordon Richards, who had the good fortune not to put on weight during the racing season, Lester has to be careful.

At Epsom on the day of the 1977 Oaks Lester had the horrific experience of being dragged towards the paddock rails by his mount, *Durtal*, after her sweat-soaked girth failed to hold and the saddle slipped. Only a miracle could save him from serious injury or death, but as mesmerised spectators watched in terror, the miracle occurred, the stirrup leather broke and Lester was released – shocked, stunned, but with no bones broken. The next afternoon he rode the runner-up in the Prix du Jockey Club at Chantilly, and at Royal Ascot a fortnight later was leading jockey with seven victories to his credit. Such is the Piggott magic.

Below: Lester Piggott on 'The Minstrel' going to the post for the King George VI and Queen Elizabeth Diamond Stakes at Ascot, 23 July 1977, prior to their brilliant victory. WALLIS PHOTOGRAPHERS

Right: Two illustrations of Lester Piggott leaving the paddock at Newmarket on his way to the start. WALLIS PHOTOGRAPHERS

The St Leger

THE ST LEGER at Doncaster has been the highlight of the sporting year in Yorkshire for the past two centuries.

Racing had taken place on Town Moor since the earliest years of the seventeenth century, but not until 1776 did Doncaster Corporation decide to improve the course and erect a grandstand to replace the antiquated wooden structure which had housed the judge and some of the aristocratic spectators. Amongst these aristocrats were the Marquis of Rockingham and Lieutenant-General Anthony St Leger, both of whom were patrons of the Doncaster racemeetings.

In the same year that the Corporation provided £3,000 for improvements, a new sweepstake was inaugurated for three-year-old colts and fillies – to be run over two miles. In 1778 the Marquis of Rockingham proposed that the race should be named after his friend, St Leger, who lived at nearby Park Hill. The proposal was accepted and the first of the five English Classic races was born. It was the success of the St Leger Stakes which inspired Lord Derby and other members of the Jockey Club to organise the first Epsom Derby two years later.

In those early years of the St Leger the Corporation organised balls at the Mansion House and arranged plays at the newly built theatre during race week. The town was *en fête* and in the mornings crowds followed the local hunts, including the Badsworth, of which the Marquis of Rockingham was the Master.

The nobility attended the races every afternoon, often accompanied by an entourage of liveried servants. The Duke of Devonshire would come from Chatsworth and the Duke of Portland from Welbeck Abbey, but neither attempted to match the magnificent splendour of the cavalcade that brought Earl Fitzwilliam to the races. His coach was drawn by six bays, decorated with orange-coloured favours and rosettes, and attended by twenty outriders. In complete contrast was the elderly and eccentric Mr James Hirst, who lived at Wakefield and drove a rickety hand-made carriage to the races, the contraption frequently being drawn by a bull.

During raceweek the local shopkeepers and hostelries did a roaring trade, and took the opportunity of increasing their prices outrageously. One foreign visitor complained bitterly and wrote:

De Yorkshire are de damned rascal, noding without de guinea. We dine at de ordinary of de hotel, and have a dinner execrable! for which we pay a guinea. When we got to de stand to see the race, encore une guinea, and now that we go, dey charge a guinea for de stand of a carriage at the inn, et pour le lit de mon domestique, encore une guinea! Oh, foutre, noding without der guinea!

In 1806 the largest crowds ever known on Town Moor watched the St Leger, but the centre of attraction was not the favourite but the Prince of Wales, later King George IV, who was visiting Doncaster with his brother the Duke of Clarence. It was the first occasion upon which Royalty had attended the St Leger.

In 1813 the distance of the race was reduced from 2 miles to 1 mile 6 furlongs 193 yards. The winner was *Altisidora*, a tough filly who proved her fitness by winning a two-mile race an hour after her St Leger triumph.

Six years later the St Leger provided an astonishing fiasco – for the race was run *twice*. There were nineteen starters, but when the flag fell four took no part. *Antonio* was first past the winning post, but the Stewards immediately declared a false start and ordered the race to be re-run. On the second occasion there were only ten starters, with the exhausted *Antonio* not amongst them. A fortnight later the Stewards of the Jockey Club published their decision:

The Stewards of the Jockey Club having taken into consideration the case laid before them by the Stewards of Doncaster races respecting the St Leger, and having examined Mr Lockwood, the person appointed by the Stewards of Doncaster to start and judge the race, are decidedly of the opinion that the race should have been given to *Antonio*; and consequently that the Stewards should not have allowed a second race.

Perhaps the most interesting feature of this notice is the fact that the judge and the starter were the same person!

There is little doubt that at this time in Turf history nobbling, doping and nefarious practices were rife, and that the St Leger was no exception to the practice of rigging races. In 1827 the Derby winner, *Mameluke*, was backed by John Gully and his supporters to win a fortune, but no matter how much money was wagered upon him, the price never shortened. It was rumoured that Gully's great rival Crockford had arranged that, whatever else happened, *Mameluke* would not win. There were eight false starts to the St Leger, and when the starter finally said 'Go', *Mameluke* was left flatfooted almost a furlong behind his rivals. Gully was down at the start, a hunting whip in his hand, and in exasperation he urged his horse in the direction of the fast-disappearing rivals. The task was hopeless and *Mameluke* was beaten. The starter was subsequently sacked, but this was small compensation to Gully.

Although the Two Thousand Guineas had been inaugurated in 1809 it was not until 1853 that a horse won the Triple Crown. *West Australian*, bred by his eccentric owner John Bowes, was trained by the famous John Scott at Malton, and was described by Scott as 'a yellowish bay, rather long in the body, with a low stealing action that gave nothing away'. *West Australian* won the St Leger in a canter, and afterwards his jockey said, 'I only touched him once with the whip and I was glad to get him stopped'. The great champion was a very hard puller and even as a four-year-old, when he won the Ascot Gold Cup, his jockeys found him a handful to control.

John Scott trained fifteen St Leger winners during his distinguished career, in addition to five Derby winners and nine Oaks heroines. Unlike some of his contemporary trainers, he never galloped his fancied runners on the day before a Classic race. He invariably arrived at the races in a brougham, and wore a broad-brimmed hat, black coat, drab knee-breeches and gaiters, and a spotless white handkerchief. No man in England was more respected than Scott, who was often labelled 'The Wizard of the North'.

Before the end of the nineteenth century eight more horses had been acclaimed as Triple Crown winners. Two of them, *Ormonde* and *Flying Fox*, were owned by the Duke of Westminster and trained for him by John Porter at Kingsclere. Porter could well have been called 'The Wizard of the South'. He trained seven Derby winners and six St Leger victors.

In 1886 *Ormonde* followed up his Derby triumph, when he was ridden by Fred Archer, with two scintillating victories at Royal Ascot. He was then rested until Doncaster, although he had engagements at Goodwood. Porter held the belief (contrary to that of some modern trainers) that any colt who was being seriously trained for the St Leger should not have a race between Royal Ascot and Doncaster. He was convinced that it was not feasible to keep a horse at concert pitch for so long, and thought that there should be a period during which the horse could ease off and pick up something to work on in the ensuing months.

A few days before the St Leger, Porter was horrified to discover that there appeared to be something the matter with *Ormonde*'s wind. Despite this infirmity the great colt, starting at 7 to 1 on, won the St Leger with consummate ease. After the race *Ormonde*, his owner and his trainer were mobbed by the Yorkshire crowd, who have always venerated a true champion.

Later the Duke asked Porter if he would prefer £500 or a racehorse named *Kendall* as a present. *Kendall*, a chestnut colt by *Bend Or*, was the same age as the mighty

Ormonde, and as a two-year-old had won six races before breaking down. In trial gallops at Kingsclere he had beaten *Ormonde* by a length, only receiving one pound – which illustrated his ability: Porter had always thought *Kendall* to be a very honest tough colt who would have had a bright future if he had remained sound. He had no hesitation, therefore, in choosing to accept *Kendall* rather than a cheque.

The horse's subsequent career vindicated

Porter's decision in no uncertain terms. He was leased to Lord Wolverton, who was forming a stud near Blandford, for £300 a year. Before the lease was up Lord Wolverton died and his widow asked Porter to take back the stallion. Porter agreed, and then sold *Kendall* to Mr John Gubbins for £3,000. The stallion was sent to the Knockany Stud, Co Limerick, where he sired many top-class horses, including *Galtee More*, the Triple Crown winner of 1897.

Above: Colonel Anthony St Leger, from a print after a painting by Gainsborough.
DONCASTER MUSEUM

After *Galtee More*'s easy victory in the St Leger it was suggested by the executive of Lingfield Park that they would be willing to put up a huge prize for a match between him and the Prince of Wales' colt *Persimmon*, who had won the Derby and St Leger the previous year. The proposal

came to nothing, as *Persimmon* had already had a strenuous season.

The early years of the twentieth century saw the St Leger victories of two brilliant fillies – *Sceptre* (1902) and *Pretty Polly* (1904).

Within twelve years of *Pretty Polly*'s triumph the St Leger had been won by three colts who were to have an immense influence upon the future of bloodstock breeding. Curiously, two of these great horses, *Bayardo* and *Swynford*, failed even to gain a place in the Derby, whilst the third of the trio, *Hurry On*, never ran at Epsom.

Bayardo was owned by Mr A.W. Cox, who raced under the pseudonym of 'Mr Fairie', and had departed for Australia as a young man after failing to pass entrance exams to the Army. The founding of his immense fortune came about in extraordinary fashion. One evening he played poker. One of the losers could not pay his modest debt and offered to settle by giving shares in an apparently worthless Australian mining company. Mr Cox took the shares, which years later became worth a king's ransom.

Bayardo, as a three-year-old, suffered from sore shins and shelly feet, and consequently could not be trained on the firm ground which prevailed in the spring and early summer. By July conditions underfoot favoured him, and he won eleven races in succession, including the St Leger in which he trounced his Derby conqueror, *Minoru*, by more than six lengths. At stud *Bayardo* sired *Gainsborough*, sire of *Hyperion*, before his untimely death at the age of eleven.

The second of the trio was Lord Derby's *Swynford*, who won the St Leger in 1910, twelve months after *Bayardo*'s victory. *Bayardo* had taken his revenge on *Minoru*, and in a like manner *Swynford* turned the tables on *Lemberg* who had beaten him at Epsom. Sent to Lord Derby's stud, *Swynford* influenced the bloodstock industry through his son *Blandford*, sire of four Derby winners.

The last of the trio was *Hurry On*, who won the 1916 St Leger. He was trained by Fred Darling, who thought the massive colt was the best horse he ever trained. At stud *Hurry On* revived the line of the Godolphin Arabian and *Matchem*, his best son being *Precipitation*. Ten years after *Hurry On*'s Doncaster victory his son *Coronach* won the St Leger equally impressively.

The previous year it was again forcibly shown that by the autumn of their three-year-old careers some colts are only just coming to their best. *Solario* had been unplaced to *Manna* in the Derby, and although some onlookers thought him unlucky in losing a great deal of ground at the start, when he was caught up by a loose tape in the starting-gate, it is probable that at Epsom *Manna* was the better colt. Just over three months later *Solario* was infinitely superior; he won the St

Left: Emil Adam's painting of the Duke of Westminster's 'Ormonde', Fred Archer up, with his trainer John Porter.
THE JOCKEY CLUB (JOHN SLATER PHOTOGRAPHY LIMITED)

Leger comfortably, and went on to win the Ascot Gold Cup the following year. At stud he sired two Derby winners.

Before the outbreak of the Second World War other champions to triumph at Doncaster included *Fairway*, *Hyperion*, *Windsor Lad* and *Bahram*, the first Triple Crown winner for thirty-two years. This long period without a Triple Crown winner can be explained by countless factors – Derby winners subsequently breaking down, St Leger winners not acting on the Epsom gradients and a host of other reasons have been put forward by those wishing to interpret facts to prove some theory or hobbyhorse.

Despite such reasoning the inescapable fact remains that a truly great horse, trained by an able trainer and ridden with outstanding skill, can be, and should be, hailed as a Triple Crown winner. No three-year-old between the wars could achieve a greater feat. Today the achievement can be overshadowed by other considerations.

Since the end of the Second World War *Airborne*, *Tulyar*, *Never Say Die*, *St Paddy* and *Nijinsky* have won both the Epsom Derby and the Doncaster St Leger, whilst the filly *Meld* won the Oaks at Epsom and the final Classic at Doncaster. Only five such heroes and one heroine in thirty years!

There would seem to be two major reasons for this record, which in the eyes of some is lamentable. The first is the prestige, prize money and date of the Prix de l'Arc de Triomphe at Longchamp. Coming so soon after the running of the St Leger, it is inevitable that many owners and trainers set their sights on the French race, the richest in the world.

Secondly, the monetary value placed upon an Epsom Derby winner is so great that there is the temptation to move heaven and earth to ensure that he remains undefeated in any future race. There is no doubt that by early September many colts who were still backward in June are fulfilling the hopes and dreams of their owners and trainers. *Ragusa*, third in the 1963 Derby, was born so late in the year that on Derby Day he was in reality still a two-year-old. Four months later he won the St Leger by six lengths. Against such improving horses many owners of Derby winners are loath to risk the reputation of their supposed gold mine, for defeat can halve the potential value of a horse.

In some respects, therefore, the Doncaster St Leger is the loser in modern times, as a number of the best three-year-olds omit the race from their season's programme.

Yet the people of Yorkshire are great horse-lovers; it has been claimed that if a bridle is waved above a Yorkshireman's grave he will rise up and search out a horse. When a Yorkshire-bred horse, such as *Peleid* in 1973, wins the St Leger the cheers of the crowd almost take the roof off the grandstand, for no victory can be more popular. Whatever the future prestige of the St Leger, historically it is of the utmost importance, not only as the final leg of the Triple Crown but also as the inspiration which resulted in the establishing of the Epsom Classics.

21

Prix de l'Arc de Triomphe

OVER THE YEARS the value of all-age competition in racing has rightly gained in stature and importance. There was a time when the five English Classics were regarded as the supreme races of each season and of course they still hold a major part of the stage. But part of the essence of racing has always been the chance to compare horses of different generations. That is why the most valuable all-age races have an extra and undeniable significance.

It is justifiable for a Derby winner to be considered the best colt of his generation, but a far better yardstick of his ability comes from a battle between him and the Derby victor of the previous year.

Furthermore, the provision of top prize-money provides an extra and important incentive for owners to keep their horses in training after the age of three, with the chance to establish their reputations further.

Such increased prestige, apart from adding more stake-money to his owner's coffers, is bound to result in the horse being in high demand when he goes to stud. Such demand is likely to mean better quality mares, with the consequent chance of getting better quality winners and the whole thing – if it goes correctly – can be a permanently successful progression.

All racing countries have their star race for horses aged three and over. In England it is the King George VI and Queen Elizabeth Stakes and in France the Prix de l'Arc de Triomphe, while countries such as America, Italy, Germany and Australia have their own races of equal significance.

Even those who yield to no one in their chauvinistic support for anything English may find that it is difficult to get away from the conclusion that no single race carries more world-wide prestige than the Prix de l'Arc de Triomphe. It is the most valuable race in Europe, it invariably attracts top-class horses from many countries and has the big advantage, over other pretenders for that title, that its timing means trainers and owners are not unduly concerned about where to run their horses afterwards.

A trainer might be inclined to miss the King George VI and Queen Elizabeth Stakes with his colt if he feels, for example, that ground conditions are not quite right and that if the horse runs he could be out for the rest of the season should something go wrong. But with the Arc, which normally takes place on the first Sunday in October (it seldom varies from that day) the season is instantly over for many horses and any trouble they may incur can be allowed to fade away during the winter.

The Arc is run over the 'classic' distance of a mile and a half at the best-known Paris course, Longchamp. It would be over-stating the case in some ways to claim that Longchamp is the premier French track, for both the Prix du Jockey Club and the Prix de Diane (equivalents of the Derby and the Oaks) take place at Chantilly. For all that, Longchamp is almost certainly better known internationally.

For all its prestige the race is not outstandingly old, for it was first run in 1920, compared with 1836 for the Prix du Jockey Club and 1843 for the Prix de Diane. Even so it is considerably senior to the King George VI and Queen Elizabeth Stakes, which was started only in 1951 to coincide with the Festival of Britain.

Another aspect in which the Arc has almost invariably had the edge over the King George is the one of prize money. In the first year of the Ascot race when it did not have the Festival of Britain tag it was worth £23,302 for *Tulyar*'s owner, the Aga Khan. The Arc that autumn brought the same lucky owner another £29,704 via the three-lengths win of *Nuccio*.

By the mid-sixties, however, the balance of money power had tipped very firmly in France's favour. In 1966 *Aunt Edith*'s King George victory collected £29,167 for Colonel John Hornung, while *Bon Mot*'s earnings for Mr Walter Burmann were £86,531, nearly three times as much. The generous sponsorship from de Beers has in the last few years made a big difference to the King George and *Dahlia*'s second win in 1974 netted £81,240 for Mr Nelson Bunker Hunt, but even so that was some way behind the £128,363 which *Allez France* earned for M Daniel Wildenstein.

The huge amount of betting money diverted back into racing by the French government enables this vast prize money to be provided, and it is the Tiercé betting which makes such huge funds available.

The Tiercé – a pool competition to forecast the first three in a nominated major race each weekend (the Arc is obviously the one on its day) – is a direct benefit of the French tote monopoly and attracts a high percentage of the population who know little about racing but are attracted by the lure of winning a lot for a little. On that basis it is the equivalent of the British football pools.

The very first Prix de l'Arc de Triomphe, in 1920, was won by the three-year-old *Comrade* and then one of the many famous equine names made its appearance on the Arc's roll of honour. *Ksar*, who had cost the then vast sum of 151,000 francs as a yearling in 1919, won not only in 1921 but also the following year, besides taking the

Prix du Jockey Club, the Prix du Cadran and the Prix Royal Oak.

And *Ksar*'s name has been well perpetuated by the exploits of his progeny, headed by *Tourbillon*. In the 1962 Register of Thoroughbred Stallions *Ksar*'s name appears in twelve different pedigrees including *High Lupus*, *Right Royal* and *Tyrone*, while *Tourbillon* features in a dozen pedigrees in the 1972 issue.

In 1923 came the first Arc success for an English-trained horse when *Parth*, who had been third to *Papyrus* in the Epsom Derby, was successful; but, rather remarkably, in the first ten runnings of the race only *Massine*, apart from *Ksar* the second time, was successful as a four-year-old. All the other winners were second-season horses.

There were other famous names in the list of winners around this time. *Motrico*, who won in 1930 and 1932 (when he was seven), later became the maternal grandsire of that magnificent jumping stallion *Vulgan*. *Brantome*, who has been described as the best of *Blandford*'s many good sons, also took the Poule d'Essai, the Prix Royal Oak, the Prix Lupin and the juvenile Triple Crown in France. The third dual victor, *Corrida*, who was successful in 1936 and 1937, must be considered one of the greatest race mares in Turf history. Owned by M Marcel Boussac, this gallant filly almost established a unique record, for in 1935 she was third in the Arc, beaten by a neck and a neck after being unlucky in running. During the war, tragically, she vanished and her disappearance and ultimate fate still remain an unsolved mystery.

There was no race during the early part of the Second World War but the Arc was back on schedule in 1941, when it was won by *Le Pacha*. In 1943 and 1944 it took place at the now defunct track of Le Tremblay and in 1948 *Migoli* provided another triumph for England.

Two years later another of the great names reached the Longchamp winner's circle. This was M Francois Dupré's *Tantième*, who was also successful in 1951. He achieved high rank as a stallion, thanks to the splendid exploits of the full brothers *Match* and *Reliance*, their three-parts brother *Relko* (all three being out of that superlative broodmare *Relance*), *Tanerko* and *Danseur*.

But even *Tantième*'s fine record has to give best to another dual Arc hero of only a few years later – *Ribot*, one of the greatest racehorses and stallions of all time, who raced in the colours of the Italian genius

Right: 'Allez France', winner in 1974, with Yves Saint-Martin up. P. BERTRAND ET FILS

Signor Federico Tesio. He won in 1955 and 1956, and at stud more than just followed up his unbeaten sixteen-race career which also embraced the King George VI and Queen Elizabeth Stakes, the Premio del Jockey Club and the Gran Premio di Milano.

Ribot sired winner after winner after winner – *Molvedo*, who followed in his sire's Arc hoofprints, though not as a stallion, *Ragusa*, *Romulus*, *Tom Rolfe*, the full brothers *Ribero* and *Ribocco*, *Arts and Letters* and *Graustark* are just some of them.

In 1958 *Ballymoss* won the Arc for Ireland and the following year produced one of the race's most dramatic and controversial finishes when *Saint Crespin* and *Midnight Sun* passed the post inseparable, even with the aid of the camera. *Midnight Sun* was relegated to second and the race awarded to *Saint Crespin* outright.

Like every other important race the Arc has had its share of shock results. *Oroso* (54 to 1) in 1957 and *Soltikoff* (40 to 1) five years later come into that category, while the victory of another of *Ribot*'s sons, *Prince Royal* in 1964, was not well received in some quarters; he had finished last in his previous race, the Prix Royal Oak.

Prince Royal came between two of the race's top winners, the all-quality chestnut *Exbury* in 1963 and the spectacular *Sea Bird*. *Sea Bird*'s dismissal of a top-class field with an ease which bordered on contempt entitled him to be put on the same mark as *Ribot* as a racehorse. *Sea Bird*'s stallion career, which effectively was spent entirely in America, never scaled the

heights of his racing, but he got some good winners in the States and made a real mark with his magnificent daughter *Allez France*, who followed her sire's example and took the Arc in 1974.

Topyo carried the famous Volterra colours to another of the shock wins in 1967 – he returned 80 to 1 on the Pari Mutuel – but *Vaguely Noble*'s resounding triumph in the colours of the American Doctor Robert Franklyn the following season was widely foreseen. It made the huge gamble of paying a British record of 136,000 guineas for him the previous December seem a tip-top investment.

Vaguely Noble had spent his early days in England and by the time of his success there was an almost permanent challenge from the British Isles in an attempt to make good the long gap since *Migoli*'s victory. In 1969 there were high hopes that the splendid filly *Park Top* might do just that. But in a race which brought widespread criticism of her jockey, Lester Piggott, she went under to the Ascot Gold Cup victor *Levmoss*, who raced for the McGraths. This gave Ireland their second victory in a dozen years.

The following season it was the turn of *Ballymoss*'s trainer Vincent O'Brien to send over the apparent good thing. This was the unbeaten *Nijinsky*, the first winner of the English Triple Crown since *Bahram* in 1935. But *Nijinsky*, tasting defeat for the first time, was beaten very narrowly by *Sassafras*, and talk began that the Arc was a hoodoo race for Piggott.

In 1971 there was another very strong claimant from English shores and this time the army of supporters who make an annual pilgrimage to Longchamp were not disappointed. *Mill Reef*, trained by Ian Balding for his breeder Mr Paul Mellon,

and ridden by Geoff Lewis, followed up his successes in the Derby, the King George and the Eclipse by storming home to the exultant shouts of his British fans and to generous applause from the French as well.

Fillies took three of the first four places in 1972 when only the third home, *Homeric*, stood up for the colts against *San San*, *Rescousse* and *Regal Exception*. It was the first time they had done so well since *Samos* won from *Peniche* and *Corrida* (who went on to take the next two runnings) in 1935.

In 1973 Lester Piggott firmly eliminated any Arc hoodoo theory when he brought home *Rheingold* a clear-cut winner. The first prize thus left France for the third time in five seasons.

Excitement was added to the 1974 Arc by the fact that the injured Yves Saint-Martin had to have pain-killing injections before the race. They evidently worked, for he and *Allez France* won narrowly from *Comtesse de Loir* – a highly popular victory. This was yet another of the many dramas in the history of the race, for a contest as celebrated and important as the Prix de l'Arc de Triomphe can be guaranteed to provide its share of thrills.

In 1975 the race produced its biggest surprise in its history when the German-trained *Star Appeal* won at the odds of 119 to 1. *Star Appeal*, who had won valuable races in Italy and England that year and raced in five countries during the season, was ridden at Longchamp by his regular partner the English jockey Greville Starkey.

Freddie Head, who won on *Bon Mot III* in 1966, and *San San* in 1972, had his third Arc triumph in 1976 on the filly *Ivanjica*, trained by his father, Alec, earlier successful with *Nuccio* (1952) and *Saint Crespin*.

Below: Heroine 'Allez France' in her moment of glory. P. BERTRAND ET FILS

22

Racecourse
Technical Services

Above: Handlers loading runners into the stalls at Newmarket. RON HAMMOND

WHAT HAS BEEN the most popular introduction or improvement to British racing since the end of the Second World War? Is it starting-stalls? Is it the photo-finish? Is it the running commentary which enables every one to know what is happening in a race? Is it the camera patrol, which does away to a large extent with the ill-will which used to come from objections?

Former generations of racegoers would have been amazed at and highly appreciative of all the technical developments which are part of today's racing scene, and which we tend to take too much for granted. These improvements have only come about through much hard work, experiment and planning, and are costly to provide because British racing is decentralised and takes place on more than sixty courses spread throughout the kingdom.

The financial cost of providing photo-finish and race-timing, camera patrol, public address, race commentaries and starting-stalls is borne by the Horserace Betting Levy Board through a subsidiary company, Racecourse Technical Services, whose headquarters are at Raynes Park, while the cost of closed circuit television is borne by the racecourse itself. The company, whose Board is appointed by the Levy Board with representatives from the Jockey Club, the Levy Board and the Racecourse Association, has more than a hundred technical employees. During 1976 it has been responsible for a wide variety of technical services including race commentaries on 958 days on 61 courses, starting-stalls on 460 days on 38 courses, photo-finish on 895 days on 57 courses, camera

patrol on 649 days on 46 courses, and race-timing on 238 days on 16 flat courses. All this is in addition to exporting equipment to South America, Yugoslavia, Saudi Arabia, Jamaica, Sudan, Qatar, Iraq, Bahrain, Thailand, Malaya and Singapore. It is a prodigious undertaking which is successfully carried out for the benefit of British racing, in spite of the wide variety of factors involved.

It is generally considered that racing in Britain is more attractive than racing in America, and that is why many Americans cross the Atlantic to see their horses run at Newmarket, Epsom, York and Ascot. In the United States practically all racing is on 'dirt' tracks, and consequently there is

77

Above: Moments before the start at Chester. English handlers are considered the best in Europe. RON HAMMOND

no difficulty about racing six days a week for six weeks. It may make the racing singularly monotonous, but it has the advantage that technical services can be permanently installed. It becomes economic for individual racecourses to buy their own sets of starting-stalls and photo-finish equipment and to employ specialist sub-contractors to run these technical services. It is interesting, however, that Canada is moving away from sub-contractors to a central organisation like Racecourse Technical Services, despite Canada's great size.

It would be impossible for such a state of affairs to exist in Britain, because the racing is decentralised. The result is that the men and machines provided by Racecourse Technical Services are constantly on the move. Starting-stalls have to be specially designed so that they are sufficiently strong

to hold a Thoroughbred securely before the start of a race, but light enough to be towed long distances on special trailers from course to course at a speed which will enable them to be in action at Chester, perhaps, one day and York the next. The team must be prepared, during the Flat season, to be away from base for long periods, in sharp contrast to their American counterparts.

All races in Britain were started by flag until, at Newmarket in the autumn of 1897, a new-fangled starting-gate with tapes across it was introduced – much to the disgust of the reactionaries. The first trials of starting-stalls were carried out at Newmarket sixty-eight years later. Further trials were staged the following year and in October the Jockey Club and the Levy Board agreed to initiate a joint scheme which enabled starting-stalls to come into general use in 1967.

Today there are four starting-stalls teams – one for the south based at Kempton

Park, one for the Midlands based at Newmarket, one based at York and one in Scotland. The northern team of nine handlers is under the leadership of Peter Hickling.

Peter Hickling, born in Nottinghamshire, first went into racing as an apprentice. He joined the famous trainer Joe Lawson after he moved from Manton to Newmarket, and he was working in the stable when they sent out *Never Say Die* to win the Derby. Later he worked for Dick Perryman before increasing weight put paid to his chances of becoming a jockey.

When the first starting-stall team was formed in 1966 he became a recruit. The pay was good, he was still with horses and, although during the seven months of the Flat season he was often away from home, there was always the compensation of spending the winter months working a five-day week at Newmarket, carrying out starting-stall maintenance.

The qualifications required by handlers

bers allocated to them, with the odd numbers usually being put into the stalls first.

Some horses walk straight into the stalls of their own accord, or are led in by the handlers; a few dig in their toes and will not take the final few steps. Then the handlers' 'strong men' come into action. One man leads the horse and two, or even four, push from behind using a rope quoit so that they can keep out of the way of the rear hooves. If the horse is persistently reluctant he is blindfolded, usually walked around for a moment so that he temporarily loses his sense of direction, and then led into the stalls. If he still refuses – which seldom happens, except with a very green two-year-old – the starter may start the race without him. He will not have been 'under starter's orders' and consequently bets made upon him will not be lost (save any made ante-post).

The work of the starting-stall handlers is important, and requires a high degree of skill; so too does that of operating the photo-finish and camera patrol services. A system of photo-finish was introduced into American racing at the outset of the Second World War. In June 1944 the Jockey Club set up a committee to investigate whether photo-finish equipment of the

Below: Camera patrol ready for action.
RON HAMMOND

necessary precision and reliability could be designed and manufactured in England to satisfy the need for a photographic aid to the judge.

During the war enormous strides had been made by the RAF in the development of aerial photography, and by 1946 they had amassed a vast store of specialist knowledge on this complicated subject. In command of this sphere of technical photography was Group Captain F.C.V. Laws, the Deputy Director of Photography under the Directorate of Operations at the Air Ministry. Group Captain Laws was seconded to the Jockey Club as a technical adviser, thus enabling racing to benefit from his immense practical knowledge and wisdom where photography was concerned. In 1947 the photo-finish first was introduced into British racing, and was a direct application of a special camera used by the RAF for high-speed low-level photographic reconnaissance.

Its introduction meant that not only had

photo-finish control rooms to be sited high up in the main grandstand, but that the judge's box had to be immediately below, so that the image of the photo-finish film could be projected immediately and directly to the judge.

The very earliest trials were conducted on racedays at Epsom, using a darkroom tent in the stands. Much interest was taken in the results, but there was considerable confusion when, on one occasion, the operator produced a piece of clear film, and apologised to the expectant judge and committee for having accidentally put it into the wrong solution in the darkness of the tent! When the photo-finish was first tried at Newmarket there was no running water to develop the films and the necessary water had to be brought to the developing-room in buckets. Since these early days steady strides have been made and the most modern and exact equipment is used. The photo-finish is now also operated on National Hunt racecourses, and an additional bonus has been introduced in the form of a modern electronic timing system, which automatically records the time of each race on the film.

In 1957 the Jockey Club considered the possibility of introducing a picture surveillance system similar to that used in America, which is known as film patrol. The first British camera patrol unit was formed three years later. Thanks to the camera patrol there are now far fewer cases of dangerous and unfair riding, for a jockey knows perfectly well that if he bumps or bores another jockey, or rides dangerously, not only will the camera patrol show up his actions, but he will also be liable to lose the race in the Stewards' room and may be suspended for days, weeks or even months.

In 1965 the camera patrol service was further improved by introducing a 'scout' camera mounted on a smaller mobile tower which could be re-positioned on the course between races. Another innovation came in 1966 when long-range zoom lenses were taken into use to give greater continuity of viewing and consistency in image size. At the same time the Jockey Club decided to appoint a second Stewards' Secretary at meetings covered by the camera patrol to ensure that all films were viewed and the best use made of the valuable information provided. There are now four patrol teams (three film and one video, the latter being introduced in 1968). Recently the film units have been modernised to provide a much higher quality film, and the video was equipped with colour cameras. The patrol film was never of greater value than at Royal Ascot in 1974 when, having watched the film of the Queen Anne Stakes, the Stewards made racing history by disqualifying the first three!

Racecourse Technical Services, under the Managing Directorship of Colonel J.C.S. James, CEng, MIMechE, FIProdE, MBIM, also provides the public-address system on racecourses and a team of experts to give a running commentary on each race. Modern British racing, considered the best in the world, owes much of its reputation to the work performed by every branch of Racecourse Technical Services Ltd.

go far beyond the bounds of being able to pacify horses at the start. They must be mechanically minded and be able to tow the stalls by Landrover on an articulated trailer from racecourse to racecourse, in addition to moving them from the various starting gates during an afternoon's racing. Recently one of the green-coated handlers remarked, 'the whole thing is a matter of team work. One has got to go about it in a quiet unworried way. The horses can be a bit "geed up" when they arrive at the start. While we are checking their girths and putting them into the stalls most of us chat to them all the time. It is a good thing to talk to them, it gives them confidence to hear a friendly voice murmuring small talk. It amuses some of the spectators, but I know it helps.'

Once the girths are checked the starter calls the roll in front of the stalls and the numbers of the stalls for each horse. As the jockeys take their horses to the rear of the stalls the assistant starter calls out the num-

23

'Mill Reef'

BRITISH racing had its first sight of *Mill Reef*, the American-bred colt who was to prove the best home-trained middle distance horse for a great many years, on 13 May 1970. On that memorable afternoon the Salisbury Stakes was widely regarded as a certainty for *Fireside Chat*, another American-bred colt who had won in impressive style on his début at Newmarket. At the time the Salisbury race attracted little attention but in the light of subsequent events it should have done so, for *Mill Reef* won with consummate ease in the manner of a future champion.

Rather more than two years later *Mill Reef*'s career came to a sad and premature end, but during that time he had swept virtually all before him. Wins in the Prix de l'Arc de Triomphe at Longchamp, the King George VI and Queen Elizabeth Stakes at Ascot, the Epsom Derby and the Eclipse at Sandown had sent his reputation to a marvellous pinnacle, before he went to stand at the National Stud at Newmarket.

Mill Reef was one of the horses bred by the American Mr Paul Mellon and sent across the Atlantic from his stud at Rokeby in Virginia to be trained by Ian Balding in the small Berkshire village of Kingsclere. Over the years Mr Mellon had shown himself to be a true Anglophile and *Mill Reef*'s successes, followed by the decision to keep him at stud in England, made his owner-breeder more popular than ever.

Although *Mill Reef*'s sire, *Never Bend*, was not particularly well known in England – a situation which was soon to change smartly – his dam's line was much more familiar. She was the *Princequillo* mare *Milan Mill*, a half-sister to the One Thousand Guineas and Oaks runner-up, *Berkeley Springs*, and the useful handicapper *Goose Creek* – subsequently the sire of the brilliant steeplechaser *Tingle Creek*.

After Salisbury, *Mill Reef* went to Royal Ascot for the Coventry Stakes, a race which had been won by many future Derby winners. As the opposition consisted of only four sub-standard rivals *Mill Reef*'s eight lengths win in a canter was no more than expected. Anything else would have been a disaster.

A month later he went to France for the valuable Prix Robert Papin at Maisons Laffitte in which he was to clash with the English owned and trained *My Swallow*, another brilliant two-year-old. Fortune did not smile on *Mill Reef*. He had a rough journey over from England, had much the worse of the draw compared with *My Swallow*, and finally after a tremendous battle was beaten by a short head.

The hard race and the generally luckless experience left no mark on *Mill Reef*, as he showed four weeks later in the Gimcrack Stakes at York. Despite the fact that his

Above: A jubilant Geoff Lewis returning to the winner's enclosure at Epsom on Mr Paul Mellon's champion 'Mill Reef' after his Derby triumph in 1971. Lewis's partnership with 'Mill Reef' was the highlight of a career that began when Lewis was working as a diminutive page-boy at the Waldorf Hotel in London. Lewis, who was born four days before Christmas 1935, has had a long and successful association with the Kingsclere stable where Ian Balding trained 'Mill Reef'. At Epsom in 1971 he completed a unique treble riding the winner of the Derby, the Oaks and the Coronation Cup.
SPORT AND GENERAL

trainer feared the overnight storm would have made the going much too soft for him, *Mill Reef* simply annihilated his opponents. Floating over the rain-sodden ground as if he was skating, he came home on his own to win unchallenged by ten lengths.

By this victory *Mill Reef* was establishing himself as one of the very top two-year-olds in the country, so it was a rude shock to his ever-increasing army of admirers when he scrambled home by only a length in the Imperial Stakes at Kempton. His supporters were happier after the Dewhurst at Newmarket in which he had no difficulty in defeating two Irish colts, and equally content when the publication of

the Free Handicap saw him in second place, 1lb behind *My Swallow*, for this was a strict interpretation of the Prix Robert Papin form.

As a three-year-old *Mill Reef* resumed in the manner and supremacy that he had shown in 1970 by winning Newbury's Greenham Stakes at his leisure. Now the stage was set for a second clash with *My Swallow* in the first of the season's Classics. The field for the Two Thousand Guineas was small – only six went to the start – but it was assuredly select. Apart from *My Swallow* and *Mill Reef* the line-up included *Brigadier Gerard*, unbeaten in four starts the previous season climaxed by the Middle Park Stakes, and rated just 1lb behind *Mill Reef* in the Free Handicap. *Mill Reef* and *My Swallow* dominated the Guineas betting, but in the event both were defeated by *Brigadier Gerard* who took command inside the last quarter-mile and ran on powerfully to beat *Mill Reef* by three lengths.

This defeat did *Mill Reef*'s reputation no good at all and his chance in the Epsom Derby – in which neither *My Swallow* nor *Brigadier Gerard* were to compete – seemed temporarily to slump. But gradually others who had been put up as alternatives fell by the wayside, and on Derby Day *Mill Reef* was a clear favourite. Opinion held that if he stayed then he must win.

Such opinion proved correct. Approaching the final quarter-mile *Mill Reef* was clearly going so much better than his rivals that his stamina was the only doubt. This doubt was soon pushed aside as he stormed into the lead to win by two lengths.

The Derby began *Mill Reef*'s rocketing rise to real equine stardom and by the end of the season he was little short of a national hero. At Sandown in early July he pulverised his high-class opponents to win the Eclipse in record time, and three weeks later was splendidly impressive with a six-lengths triumph in the King George VI and Queen Elizabeth Stakes.

By this moment there cannot have been a racing man in England who did not think that *Mill Reef* had an outstanding chance in the Prix de l'Arc de Triomphe. Yet this was not the first time that such thoughts had apparently been fully justified only to come to nothing on the day. There had not been an English-trained winner of the Arc for twenty-three years, since *Migoli* in 1948. On Sunday 3 October 1971 the long disappointing gap was erased from memory.

It seemed as if half England had gone to Longchamp that day and as *Mill Reef* burst into the lead just inside the last quarter-mile the cheers went with him all the way to the winning post. Not just English cheers but also the cheers of the home spectators, for the French crowd, to their eternal credit, gave *Mill Reef* the sort of reception a horse of his quality deserved. As far as the English were concerned he was king of the world.

Nor was there any sign of his abdicating his kingdom the following year, which was resumed at Longchamp with a sparkling victory in the Prix Ganay. Now all the talk was about the possibility of a clash of the two champions, *Mill Reef* versus *Brigadier Gerard*. Such a clash would undoubtably be one of the races of the century. Then suddenly and inexplicably things started to go wrong. In the Coronation Cup at Epsom in June *Mill Reef* just managed to win in unimpressive fashion. A day or two later it became evident that he, like many of Ian Balding's other horses, was suffering from one of those accursed viruses which have plagued British racing so much in recent years.

Gradually *Mill Reef* recovered from this set-back, but the blows from the unkind Fates were anything but over. Various mishaps in training had ruled out any possibility of a second battle with *Brigadier Gerard*, and consequently stable sights were set firmly on a second Arc victory in the autumn.

Then remorseless cruel luck struck once more. One morning at the end of August *Mill Reef* was working on the gallops at Kingsclere when, for a reason that no one has been able to name, his near foreleg shattered. These tragic circumstances might have ended both his career and his life, but fortunately he was spared. There could be no more racing, but during an operation lasting seven hours *Mill Reef*'s near fore cannon-bone was screwed together by the veterinary surgeon Mr James Roberts. The operation was as great a success as anyone dared to hope.

Later *Mill Reef* was moved from Kingsclere to the National Stud at Newmarket, and syndicated at £50,000 a share (which placed a capital value upon him of two million pounds). Mr Mellon kept eight shares, and the Levy Board bought the same number. These eight shares are allotted by ballot at a fee of £15,000 (£7,500 non-returnable, plus £7,500 no-foal-no-fee).

Buyers hotly contested the sale of every yearling sired by *Mill Reef* who entered the sale ring, and the price of 202,000 guineas paid in the autumn of 1975 by Lady Beaverbrook for a colt by *Mill Reef* submitted by the Hon J.P. Philipps from his Dalham Hall stud showed the regard in which Mr Paul Mellon's colt was held.

Below: 'Mill Reef', one of the greatest champions of the Turf. FIONA VIGORS

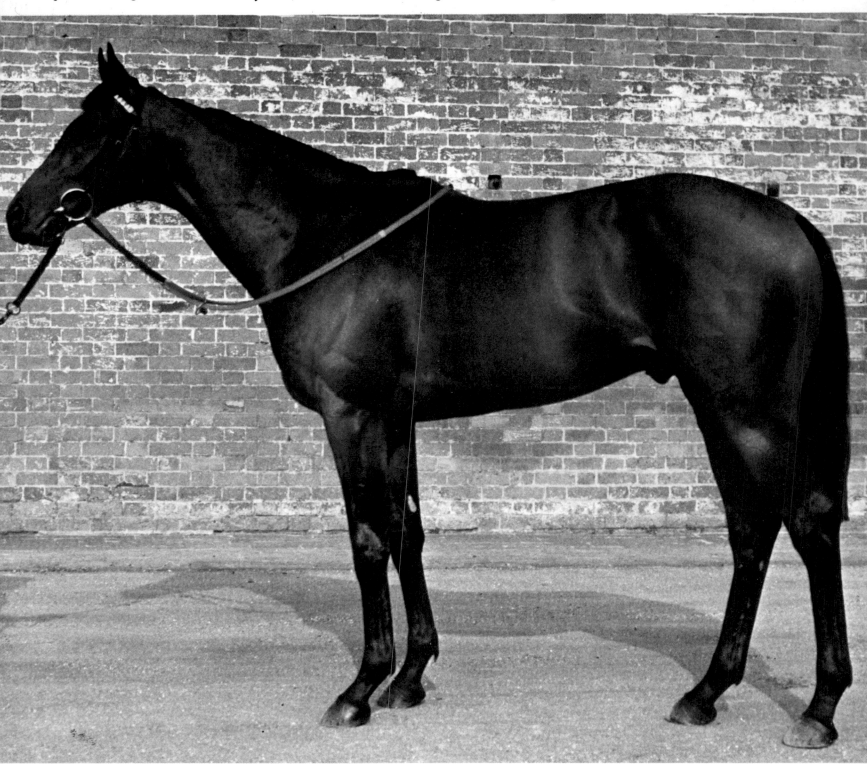

Two Centuries of Australian Racing

IN THE FINAL DECADE of the eighteenth century shipments of brood-mares arrived in Australia having crossed the Indian Ocean from the Cape of Good Hope. These broodmares, a very mixed collection in quality, were to become the nucleus from which modern-day Australian racing evolved. Thoroughbred stallions were also imported with the object of strengthening the breed, and the English-bred *Rockingham* was landed at Sydney in 1799 having made the journey from South Africa. Three years later *Northumberland*, the first stallion to be imported direct from England, arrived aboard SS *Buffalo*. Other stallions were imported from Persia and India and it was these horses who became the dominant influence when Australian racing was in its infancy.

Racemeetings were held at Parramatta and Sydney in the early years of the nineteenth century but they were crude events and often shared the afternoon with other sporting activities. Some of the meetings were organised by serving officers, others patronised by the Governor of New South Wales, Sir Thomas Brisbane, who was once described as 'the patron saint of the Australian Turf'. The Sydney Turf Club was founded in 1825, only a few years before the arrival of Captain Henry Rous RN, who visited Australia in his frigate HMS *Rainbow*. Rous, later to become the benevolent dictator of the British Turf, imported a stallion known as *Rous' Emigrant* and an Arab stallion which he called *Rainbow*. He was delighted to be lionised by the Australian Turf authorities and in return encouraged them to establish an Australian Jockey Club modelled upon its English counterpart, and with similar Rules, and in addition advocated that a greater number of English stallions should be imported. Nevertheless it was not until 1840 that the Australian Race Committee was formed. At that time a declaration was published which stated that

the nature of this country is eminently adapted to meet the purposes of the horse breeder, and there can be little doubt in the minds of those who have considered the subject with attention that as soon as the number of horses bred here shall be sufficiently extensive to supply our colonial demand, we shall find in the neighbouring settlements and in India a sure and steady market for all our surplus . . .

To advance horseracing the new Committee organised racemeetings at Home Bush outside Sydney. These races included the Metropolitan Plate and the St Leger

which became acknowledged as the first Australian Classic. By 1860 a new race-course had been opened at Randwick and the first Australian Jockey Club Derby contested. Originally the race was run in September but to please owners, breeders and trainers who complained that the date was too early in the spring it was changed to October. However, racing was not confined to New South Wales, for the middle of the century saw the establishment of racing in Victoria and South Australia. The first Melbourne Cup was held at Flemington, once little more than marshy ground alongside the Saltwater river, on 7 November 1861, and was won by *Archer*. Today this two-mile handicap is famed as the most important handicap contested in

the Southern hemisphere and the betting turnover from Darwin to the Australian Bight is prodigious, and the day tanta-mount to a national holiday. *Archer*, winner of the first two Melbourne Cups, had been bred in 1856 by Mr Charles Roberts of the Exeter Stud Farm in New South Wales. A bay horse of 16.2 hands, which was unusually large for the era, he had powerful hindquarters and the curious habit of letting his tongue loll from his mouth when galloping. Due to his powerful appearance he was known as 'The Bull'. After his two Melbourne Cup victories he was thought to be invincible, and when the weights were published for the 1862 race he was given the enormous burden of 11st 4lbs. He broke down in training and

was scratched, thus preventing the achievement of a unique treble. In October 1960 to commemorate the 100th Melbourne Cup a sepia 5p postage stamp was issued which bore a picture of *Archer*.

In 1859 the first Stud Book of New South Wales was published and twenty years later the Victorian Stud Book made its appearance, at a time when six enthusiasts who had originally met at Craig's Hotel in Ballarat formed the Victoria Amateur Turf Club. One of the first races organised by the Club was the one and a half mile Caulfield Cup. The first running took place on Saturday, 5 April – a day made miserable by strong winds which brought a pall of red dust which stunned and shocked spectators. There were fifty-five entries for the Cup but only fifteen starters. The winner was a very useful horse, *Newminster*, who had been favourite for the 1876 Victorian Derby but had been nobbled and found in his box in acute agony a few days before the race. In the Caulfield Cup *Newminster* was buffeted, baulked and consistently impeded, but still managed to win by a neck, much to the chagrin of those who had wagered heavily against him. By the middle of the century horseracing was firmly established and much of its history can be traced through the careers of successful stallions. One of the best English horses imported was *Fisherman*, who had won the Ascot Gold Cup in 1858 and 1859. An incredibly tough colt, he had won sixty-seven races before he was bought for the high price of 3,000 guineas by Mr Hurtle Fisher and sent to his Maribynrong Stud in Victoria. *Fisherman* died after only five seasons in Australia but he established a dynasty through his sons *Angler* and *Maribynrong* and his grandsons *Robinson Crusoe*, the leading sire of the 1886-7 season, and *Goldsbrough*.

Another influential stallion was *Musket*, bred in England by the eccentric Lord Glasgow, who bet in astronomical sums, changed his trainer once a month and thought nothing of chasing his huntsmen if no foxes were available! *Musket*, mated with a *Goldsbrough* mare, sired the mighty *Trenton* whose career was brilliant. On the racecourse he won eight of his thirteen starts – and two of his defeats were in Melbourne Cups. In 1885 he finished third, beaten a head and a head, and the subsequent year was second carrying the huge weight of 9st 5lbs. At stud he proved an outstanding success, was twice leading sire, second on three occasions and four times third on the Winning Sires List. Two of his sons were acclaimed as Melbourne Cup winners. In 1896, at the age of fifteen he was exported to England where one of his daughters, *Rosaline*, became the dam of *Rosedrop*, the dam of *Hyperion*'s sire *Gainsborough*, thus repaying to some extent the debt that Australian bloodstock owed to England. Another of *Trenton*'s daughters became the granddam of the renowned American racehorse *Bull Lea*, whilst his son *Torpoint* sired the dam of *Buchan*.

Four years after the birth of *Trenton*, *Musket* sired an even greater horse – the legendary *Carbine*. As a two-year-old, *Carbine* raced in New Zealand and proved the best of his generation, after having

been sired, foaled and reared at the Sylvia Park Stud near Auckland. In 1888 at the end of his three-year-old career he was sold for 3,000 guineas and the following year won the Sydney Cup. The next season he set up a record by winning the Melbourne Cup carrying 10st 5lbs. The Cup was worth £10,080 to the winner as compared to the £5,940 of the Epsom Derby. In total *Carbine* ran in forty-three races, won thirty-three, and was only once unplaced. The reason for this lapse was that he was lame. At stud in Australia he sired many top-class horses before being sold to the Duke of Portland for 13,000 guineas and shipped to England where he joined *St Simon*, *Ayrshire*, and *William the Third* at the Duke's Welbeck Stud in Nottinghamshire. It is of interest to note that *Carbine*, *Ayrshire* and *William the Third* commanded a stud fee of 200 guineas whilst the incomparable *St Simon*'s fee was 500 guineas. In England *Carbine* sired *Spearmint* who sired *Spion Kop* who sired *Felstead* – all three being the best of their generation at Epsom on Derby Day.

When *Carbine* was sold to the Duke of Portland the stipulation was made that the horse should be examined by a veterinary surgeon. In his report the vet stated that the horse was sound in body and limb but did not mention his wind. When attention was drawn to this omission the vet explained 'We never examine horses for their wind in Australia because roaring or wind ailments do not exist here.' *Carbine* was undoubtedly a champion racehorse and the eminent Dr W.J. Stewart McKay wrote:

> *Carbine* won at all distances, but was essentially a stayer and, like *St Simon*, he represents the horse changing from the old slow long distance horse with the endurance heart to the horse that was soon to acquire greater speed and the new true staying heart. In most of the races *Carbine* took part in the first part of the race was dawdled away and the horses did not begin to gallop until they reached the five-furlong post; then they began in earnest and often did the last four furlongs in fifty seconds . . .

An amusing story concerns the great Australian champion soon after his arrival at the Welbeck Stud. There was a heavy fall of snow, the like of which *Carbine* had never seen in Australia. When the door of his box was opened and *Carbine* saw the snow he pawed it with both feet, smelt it, shook his head and refused to leave his box. Finally he took a mouthful of the snow, bounded from his box and rolled in the snow for a full five minutes enjoying every second of the new experience. *Carbine* died at Welbeck at the age of twenty-seven after breaking a blood-vessel in his brain. His skeleton was presented by the Duke of Portland to the Museum in Melbourne and his skin to the Museum in Auckland.

Right: Australia's Racehorse of the Year 1975–76, 'Lord Dudley', painted by Michael Jeffery in 1976. VICTORIA RACING CLUB

A vivid description of Australian racing at the end of the nineteenth century is given by the novelist Nat Gould who lived in New South Wales and Victoria for eleven years:

There is no cramping on Australian courses; crowds are not driven into enclosures, much too small for them, like sheep, there is ample room for all. At Randwick and Flemington racing is carried on in a way that would astonish English racegoers. The charges are moderate. You can enter the lawn, ring and paddock for a couple of pounds for the four days on either course . . . and what of *Carbine*'s Melbourne Cup victory – he came along like a giant. He might have had 7st 5lbs instead of 10st 5lbs by the way he galloped. The cheers were deafening and there had never been such a crowd at Flemington before. People went frantic. They sent hats up in the air, and thousands of handkerchiefs and gaily coloured parasols were waved furiously . . . What a spectacle . . . he won. 'Old Jack' the popular hero, the best horse Australia had ever seen, the favourite – rolling home, victory never in doubt from the moment he made his run. Truly a magnificent exhibition of courage and a tribute to his sire *Musket* . . .

There was no doubt that by the end of the nineteenth century Australian-bred horses were tough individuals some of whom raced more than fifty times over extended distances. No horse was considered a hero merely because he had one or more Classic victories to his credit, and success under a welter burden in a Melbourne or a Caulfield Cup constituted a far greater triumph. Environment enabled a strong breed of horse to be reared in paddocks which basked in sunshine for most of the year, and Australian breeders attempted to raise horses whose principle characteristic was endurance. Only in the past sixty years has this policy altered.

It should not be overlooked, however, that one of the chief differences between European and North American horses and those bred in the Antipodes is the contrast in the seasons. Horses born in Europe and North America take their official birthday as 1 January each year, whilst in Australia and New Zealand their birthdate is considered to be 1 August – and consequently in International races it was difficult to assess the rival merits of horses from the three continents supposedly of the same generation. The Australian filly, *Mons Meg* won the Ascot Vase and *Merman* the 1895 Ascot Gold Cup in the colours of Lily Langtry; *The Grafter* was successful in the 1898 Melbourne Cup and two years later won the City and Suburban handicap at Epsom, but such examples prove little. Curiously, however, the records prove that in the first hundred years of racing in Australia the majority of the most influential horses were bred in New Zealand, even if they raced in Australia where prize-money was higher.

No racehorse has ever captured the imagination of the Australian public more than *Phar Lap*, the wonder horse whose fame rivals that of *Brown Jack* in England. *Phar Lap* was bred at Timaru in the South Island of New Zealand in 1926 and was sired by *Night Raider*, an undistinguished stallion who was a grandson of the champion *Bend Or*. *Phar Lap*, not being fashionably bred, attracted little attention in the sale ring as a yearling and was acquired for a paltry 160 guineas. As a yearling he was so big and backward that he was gelded. He won only one race as a two-year-old but improved to such an extent that in his second season he triumphed thirteen times, his victories inclu-

ding the Australian Racing Club and Victoria Racing Club Derbys and St Legers (the Rules did not preclude geldings running in the Classics). In 1930 he won the Melbourne Cup over two miles and the Futurity Stakes over seven furlongs to prove his versatility. Known to his adoring public as 'The Red Terror' he won thirty-six races before being sent to America to contest the Agua Caliente Handicap which he won easily to add to his legendary fame. Tragedy occurred a fortnight later when he died, struck down by a mysterious illness probably caused by eating poisoned grass. In Australia his death was considered a national calamity. His heart was sent to Australia where it was examined by leading veterinary surgeons. They pronounced that the thickness of the wall of the left ventricle was 4.2 centimetres – almost twice as thick as that of other horses. In their opinion the thickness of the wall of *Phar Lap*'s heart gave him an enormous advantage over his rivals due to its tractile power.

Since the era of *Phar Lap* Australian racing has produced many more champions including the New Zealand bred *Tulloch*, who at one time was an intended runner in the prestige English races for four-year-olds, *Todman*, *Star Kingdom*, *Vain* and *Rain Lover*. Australian horses have competed with success in the Washington International and at least one breeder with a world-wide reputation is contemplating sending his top stallions to serve mares in Australia during the breeding season in addition to his stud duties in Europe. As one looks to the future there is no doubt that where horseracing is concerned the sky is the limit in Australia.

Below: 'Swell Time', leading 'Gala Supreme', wins the Caulfield Cup in heavy conditions.

Horseracing in the USA

'Diomed', winner of the 1780 Derby, who found a new lease of life in America and founded a dynasty. THE JOCKEY CLUB

IT IS AN accepted fact, incredible though it may seem, that until 1519 when Cortes landed in Mexico with a dozen stallions and mares there had been no horses on the continent of America for thousands of years. The progeny of the horses imported by the Spanish conquistador began a new era in American equestrian history, and although some of the horses died, and others were stolen by the Indians and Incas, the breed survived. One hundred and fifty years later a racecourse was laid out on Long Island by Richard Nichols, Governor of the newly named New York State. Racing in New York and Virginia flourished, with Governor's prizes, plates and purses as rewards for the winners. The majority of the races were matches over distances of four miles or more, with the contestants relying upon stamina rather than speed to provide them with victory. By the middle of the eighteenth century racing was also taking place in Maryland where the sport was encouraged by Samuel Ogle who founded the Maryland Jockey Club in 1743.

Certain enterprising breeders in these States went to the lengths of importing English stallions, including *Bulle Rock*, a much vaunted son of the Darley Arabian, but the mares that they served were of little consequence. The first stallion to dominate bloodstock breeding in America was *Diomed* who deservedly has immortality in Turf history. In 1780 he won the

inaugural Derby at Epsom before standing at stud, firstly in Hampshire and subsequently on the Suffolk estate of his owner Sir Charles Bunbury. Unsuccessful as a stallion his fee eventually sank to the paltry sum of two guineas. At the age of twenty he was sold for fifty guineas to John Hoomes of Virginia for export to America. Shortly after crossing the Atlantic the stallion was resold for one thousand guineas to Colonel Selden. Curiously *Diomed* suddenly acquired a new lease of life, served his mares with alacrity and founded a dynasty before his death at the age of thirty. Such a new lease of life astounded breeders in England. The entire transaction, with *Diomed* changing from an unsuccessful stallion lacking in virility to a flamboyant character with a high percentage of success with his mares, has caused at least one Turf historian to puzzle as to whether or not an error was made and intentionally or unintentionally another stallion substituted for *Diomed*. The fact remains, however, that the stallion renowned as *Diomed* dominated American breeding for a decade, and his great-great-grandson, *Lexington*, headed the Winning Sires List from 1861 to 1874 and again in 1876 and 1878 to give him the unique feat of sixteen championships. *Lexington*, foaled in 1850, became the first champion American-bred Thoroughbred and sire and like *Diomed* is assured of a permanent place in the annals of the Turf. Yet the

story of *Lexington*'s career and that of his descendants is not entirely a success saga. The influence of *Lexington* saturated the pedigrees of American racing stock to the virtual exclusion of other blood-lines, and ultimately the passing of the 1913 Jersey Act in Britain caused *Lexington* to be excluded from the General Stud Book on the grounds that the pedigree of his dam, *Alice Carneal*, was not totally substantiated. The fundamental principle of the Jersey Act, brainchild of the Earl of Jersey, was that 'no horse or mare can, after this date, be considered as eligible for admission to the General Stud Book unless it can be traced without flaw on both sire and dam's side of its pedigree to horses and mares themselves already accepted in the earlier volumes of the Book'. The Jersey Act caused resentment amongst American breeders who considered it to be a deliberate attempt to protect the English Thoroughbred export trade. They continued with their bitter animosity until the repeal of the Act in 1949.

Horseracing in America came to a standstill throughout the Civil War but once re-organised at the end of hostilities took on a new aspect. By 1870 horses were no longer matched against each other at the

IROQUOIS.

private whim of their owners and the sport took on the role of entertainment for the general public, with bookmakers and betting playing a major part. Racing had taken place at Saratoga in New York State in 1863 and a decade later the Kentucky Derby was contested for the first time at Churchill Downs, Louisville. Breeders began to concentrate upon producing precocious two-year-olds and speedy three-year-olds as opposed to their pre-Civil War efforts to produce horses whose success depended upon endurance and staying power. Their efforts bore fruit and less than a decade later tobacco millionaire Pierre Lorillard sent some of his American bred yearlings to be trained at Newmarket. One of them, *Iroquois*, won the 1881 Epsom Derby and St Leger to prove to the world that American bred horses had arrived.

Throughout the subsequent thirty years racing took place all over the United States even if it did not always flourish. There were far too many racetracks (at one time as many as three hundred operated) and on many of them disreputable malpractice brought them dubious reputations. At the other end of the scale were the pretentious meetings organised by such men as Leonard Jerome, future grandfather of Sir Winston Churchill, and August Belmont, both of whom were men of initiative and integrity, and ambition for the future prosperity of American racing. Belmont, whose fortune had been founded by his association with the banking house of Rothschild whose interests he represented in the United States, inaugurated the Belmont Stakes in 1867. Men of his affluence raised the status of racing as owners, breeders and racetrack proprietors and their memory is perpetuated by races named in their honour. But the problem they faced was lack of centralisation of racing. Pierre Lorillard, James R. Keene, August Belmont and others eventually persuaded various vested interests to agree to the formation of a Jockey Club with seven Stewards and fifty members. The Club was established in 1894 and combined legislative, judicial and executive functions, wrote the Rules of Racing, and enforced them. It also licensed jockeys and trainers, appointed officials, allotted racing fixtures, maintained the forfeit list and took over the American Stud Book in 1896. The power of the Jockey Club became absolute, but it did not prevent racing declining into the doldrums in the years immediately prior to the First World War. In New York State an Act was passed prohibiting all betting and making each racetrack responsible for the enforcement of the new law. It was the death knell for many racetracks; bloodstock prices shrank to bargain basement figures and the Jersey Act became the

Above left: The American-bred horse, 'Iroquois', who won the Derby in 1881. KEENELAND LIBRARY, LEXINGTON, USA

Left: August Belmont II, a leader of the revival of American bloodstock breeding, from a painting by Chartran. NATIONAL MUSEUM OF RACING, SARATOGA SPRINGS, NEW YORK

final straw in the coffin of American breeders.

Steadily, however, a renaissance occurred, led by men of the calibre of August Belmont II who inherited the renowned Nursery Stud near Lexington, Kentucky, on the death of his father in 1890. When Sir James Miller died in 1906 Belmont purchased his Epsom Derby winner *Rock Sand*, who was shipped to America where he remained until his sale to a French syndicate in 1912. Belmont loved horses and saw in racing an opportunity for raising the standard and improving the quality of the Thoroughbred. A brilliant organiser, he arranged the unprecedented match in 1923 between *Papyrus*, the Epsom Derby winner, and *Zev*, who represented the best that America could produce to challenge his supremacy. Sadly the match, at Belmont Park, was a farce with the American champion winning easily as Steve Donoghue and *Papyrus* were totally unable to cope with underfoot conditions on the muddy rainsoaked track. Nevertheless the hospitality shown to the English party representing *Papyrus* was on a lavish scale and did much to cement Anglo-American racing relations.

Since the end of the First World War America has produced many champion Thoroughbreds, although significantly it was not until the mid-1930s that she seriously and consistently challenged the supremacy of European-bred horses. In the 1920s her outstanding hero was *Man O'War*, bred by August Belmont II, who won twenty races including the Preakness and the Belmont but had not been entered for the third leg of the Triple Crown, the Kentucky Derby. Idolised by the American public, and nicknamed 'Big Red', the mighty horse proved his influence at stud in no uncertain manner and Epsom Derby winners, *Never Say Die*, *Relko* and *Sir Ivor* can be traced back to him.

In the 1950s and 1960s other great champions have been hailed throughout America. *Citation*, *Tom Fool*, *Native Dancer*, *Hasty Road*, *Hail to Reason*, *Never Bend*, *Round Table Kelso*, *Nashua* and *Swaps* – the list is endless. No influence has been greater upon American breeding than the importation of HH Aga Khan's bloodstock through *Blenheim*, *Mahmoud*, *Bahram*, *Alibhai*, *Khaled* and above all *Nasrullah*. This colt, foaled in 1940, and sired by *Nearco*, had a racing career which was frustrating in the extreme. He should never have been defeated, but due to his temperament and apparent lack of resolution he failed on more than one occasion. Fourth in the war-time Two Thousand Guineas, third in the Derby and unplaced in the St Leger, he finally condescended to show his best form in the Champion Stakes which he won in the style of a brilliant colt. After one season at stud in England he was bought by Mr Joseph McGrath to stand at his Brownstown Stud in Ireland. Years later Arthur B. Hancock acquired him for his Claiborne Farm Stud at Paris, twenty miles from Lexington. Later Hancock was to write:

Right: HH Aga Khan's 'Nasrullah', who as a stallion had immense influence on American bloodstock breeding, photographed in 1951. KEENELAND-MEADORS, LEXINGTON, USA.

Below: 'Man O'War' who won twenty races in the colours of August Belmont II winning the Dwyer Stakes in 1920. KEENELAND-COOK, LEXINGTON, USA

I tried three times to buy *Nasrullah*. The first time was when he was first off the racetrack, and I was about two weeks late. Mr McGrath had bought him for Ireland. Then, several years later we were rather impressed with the horse and I formed a partnership between Mr Guggenheim, Mr Woodward, Mr Edward Taylor and myself, and we agreed to pay £100,000 for the horse . . . but the pound was devalued and the deal fell through . . . Eventually Mr McGrath and I worked the thing out whereby I gave him a service to the horse each year and paid him 340,000 dollars . . .

The deal was one of the greatest bargains in Turf history. *Nasrullah* proved an outstanding success before his death in May 1959 and the list of his famous progeny on both sides of the Atlantic reads like an equine Debrett. He has the distinction of being the only stallion to head the Winning Sires List in America and Britain, and must be considered one of the most influential sires of the century.

Two supreme champions in recent American Turf history are *Secretariat* and *Seattle Slew*. *Secretariat*, hailed in the USA as the greatest horse of the century, was foaled at the Meadow Stud in Virginia on the last day of March 1970. Sired by *Bold Ruler*, a son of *Nasrullah*, *Secretariat* was out of the mare *Something Royal* who only raced once and failed to win.

Below: The champion 'Secretariat' who, as a two-year-old, was voted American Horse of the Year. PACEMAKER MAGAZINE

After a stupendously successful career as a two-year-old *Secretariat* was voted Horse of the Year – the first two-year-old ever to be so highly honoured. Prior to his season's début as a three-year-old he was syndicated for a world record price of 6,080,000 dollars. It seemed an extraordinarily high and expensive price-tag,

Below: Another contemporary champion: 'Seattle Slew', the tenth winner of the American Triple Crown. DAN BALIOTTI-CLASSIC MAGAZINE

but six months later looked a bargain – for *Secretariat* had won the Kentucky Derby in record time and followed this triumph by winning the Preakness and the Belmont stakes. These victories enabled him to be acclaimed as the first Triple Crown winner since *Citation* in 1948 and as 'Super Horse' whose action was so perfect that he seemed to glide past his rivals in a style as effortless as that of a ballet dancer.

In 1977 *Seattle Slew* also achieved the distinction of winning the Triple Crown, becoming the tenth Triple Crown hero, but the first in American Turf history to

have attained this pinnacle of fame without ever having suffered defeat, and having won 717,720 dollars in the process. There is a possibility that *Seattle Slew* will contest the 1978 Prix de l'Arc de Triomphe and should he be victorious he too will become a Turf immortal and the story of his career a fairy-tale, for he was bought at auction as a yearling for a mere 17,500 dollars, and his trainer thirty-seven-year-old Billy Turner was a virtually unknown ex-steeple-chase jockey prior to the advent of his champion. Such is the fascination of Racing!

26

Three Great Australian Champions

THREE OUTSTANDING champions, *Phar Lap*, *Star Kingdom* and *Leilani*, highlight the greatest horses in Australian Turf history. The first of them, *Phar Lap*, became a legend in his lifetime and was described by his adoring fans as the most phenomenal racing machine ever seen, with immense courage, boundless stamina and a wonderful constitution. He was born on 4 October 1926 at Timaru in the South Island of New Zealand where the soil is rich in limestone and horses can be reared with strong sound bones and limbs. His sire, *Night Raider*, was an undistinguished grandson of the English Derby winner of 1880, *Bend Or*, owned by the Duke of Westminster. His dam, *Entreaty*, was by *Winkie* an imported son of *William the Third* who had won the Ascot Gold Cup in the colours of the Duke of Portland. *Entreaty* had broken down after only one race and had been sold for a paltry sixty guineas, but nevertheless was sufficiently well bred to produce a top-class horse, for *Winkie* was a brother of a One Thousand Guineas winner and was out of Lord Astor's renowned foundation mare *Conjure*.

The name *Phar Lap*, meaning lightning in the Thai language, was given to *Entreaty*'s second foal who was to become Australia's most famous racehorse. In January 1928 *Phar Lap* came under the auctioneer's hammer at the New Zealand Yearling Sales. When he appeared in the sale ring he seemed so gangling and unprepossessing a colt that no one spared him more than a cursory glance. Only one potential purchaser, Hugh Telford, was interested in him – and he was acting on behalf of his fifty-one-year-old brother Harry, who trained across the Tasman Sea. For the ridiculously low sum of 160 guineas *Phar Lap* was knocked down to Telford and shortly afterwards was shipped to Sydney, New South Wales. Harry Telford had bought the colt ostensibly for American Mr David J. Davis who had one look at him as he was disembarked before promptly stating that he thought the yearling seemed so undeveloped that he had no wish to buy him; he added that he would not contribute a shilling towards his keep. Such remarks put Telford in a quandary, for he could not afford to buy the horse himself. A compromise was reached that Davis would purchase *Phar Lap*, lease him to Telford for three years and take a third of any prize-money.

The yearling was gelded and subsequently was trained by Telford up and down the coastal sandhills outside Sydney. *Phar Lap* thrived on this unorthodox training which strengthened his legs as he laboured through the soft and sinking sand. As a two-year-old *Phar Lap* ran without distinction in four races before he won the Rosehill Maiden Juvenile handicap over six furlongs. No one watching this modest victory could have guessed the future triumphs that were in store!

His rise to stardom began the following season, when he won the AJC Derby, the Victoria Derby, the VRC St Leger, the AJC St Leger and finished third in a field of fourteen in the Melbourne Cup – the smallest in number for sixty years – after a race run at a muddling pace. His phenomenal record as a four- and five-year-old which resulted in a total of thirty-six victories made him a legend in his lifetime and brought from his countless admirers the name 'The Red Terror'. His victory in the 1930 Melbourne Cup, which he started

as the shortest-priced favourite in the history of the race despite the huge burden of 9st 12lbs, brought him immortality. A few days before this record achievement it was rumoured that an eccentric crackpot had fired a gun at him as he was returning from morning exercise. The rumour had been started by a group of newspaper reporters hoping to gain a sensational scoop from their misconceived hoax.

A year later *Phar Lap* was given the colossal weight of 10st 10lbs in the Melbourne Cup, and there were exaggerated rumours that if the mighty horse did not compete the race would be cancelled. Without doubt racecourse attendances were falling and the Flemington executive were afraid that *Phar Lap*'s non-appearance would adversely affect the attendance. He was not at his peak of condition on Cup day and it is feasible that without official pressure he might have been scratched. He finished eighth to *White Nose*, having been eased by his jockey nearing the end of the race when all hope of success had faded. The Melbourne Cup was his last race in Australia, for weeks later he was sent to New Zealand en route for San Francisco. A month after arriving in America he was sent 500 miles south across the border to contest the valuable Agua Caliente Handicap in Mexico. Huge crowds flocked to see the champion and when he won impressively under the top weight of 9st 3lbs many spectators announced that he was the greatest horse that they had ever seen in action. The executive Secretary of the New York Jockey Club acted as starter for the Agua Caliente Handicap and later commented:

. . . until passing the six furlong pole *Phar Lap* was restrained at the rear of the field. He was then urged forward, raced past rival after rival without effort and was in front three furlongs from home . . . maintaining his magnificent run and stride right to the line, he won with something in reserve . . . it was the finest and gamest performance I have ever been privileged to see in a lifetime of racing. There will never be another *Phar Lap* . . .

A fortnight later, on 5 April 1932, *Phar Lap* died in agony at Mento Park, California. His tragic death will always be surrounded by mystery and conjecture that he had been poisoned by hooligans and gangsters. In Australia his death was viewed as a national disaster. Australia was stunned beyond belief, but the probable true facts of the calamity were explained by the Australian veterinary surgeon who was with him at the time of his death and who carried out a post-mortem when he stated:

. . . it was a mixture of arsenate of lead and caustic soda that he swallowed with his food. A tree surgeon had sprayed trees in the area with this mixture using a high-pressure pump. He had done the job during a very high wind and the spray had penetrated a long distance. Analysts found the poisons in the straw on the floor of *Phar Lap*'s stable, in his chopped hay and oats, which had been imported from New Zealand, in his wheat bran and in the grass of the paddock in which he grazed. Because only small quantities were found in *Phar Lap* this has resulted in some people saying that poison was not the killer. But I say that the horse excreted most of the poison before he died . . .

After his death his heart was sent to Australia where it was examined by leading veterinary surgeons. They pronounced that the thickness of the wall of the left ventricle was 4.2 centimetres – almost twice as thick as that of any other horse. In their opinion the thickness of the wall of *Phar Lap*'s heart gave him an enormous advantage over his rivals due to its tractile power. Whether this is correct or not makes no difference. The truth is that *Phar Lap* was as beloved in Australia as was his contemporary in England, *Brown Jack*.

Star Kingdom, the second of the heroes, was bred by Mr Richard Ball at his Moorside and Reynoldstown Stud in Co Meath. Sired by HH Aga Khan's stallion *Stardust* out of an unraced mare, *Impromptu*, *Star King* (the name of the colt until he arrived in Australia) was bought as a yearling by publisher Mr Wilfred Harvey for 3,100 guineas. A neat and dapper colt who seemed slightly less robust than some of his contemporaries, *Star King* proved himself to be a flying machine in the spring of 1948 and in his two-year-old career won five of his six races including the historic Gimcrack Stakes at York. His only defeat came at Sandown when he was beaten a short head by another flying machine, *Abernant*, in one of the most epic two-year-

old races seen in England this century. As a three-year-old *Star King* won the Jersey stakes at Royal Ascot and two races later in the season, and added to his reputation in 1950 by winning at Chester before being bought by Mr Stanley Wootton.

The famous Wootton family had originally lived in Australia before making their home in England. Stanley Wootton, born in Sydney in 1897, was never as great a jockey as his brilliant elder brother Frank who was considered by many to be the equal of Fred Archer in the saddle, but he rode many winners before setting up training at Treadwell House, Epsom. A great trainer of apprentices in addition to horses, Stanley Wootton was responsible for putting Charlie Smirke, Staff Ingham and J. Sirett upon the road to fame.

In 1951 Stanley Wootton sent *Star King* to Australia where he was renamed *Star Kingdom*, and took up his duties as a stallion at Mr A. O. Ellison's Baramul Stud at Kerrabee in the Widden Valley, an offshoot of the Hunter Valley where the majority of Thoroughbreds are raised in the lush and fertile paddocks. The Baramul Stud, which extended for nearly fifteen miles along the Valley, had originally been a dairy farm before being acquired by Sydney solicitor Alwen Ellison in the early 1930s. When *Star Kingdom* first arrived at Baramul Ellison was unimpressed, for the horse looked bedraggled and lacking in condition after a lengthy and hazardous journey from England. Other breeders in the area were equally unimpressed and it appeared probable that no one would send fashionably-bred mares to be covered by the new arrival, particularly as he seemed to be on the small side. However he soon began to pick up condition in the warmth and sunshine of the Valley and served his mares efficiently. Less than a year later Ellison and Wootton were delighted with *Star Kingdom*'s first crop of foals for all seemed to have inherited the good qualities of their sire, had bold heads, excellent shoulders and an air of *joie de vivre* which stamped them as potential top-class horses.

No stallion has ever made a more promising start to his stud career than *Star Kingdom*, for his first crop included *Kingster* who won the AJC Breeder's Plate and *Ultrablue* who won the AJC Gimcrack Stakes, the fillies' equivalent. *Star Kingdom*'s achievement in siring the winners of both these two-year-old Classics was only the second occasion in Australian Turf history that the unique double had been completed in the same season. At the end of the year *Kingster* was rated the best two-year-old in Australia. Such success made *Star Kingdom*'s second crop much sought-after and at the annual Sydney Sales one of his yearling colts fetched 6,500 guineas, only 250 guineas below the record price ever attained for a yearling. The victories of *Kingster*, *Ultrablue*, *Starover* and *My Kingdom* made *Star Kingdom* the most coveted stallion in Australia and his great reputation even increased with his third crop which included *Todman*, *Concert Star* and *Gold Stakes*. *Concert Star* won the Gimcrack Stakes at Randwick by five lengths, the Débutante Stakes at Caulfield by the same margin, and then

won two races at Flemington in the first of which she numbered *Tulloch* amongst her defeated rivals.

Todman made his début at Randwick in December 1965, won by ten lengths and broke the track record in so doing. Later in the season *Todman* won the Golden Slipper Stakes by eight lengths and caused ace jockey Neville Selwood to state that *Todman* was the best two-year-old he had ever ridden, and possibly the best horse of any age that he had ever ridden. At the end of the season *Star Kingdom* finished second on the List of Winning Sires to Delville Wood, and if *Starover* and *Star Realm* had not been shipped to the USA early in

the season the placings would probably have been reversed.

In October 1958 *Star Kingdom* scored his first Classic success as a sire when *Skyline* won the AJC Derby. This victory repudiated the assertion that *Star Kingdom* could only sire sprinters. In his next crop *Star Kingdom* produced *Queenstar*, *Endure* and *Fine and Dandy* who headed the two-year-old Free Handicap after winning seven races, and the brilliant *Noholme*, a full brother to *Todman*. The victories of these horses enabled *Star Kingdom* to head the Winning Sires for the first time, and make Turf history by heading the Winning Two-Year-Old Sires for the fifth successive

year. Within the next twelve months the Victoria Derby triumph of *Sky High*, a brother of *Skyline*, set the seal on *Star Kingdom*'s immense reputation.

Star Kingdom died from a twisted gut in April 1967. To the end of the 1967 season his offspring had won 845 races in Australia worth 1,760,059 dollars – a stakes record for any horse who had been at stud in Australia or New Zealand. The great stallion was five times Australian Champion Sire and at the time of his death an international breeder wrote:

Star Kingdom was the greatest stallion influence, in immediate impact, in

Michael Jeffery
1975

Australian Thoroughbred history. With eighteen sons also at stud and regular high placings on the list of sires of broodmares, he seems assured, too, of lasting influence.

Alongside *Phar Lap* and *Star Kingdom* must be considered the heroine *Leilani*, whose name is a Hawaiian word meaning 'Heavenly Flower'. *Leilani*, raced on lease from her breeder Mr Ian McRae by Cabinet Minister Hon Andrew Peacock, who had been elected Federal Member of Parliament for Kooyong in 1966, and his friend Mr Ian Rice, was sired by *Oncidium*. This English-bred colt had won the 1965 Coronation Cup at Epsom from *Soderini* and a star-studded field and had started favourite for the Ascot Gold Cup before being sold by his owner-breeder, Lord Howard de Walden, to a New Zealand syndicate for a price reputed to be £60,000. Shortly after the deal was announced *Oncidium* was sent to the Te Parae stud of Mr and Mrs A. C. Williams at Masterton in the North Island. Prior to his death in July 1975 *Oncidium* rewrote the record books of racing in the Antipodes. He was twice Champion Sire in Australia and a filly from his final crop realised 120,000 dollars at the Trentham Sales. *Leilani*, his most brilliant daughter, was out of *Lei*, a mare by *Summertime*, who had won sixteen races at distances between six and ten furlongs and whom Mr McRae had bought for 400 guineas as a yearling. *Leilani* was her second foal, and was not robust as a youngster. Consequently her trainer Bart Cummings decided not to race her as a two-year-old. In the spring of 1973 she ran with some promise and later in the season won her first race – the St Clair Handicap at Caulfield – before being sent to Sydney where she won the AJC Oaks to prove herself the best middle-distance filly of her generation. Soon, however, she was to outstrip her own reputation and be hailed as the best racehorse in Australia and a mare of international class and prestige who was thought to be the finest racemare seen in Australia since *Wakeful* at the turn of the century.

After the AJC Oaks her next objective was the Caulfield Cup, but soon after her Classic victory she became lame and an X-ray examination showed that she had sustained a hair-line fracture in a hock bone during the Oaks. Six weeks later the plaster was removed and *Leilani* recommenced her training programme. In the new season she had her first race as a four-year-old in September, and within the space of five glorious weeks became a national idol. She began her scintillating campaign by capturing the Turnbull Stakes at Flemington and the Toorak Handicap which she won so convincingly on a miserably cold wet afternoon that bookmakers installed her as favourite for

the Caulfield Cup for which she was set to carry 52 kg (8 st 2 lb) – a weight too low for stable jockey Roy Higgins. Ridden by R. Mallyon she turned the valuable race into a procession on the very heavy and muddy ground to win comfortably by 2¾ lengths from *Broadway Hit* and *Turfcutter*, also sired by *Oncidium*, and thus become the eleventh mare to win the coveted Caulfield Cup. Many spectators thought that *Leilani* could add to her glory by becoming the second mare to win both Cups, thus emulating the achievement of *Rivette* in 1939. It was feared, however, that the weight she was set to carry and the distance might beat her. At Flemington, *Leilani*, the heroine of the vast crowd of nearly one hundred thousand and more fêted than a Hollywood film star, looked to have the Melbourne Cup in safe keeping a furlong from the winning post, but she was beaten by her stable-companion, *Think Big*, who swooped down without mercy to go a length clear at the line. *Leilani* was not to leave the Festival meeting empty-handed for on the final day she showed her astonishing recuperative powers after her gruelling race in the Melbourne Cup by winning the Queen's Cup, to shatter the existing record for winning stakes won by a racemare. At this moment in her wonderful career an admirer described her as 'wrought by a fine craftsman, she is lithe, feminine yet athletic, with a barrel which tapers sharply from a deep strong chest to exquisitely fine loins. Her long stride is relaxed and fluent and she is capable of instant acceleration.'

When *Leilani* returned to racing after a midsummer break it seemed at first that her outstanding ability was not impaired. She equalled the Sandown Park record for 1,400 metres and won over 1,800 metres at Caulfield. She seemed to be virtually invincible and the racecrowds adored her. She was entered for both the Australia Cup at Flemington and the Sydney Cup – both handicaps – and the thought was widely held that she might win each of these prestige events. En route for these prizes she won the Queen's Plate at Flemington but although she triumphed in the Australia Cup there was a suspicion that a little of her former fire and sparkle were missing and that she won only through sheer courage and tenacity. In Sydney she did not run for the Cup, and lost both of the two races that she contested, being second in the All Ages Stakes and defeated by a mere short half head in the Queen Elizabeth Randwick Stakes. Nevertheless, her career deservedly brought her the award of Australia's 'Racehorse of the Year' after a brilliant record of thirteen wins, six seconds, three thirds and one fourth from a total of twenty-three starts which had amassed 254,305 dollars in prize-money during the seasons when her exploits had thrilled Australians from the Gulf of Carpentaria to the Bass Straits.

Left: 'Leilani,' as a Four-Year-Old, was the Australian Racehorse of the Year for 1974-75. In that year she had nine wins and was otherwise placed four times in fourteen starts, and won $A222,150. Michael Jeffery's portrait, painted in 1975, shows the champion with Roy Higgins up. VICTORIA RACING CLUB

27

Stallions

FASHIONS IN STALLIONS change faster than in almost any other sphere. A horse can be at the top of the popularity poll one season after his progeny have carried all before them; his yearlings sell like hot cakes and people fall over themselves and their cheque-books trying to obtain nominations. Then, after a thin unsuccessful season, those notoriously short racing memories seem to forget all about the name that was on everyone's lips just twelve months earlier, and anyone who wants a share in, or a nomination to, the stallion has no problem in acquiring one.

This state of affairs is further illustrated by the details of the leading stallions each year. There is almost always a remarkable difference between one year's top twelve and the next; and when *Vaguely Noble* topped the stallion list for the second successive year in 1974 it was the first instance of such a double since *Aureole* did so in the early '60s. Contrast this achievement with records in the United States, where the brilliantly successful *Bold Ruler* topped the list for seven years in a row.

But despite the vagaries of the results there are a certain number of horses who have proved over the years that they can sire top-class stock. Assuming that the necessary finance is available, which stallions should be used to produce the best results?

Of course, much can depend on the mare and her characteristics have to be taken into account. Some mares are far more dominant than others, but it is reasonable to expect that a stallion will be able to pass on at least some of his qualities to his stock. For example, *Mill Reef*'s progeny would be expected to stay a mile and a half, but as he has had only a season and a half with runners, his reputation as a stallion has still to be made.

The top stallion in the British Isles for the last two years has been *Vaguely Noble*, who owes his position there very largely to the exploits of *Dahlia*, though the Sussex Stakes win by *Ace of Aces* was a useful back-up result for him. *Vaguely Noble*, however, stands at Gainesway in the United States where, rather curiously, he has not been anything like so spectacularly successful; and the cost of sending a mare to him is a considerable extra expense for an English stud.

His nearest rival in 1974 was *Petingo*, sire of the Irish Sweeps Derby winner *English Prince*, who is now at stud. *English Prince* is a good example of how a mare can pass on her characteristics just as much as a stallion for, whereas *Petingo*'s best trip was a mile, *English Prince* was clearly very effective over a mile and a half. So it seems justifiable to conclude that *English Prince*'s stamina came at least in part from his dam

English Miss, a daughter of the Derby winner *Bois Roussel*.

But whatever the pros and cons of that argument, *Petingo* was proving a most successful sire and a powerful member of Captain Tim Rogers' stallion complex in Ireland – he stood at the Simmonstown Stud in Co Kildare, where he retired in 1969 after winning six races, until his death in 1976.

Petingo was top of the Free Handicap in his first season after storming home in the Gimcrack and the Middle Park. The following year, though he had to give best to *Sir Ivor* in the Two Thousand Guineas, victories in the Sussex, St James's Palace and Craven Stakes came his way. His first runners in 1972 yielded five individual winners in these islands and two of that batch, *Pitskelly* and *Miss Petard*, went on to add further good successes the following year. *Pitskelly* won the Free Handicap, *Miss Petard* took the Ribblesdale and there was another good credit in the shape of *Pitcairn*.

After a useful two-year-old season in which he was placed in top-class company *Pitcairn* had a very good three-year-old career, with wins in the Blue Riband Trial and the Goodwood Mile. In general terms it seems that *Petingo*'s major successes as a stallion will have come at distances up to a mile and a quarter, though *English Prince* shows that his stock can win in top company over longer trips.

It took him no time to get up to the top part of the list. This was also the case with *Busted*, who was a close third in 1974. *Busted* has already sired two Classic winners in *Bustino* and *Weaver's Hall* and a

smart contingent of others like *Bog Road*, *Valuta* and *Cheveley Princess*. He was a top-class mile-and-a-half horse whose sizzling victory in the King George VI and Queen Elizabeth Stakes was most impressive in an impressive career.

Busted was essentially a middle-distance horse with a mile and a half his ideal trip. While he can and does sire winning two-year-olds it seems a reasonable observation that his progeny will, in general terms, be most effective over distances above a mile. He also showed conspicuous improvement from three to four, for he was really of no great account in his second season and it might be that his stock will also advance with time.

Busted is a son of *Crepello*, whose long and successful career came to an end in the autumn of 1974. His retirement from active service was followed not long afterwards by the sad news that he had had to be destroyed. After a slow start as a stallion *Crepello* began to hit the highspots in the latter half of the '60s and thereafter he went from strength to strength. *Busted* was already in high demand by owners of mares and his sire's death seems sure to increase the pressure for nominations.

One of the shock results of 1974 was the Derby victory of *Snow Knight*. He did not win before or after as a three-year-old, and the Epsom result sent his sire *Firestreak* into fourth place in the overall list. But *Firestreak* is now twenty-one years old and it seems advisable to concentrate in this review on stallions who seem likely to have rather more stud years before them.

One such is *Habitat*, who is another member of Tim Rogers' team. *Habitat*, an

Left: 'Petingo'. Above: 'Runnymede'.
UNITED PHOTOGRAPHIC LABORATORIES LIMITED

outstanding miler as a three-year-old when he took the Prix du Moulin, the Wills Mile and the Lockinge, crashed into the record books with his very first crop of runners. They included two really fast two-year-olds in *Habat* (now at the National Stud at Newmarket) and *Bitty Girl*. Mainly as a result of their exploits *Habitat* finished eighth on the overall list and set a new record for earnings by a first-season stallion.

The increase in prize money means that all such records are virtually bound to be broken in due time but to finish as high in the table as he did, with only one crop to represent him, was a notable effort. Last year, though *Habat* and *Bitty Girl* did not do as well as had been hoped (particularly the filly), their sire was right up front again after *Steel Heart* had taken the Gimcrack and the Middle Park and *Hot Spark* and *Roussalka* had also been successful.

Habitat was *par excellence* a miler – and it seems that his progeny are going to find that eight furlongs is their optimum distance. It is clearly dangerous to make too many assumptions, but distances up to, rather than over, a mile seem to be their forte so far. He always seemed firmly destined for great things and had his first classic success when *Flying Water* won the One Thousand Guineas in 1976.

Of *Reform*, who was one place below him on the 1974 list, it seems safe to say that he has already made his reputation. *Reform*'s career has been interesting in that he made a bright start with the Gimcrack victor *Wishing Star* among his first crop but his second season was, not to put too fine a point on it, a modest year.

Since then, however, he has gone from strength to strength. *Polygamy*'s Oaks win was *Reform*'s second Classic victory, following that of *Roi Lear* in the Prix du Jockey Club the previous season.

Another of *Reform*'s recent stars has been the much-travelled *Admetus*, a winner in top class in France, England and the United States last season, while *New Model*, an equally experienced traveller and now at stud in Italy, has certainly done his sire no harm. *Reform*'s most effective distance was between a mile and a mile and a quarter, but the victories of both *Roi Lear* and *Polygamy* show that his progeny can and do stay further than that even in the top level.

Fabergé II, who followed *Reform* in the 1974 table, is another example of the one who got away. So many stallions have left these shores – very often for Japan – in the middle of careers of no especial distinction and have then sired a really good horse or horses, that one ought to be inured to such an occurrence. *Fabergé*'s post-export winners were headed by the Prix de l'Arc de Triomphe hero *Rheingold*, with powerful support from *Giacometti* and the Derby Italiano winner *Gay Lussac*.

It is a curious fact that for all their importing of horses who have sired good winners, and for all the successes that those horses have in their new domain, the Japanese have yet to produce a horse capable of holding his own in international competition. Some of them, especially *Speed Symboli*, have run with credit, but we are still awaiting the first Japanese-bred major winner outside that country.

Great Nephew leapt into a high place thanks to the victories of *Grundy* in the Champagne and the William Hill Dewhurst, and should improve his position in 1975 after that colt's wins in the Irish Two Thousand Guineas, the Derbies, and that magnificent race with *Bustino* for the King George VI and Queen Elizabeth Stakes. *Grundy* could be the star to 'make' his sire, who until this new star had been doing no more than adequately – *Full of Hope*, *Red Berry*, *Alpine Nephew* and *Great Paul* have been near his best performers and none of those can be rated that highly.

Great Nephew's best trip was probably a mile, though he was second to *Busted* in the Eclipse, and he won such good races over that trip as the Prix du Moulin and Dollar and was also beaten by only a whisker by *Kashmir II* in the Guineas. On the whole his progeny seem to have been most successful at trips up to, rather than beyond, a mile, though *Grundy*'s Derby running has very much altered this impression.

Sing Sing, like *Crepello* who was one place below him, is dead, though he has some sons to represent him, including *Manacle*, *Jukebox*, *Mummy's Pet*, *John Splendid* and *Song*. Of that quintet, *Jukebox*, with *Music Boy*, *Record Token* and *Reelin Jig* among his winners, is showing considerable promise.

Queen's Hussar was transformed from a stallion in whom few people were particularly interested into one who was all the rage by the advent of one horse – *Brigadier Gerard*. The *Brigadier*'s marvellous run of success (how he was ever beaten by *Roberto* at York will always remain a mystery) focused maximum attention on his sire and there were inevitably some people prepared, indeed keen, to write off the *Brigadier*'s breeding as a fluke. Then *Queen's Hussar* struck again with the royal dual classic filly *Highclere*, who won the One Thousand Guineas and then the Prix de Diane, so that her sire's critics were finally silent.

Both *Brigadier Gerard* and *Highclere* really stayed a mile and a quarter and the *Brigadier* was successful over a mile and a half in the King George VI and Queen Elizabeth Stakes. Their sire's best distance was a mile, but it is clear that there is nothing to stop him siring horses who stay further than he did.

Further down 1974's list of winning stallions come *Nearctic*, *Aggressor* and *Sir Ivor*, none of whom is available to breeders in this country unless they are keen to send their mares to America or Italy, but *Wolver Hollow*, who comes next, is in Ireland and so easily accessible.

He sired a British Isles Classic winner in the 1974 Irish Two Thousand Guineas victor *Furry Glen* early in his career, but his real star so far has been *Wollow*. The Champion two-year-old of 1975, *Wollow* went on to take the Two Thousand Guineas, the Benson and Hedges Gold Cup and the Sussex Stakes before retiring to the Banstead Manor Stud with nine wins and more than £200,000 to his credit. *Charlie Bubbles*, who was successful in the

Newbury Spring Cup to follow up his Free Handicap success of 1974, was another useful colt by *Wolver Hollow*.

Wolver Hollow's best triumph was in the Eclipse of 1969. He may have been a bit lucky to beat *Park Top* on that occasion but both then and at other times he showed himself to be a good, game horse over distances around a mile and a quarter.

He is by *Sovereign Path*, another of whose sons, *Town Crier*, finished well up the list in 1974, thanks to the brilliant exploits of his daughter *Cry of Truth*.

It would be wrong to say that *Relko* has lived up to all that was expected of him as a stallion, though he has produced some good winners. *Relkino*, *Ranimer*, *Relay Race*, *Reload*, and *Royal Echo* are among them, though in this country at least it seems that he has not yet got a horse of his own high standard. His offspring tend to stay twelve furlongs and though he has not done it yet, there must be a chance that *Relko* will turn up with a really

classic horse in due course.

White Fire owed his place in the leading twenty solely to the shock Eclipse success of *Coup de Feu*. In any case he is in Japan, but *Bold Lad*, who was just below him, remains in Ireland where he was trained and where he has stood all his stallion career.

His racing career was dominated by sizzling speed and he romped away with the Middle Park, the Coventry and the Champagne. At stud his very first crop included the One Thousand Guineas heroine *Waterloo* and his other big successes have been *Daring Display* and *Boldboy*. At the risk of seeming a bit demanding, it could be said that he has not quite maintained the standard he set with his very first crop, when he set a new earnings record for a first-season stallion, but it would be unwise to write him down yet.

Though he was an out-and-out sprinter, *Bold Lad* has already sired stock with more stamina than he had – *Waterloo* is an obvious example, and clearly his progeny do not have to be speedsters pure and simple.

Reliance, a top-class racehorse whose only defeat was at the hands of one of the two very best middle-distance horses ever seen (*Sea-Bird*), has been rather like his close relation *Relko* at stud. There have been good winners by him, like the crack French-trained stayer *Récupére*, and others like *Proverb*, *Consol* and *Realistic*, but it seems that he has not quite landed the big breakthrough. His offspring stay well and in fact they seem to have more stamina than do those of *Relko*.

Polyfoto, who had a fine season – by far his best – in 1974, is a good example of a stallion who worked his way up the list from a humble start. His big star that year was the five-furlong specialist *Bay Express*, but there was useful support from horses like *Cave Warrior*, *Say Cheese* and *Prince Poona*.

Gulf Pearl is another horse who enjoyed his best season in 1974. Many have a high opinion of him. He stayed well, winning the Imperial Stakes at very long odds in his first season and the Chester Vase in a somewhat restricted second season, but he has already shown that he can get winners over all distances. His biggest success so far has been that tip-top sprinter *Deep Diver*, but there have also been good winners over middle distances like *Pearl Star*, *Hubris* and *Sea Life* and horses with plenty of stamina like the 1974 Ebor victor *Anji*. His fee has gone fairly smartly upwards since his good run in 1974 and he remains a horse with a bright chance of the big time.

Further down the 1974 season's list were consistent horses like *Red God*, *Tamerlane* and *Blast*, while both *Derring-Do* and *Silly Season*, who were some way off the top last time, have shown in the past that they can do better than that – particularly *Derring-Do*, a high-class miler in his racing days and already the sire of two classic winners in *High Top* and *Peleid*.

Runnymede is fast making a name for himself as a sire of useful sprinters that will in fact go up to a mile, while of those who have not yet had the seasons to reach the top rank I think that *Prince Regent* and *Balidar* could well get there.

Balidar, himself a smart sprinter, is the sire of the Two Thousand Guineas winner *Bolkonski* and so can clearly sire horses who get further than he did. *Prince Regent*, one of the unluckiest losers of the Derby, made a slow start with his first runners in 1974, but was certainly getting the results in the closing months and has been going on the right way in subsequent years.

Mill Reef and *Brigadier Gerard* had their first runners in 1976 and while their starts were far from sensational they are among the many stallions who look sure to sire good winners in the immediate seasons to come – *Grundy* and *Bustino* are two other inevitable examples. A study of the records, achievements and careers of stallions at stud is a fascinating task – but proves conclusively the 'glorious uncertainty' of the sport.

Left: 'Habitat'.
UNITED PHOTOGRAPHIC LABORATORIES LIMITED

French Stud Farms

TO MOST foreign visitors, France means the Eiffel Tower, the châteaux of the Loire and, above all, good food and wine. To a smaller, but very eager, contingent it means also the richest and possibly best racing in the world. Though American, Irish and British bred runners have gathered many valuable laurels on the French Turf, by far the largest number of horses running in France are raised on French studs.

Most of the studs are found in an area of approximately 150 square miles, which has at its centre the main National Stud in Normandy, the Haras du Pin, created by Louis XIV and designed by the great architect Mansard. This part of France was considered by the experts in those days as the best for the raising of horses, and all or most of the Sun King's horses, from hunters to draught, were bred there. In its heyday the Haras du Pin stabled some 800 stallions, including most of the breeds available in those times. Nowadays, there are less than two hundred, among which are to be found Thoroughbreds, Trotters, Cobs, 'Selle Français' – big, often common-looking, mostly chestnut, hacks up to plenty of weight.

A recent addition has been a number of ponies of the Welsh, Connemara and New Forest variety. There are also huge grey Percherons, which were a popular export order to the United States until a few years ago, but are now seldom in demand. The small, active, mostly roan, Bretons are still represented, as are lesser draught breeds.

These stallions go out to local 'stations' for the season, and the practice of walking them about their 'parish' has gradually died out. A few older breeders, however, still send out their prize sires – nearly always Percherons or Bretons – striding out on their amorous forays dressed to the nines in polished harness and plaited-up in the owner's colours. Some of them are ridden more than twenty miles a day, covering as many as ten mares with surprisingly positive results.

Every stud has its own particular methods, but in spite of the fact that the average Frenchman has no great affinity for animals, most studmen take an intense interest in their charges. It is virtually impossible to take a mare to be covered without being shown anything and everything there is time to see. Although foaling is singled out for the professionals to watch, the covering yard is also a matter for interest, often for pride and sometimes for embarrassment should the performance not be up to scratch. There is seldom, if ever, any sort of false prudery. One is cheerfully invited to witness the possible conception of a future Arc de Triomphe winner. The comments are relaxed and the presence of women accepted as perfectly natural. Jokes are not as ribald as the uninitiated might expect.

The mares receive equal attention and, breaking the old tradition of teasing first thing in the morning, many studs now opt for the more logical method of teasing during the day or when they are brought in after being in contact with the other mares. Most people realise that mares will 'show' to one another in the paddock only an hour or so after attempting to demolish the Trying board in the discouraging early-morning cold.

The trend in France today is towards the re-introduction of fast American blood, and as the new arrivals come in, so the Japanese depart with the best stayers. If they do as well with them as the Americans have done in the past, then the French bloodstock industry will be in further trouble.

Basically, the French horse is tough and has the ability to stay on when others fade. Good examples of this are *Match* (Washington DC International) and *Exbury*, both of which were effective over a distance of ground and finished like express trains. The ideal racehorse, a rare paragon indeed, is one who can win over fifteen furlongs (Grand Prix de Paris) or ten furlongs or the classic mile and a half in top company. Thus injections of speed must be balanced by the retention of stamina. The late François Dupré amply proved this obvious ideal by having his staying mares covered by the imported sprinters *Menetrier* (Canada) and *Relic* (USA), then putting his better fillies back to the great, but initially unfashionable, *Tantième*. In doing so he may have missed a possible vintage crop, but amply proved his point by subsequently turning out Classic winners such as *Tanerko*, *Relko*, *Reliance*, *Match*, *Danseur*, *Rheffic* and *La Sega*.

Breeders tend to shun long-distance winners such as *Sheshoon* and *Levmoss*, yet the first has shown he can get two-year-olds, as indeed can *Levmoss*, and this without any loss of their basic qualities.

It would be a great shame if French breeders tried for too much early speed. The whole French racing programme is aimed at the three-year-olds, so it is surely wisest to produce stoutly-bred two-year-olds with scope for improvement. Perhaps it is a question of the wheel turning full circle, for at the beginning of the century many fast American-bred horses figured in French pedigrees; they blended and are now due for a renewal.

Regardless of what people may say and write, or think, in recent years results proved that French studs are still turning out good bloodstock endowed with both speed and stamina – and the ability to improve with age. Examples in 1974 were such good winners as *Dankaro*, whose dam is entirely French-bred and who, like *Regal Exception*, traces back to *Sunny Boy*'s dam *Fille de Soleil*. *D'Arras* and *Récupéré* are others which come readily to mind.

At Ouilly, Mme Dupré's lovely place near William the Conqueror's Falaise Castle, many are lop-eared, brown, and with more size to them. At M Boussac's Fresnay-le-Buffard, far from any main roads on the edge of the Orne valley, there are to be found those Araby heads so often seen in the winners' enclosure at Epsom or Ascot just after the Second World War.

Only a mile or two away Mme Volterra's Haras de l'Orne is filled with many of the predominantly dark bay or brown progeny of the great *Vatellor*. Further south, just outside Le Mans, Mme Couturié's vast Le Mesnil – 'trinity' of studs – has sent out many top-class winners, mostly of great size and very dark brown – *Right Royal* for instance – and pre-war played host to Lord Derby's overseas contingent and to American owners like the Widners.

Among the breeders who mostly sell their yearlings and stand syndicated stallions, there is the Duc d'Audiffret-Pasquier, whose Haras de Sassy with its imposing château overlooks one of the finest gardens *à la française* and properties in the district. It was here that the Queen stayed during her informal and very popular visits to the studs of Normandy a few years ago. In the same neighbourhood is Countess Batthyany's Haras du Bois Roussel, on which Mme Volterra's Haras de l'Orne was accurately modelled. *Bois Roussel*, the 1938 Derby winner, was foaled here and the great stud-groom William Hayton, originally from the North Riding of Yorkshire, had foaled the incomparable *Plucky Liege*, dam of *Sir Galahad*, *Bull Dog*, *Vatout* and *Bois Roussel* himself.

There are also the new studs including the Aga Khan's Haras de Bonneval, close to his older St Crespin. M Henri Berlin (of La Lagune fame) owns the Haras de Boel near l'Aigle on the Paris road, and Jean-Louis Lucas owns Haras de Préaux, a family estate built up and modernised as a stud, with his partner, the journalist David Powell. Lucas shares an advantage many French studs can boast, namely the proximity of star-studded restaurants. His tame hostelry is none other than the Château de Montfort with swimming-pool and tennis courts; a useful combination indeed!

On reflection, perhaps one of the most attractive studs, combining the two extremes of ancient and modern, is the oldest established of all French private studs, the Haras de Victor, leased to M Wildenstein, with its moated manor and beautiful fish-scale-like tiled roof, the swans cruising

Left: Anglo-Arab at the Haras de Pompadour.
SALLY ANNE THOMPSON

101

serenely, surrounded by harmoniously designed stables with ultra-modern fittings inside.

The stud with one of the newest houses is Baron van Zuylen de Nyevelt's Varaville; built on the site of Clement Hobson's place which was burned down during the 1944 invasion. This is a brilliantly conceived, utterly modern building which rises out of, and blends subtly into, the surrounding trees and shrubs. All round the top floor is a balcony from which one can survey every paddock in the place.

In France there are few horses bred expressly to make future jumpers as in Ireland or England. However, with the assistance of the National Stud in the shape of accessible stallions, and a separate racing programme for half-breds, euphemistically called 'Autre que de Pur Sang' (other than TB), certain cattle breeders in the Charolais country, the west and the foothills of the Pyrenees lavish time and skill raising and training and racing these chasers, mostly over Pardubice-type cross-country courses. Some of them earn huge sums in stakes and graduate to Auteuil and even Aintree where they have jumped proficiently.

But nearly all the jumpers at Auteuil and Enghien are Thoroughbreds, some of whom started as Classic prospects. One will in fact not infrequently find winners of group races in the smart maiden hurdles

Below: French saddle-horse at the Haras du Pin.
SALLY ANNE THOMPSON

there. After all, who can afford to look down their Longchamp noses at £3,000 to the winner of a maiden race and fourth and sometimes even fifth prize money! In fact the 'right' sires head the lists under both codes.

An interesting recent development is the acquisition by a number of British owner/breeders of studs in France complementary to their British establishments. This is good sound breeding policy: Lord Derby did the same before the war and the change of soil and environment at weaning has proved advantageous.

There is a secondary, less obvious and much more important reason, which is financial. French-based breeders earn large premiums, up to twenty-five per cent of the first money in a pattern race and ten per cent of the place money up to fourth moneys won by horses of their breeding. These premiums are also paid out on winnings achieved by their produce abroad. These royalties are a very fair recognition of the skill and investment required to produce winning stock. However, they are paid only in respect of bloodstock foaled, weaned and developed up to the yearling stage, that is up to 1 June in France!

They are also, being officially 'French bred', eligible to run in every race in the French calendar, without restriction. This is a considerable concession, made even more generous when one remembers the fact that they maintain this qualification even when later trained abroad.

The picture of racing and breeding in France would not be complete without a

mention of the largely expanding trotting sport. Trotting is a vast, immensely popular facet of general racing, and therefore of studs in France. The horses show less quality, the sums involved are less unreal, but the volume of racing is nearly as great.

Trotters are easier and more economical to train than racehorses. Another peculiarity about trotting-racing in France is that by the very constitution of the rules, which still hark back to the times of cavalry and horse artillery, some races are for ridden trotters. With at least twelve stone to carry this is, on the part of the unlikely-looking jockeys, an ugly but impressive performance, and originally effectively 'killed two birds with one stone'. First, it guaranteed a supply of strong active chargers for the heavy cavalry – and cavalry charges were mostly at the trot – and, secondly, it effectively kept the invading whippet-like American-breds out of the jealously guarded French Trotting Stud Book.

Horses have always been bred in France, although it was not until 1833 that Lord Henry Seymour, encouraged by Ferdinand Philippe, Duc d'Orléans, founded the French Jockey Club and established racing at Chantilly. For this purpose men and horses were imported from England. Consequently many of the trainers and stud grooms still bear their English surnames. The majority of them are now entirely French, though a surprising number still speak their original tongue, and the mostly unprintable stable-talk is still loosely, and very basically, English!

Buying a Yearling

EVERY AUTUMN YEARLING sales are held by Tattersalls at Newmarket, by Goff's in Dublin and by the Doncaster Bloodstock Sales Company during St Leger week. Sales catalogues give comprehensive details of the racing careers of the sire and dam of each yearling, list the achievements of their ancestors for several generations, and add further information for the benefit of prospective buyers.

Today the chance of buying a future Classic winner at auction is not remote, for the era of the vast racing empires of such owner-breeders as the Aga Khan and Lord Rosebery is virtually over. Since the end of the Second World War Derby winners including *Nimbus, Pinza, Hard Ridden, Santa Claus* and *Snow Knight* have been bought at public auction, with *Hard Ridden* costing a mere 270 guineas when sold as a yearling at Ballsbridge.

At the other end of the scale there are countless yearlings sold every season for huge sums who never repay a fraction of their initial cost. At Tattersalls Sales in 1976 a yearling colt by *Habitat-Jaffa* fetched 85,000 guineas, a colt by *Relko-Noble Lassie* 76,000 guineas, and a total of seventeen yearlings brought in more than 37,000 guineas each. At Goff's, a filly by *Secretariat-Aladancer* fetched the huge sum of 160,000 guineas and four others were sold for more than 40,000 guineas each. To repay these immense sums at least one Classic or prestige race must be won to recompense the purchaser for his hope and confidence. The records prove that such hope and confidence are seldom justified!

When considering the purchase of a yearling all buyers should heed the wisdom of the late Atty Persse, one of the greatest trainers in Turf history. He once wrote:

In buying a yearling, first of all look up the dam's pedigree. If she has been a good winner herself, or has produced winners – and having satisfied yourself as to this – provided that you like the appearance of the youngster, you are entitled to take a chance, even if he is not the progeny of a fashionable sire of the day. It is a fact that really good mares nearly always reproduce themselves, although they may miss a generation or so.

It is the words 'appearance of the youngster' which causes the real problem, for no two experts will agree completely on the perfection of a horse's conformation. In broad outline, however, a Thoroughbred ought to have an intelligent and handsome head, with a long strong muscular neck. He should have well-placed, sloping shoulders; powerful loins and quarters; straight hocks; plenty of bone in the leg below the knee; good fetlocks; and should

Above: A horse being led round the sale ring at Newmarket. LLOYD PHILLIPS

generally be well proportioned. If, however, he is such a faultless individual, and comes from a renowned stud, then there is every likelihood that he will command a fortune in the sale ring.

In the days prior to the important yearling sales, bloodstock agents will examine hundreds of colts and fillies on behalf of those who have given them instructions as to their requirements. A cursory glance may be enough to eliminate some yearlings – for instance those who suffer from parrot jaw, misshapen feet, bad knees or enlargements around the fetlocks. Many will be discarded purely on the grounds that the breeding does not conform to the client's demands, for it is not difficult to assess the probable staying power and best distance of a yearling by reference to its breeding. Others may displease the agents for less obvious reasons, which are allied to experience and instinct. Some will pass the most stringent examination, which often includes elementary tests to ensure that the horse's eyesight is not impaired, whilst a few will cause the most hard-headed of agents to express rapturous

delight. It is these yearlings who will bring huge sums to their breeders.

No matter how much care and thought go into the purchase of a yearling, at least two factors both unascertainable at the time will affect his racing career in future years. The first is his ability to remain sound, the second is even more unpredictable – his courage during a rousing finish.

If prospective purchasers could foresee a horse's character, and the extent to which he would refuse to admit defeat when under the strongest driving from his jockey, then breeding and conformation would play a less important part in the acquisition of a yearling. No matter how fashionably he may be bred, a 'duck-hearted brute' is of no use to any owner or trainer, whilst a horse who walks around the paddock amidst disparaging criticisms of his conformation, and then proceeds to win his race through sheer indomitable guts, is worth the contents of a gold mine.

Sir Gordon Richards

Above: Gordon Richards at the height of his career when he was champion jockey.
SPORT AND GENERAL

SIR GORDON RICHARDS as a jockey is now only a name to the younger generation of racegoers, for he retired from race riding nearly twenty-five years ago. However, to the older generation there has never been a champion like him. He was leading jockey almost without interruption from 1927 to 1953; an exceptionally long time in a profession which requires a high degree of physical fitness and needle-sharp reactions.

Gordon was champion jockey twenty-six times, first in 1925 as a young man of twenty and for the last time in 1953 in his fiftieth year. He had intended to retire at the end of the following season but, less than mid-way through it, he suffered severe injuries after being rolled on by a horse at Sandown Park and decided to call it a day, after a long spell in hospital.

He took to training racehorses, with considerable success. Now, well into his seventies, he manages the horses of Sir Michael Sobell and Lady Beaverbrook, still rides out when so inclined and takes a very active interest in the English racing scene. Alert and keen, he looks very much younger than his years.

Sir Gordon's climb to the top of his profession is a marvellous success story, for he had no sort of help from racing relations of any kind. Douglas Smith, who succeeded Gordon as champion jockey, had an older brother to help him and a family who all rode. More recent champions Lester Piggott and Pat Eddery both had fathers who were jockeys. Gordon came from a background which had nothing to do with racing or hunting.

He was the son of a Shropshire miner

who, by dint of his industry, had become a mining contractor engaged in preparing the face of the coal seam for other miners to work. Gordon was one of a family of eight. His mother, like his father, had a good business sense and it was she who suggested that they should build three houses on the 'never never' system. The family lived in one, let out the other two and, in addition, built on some stables to house ponies which could pull a trap to meet people at the railway station and be hired out to children who wanted to ride.

Gordon started driving the trap and looking after the ponies when he was only seven. One of his daily chores was to turn out the ponies on the pit banks in the evenings and collect them each morning before going off to school. The task took time, for during the night the ponies wandered far away and it meant that he had to get up very early. However, he loved riding the ponies home before going to school and never complained. When he was thirteen he left school. He was not allowed to go down a mine because he was so small; instead, he got a job as a clerk in an engineering works near by, and used to ride to and from work on one of the family ponies.

The people in the factory where Gordon worked noticed how keen he was on his ponies and how much time he spent with them, and also how small he was. Some of them suggested that he should try to become a jockey, so one day he answered an advertisement for stable-boys in a local paper. The advertiser was Martin Hartigan, who then trained at Foxhill, in Wiltshire.

Gordon Richards was one of a very united family. Consequently, he had to persuade his parents to let him embark on a long apprenticeship with Martin Hartigan, far away in the south. His mother thought it too much of a gamble, his father was in favour if that was what the boy wanted to do, so off Gordon went at the beginning of 1920, to his first training stable. He was only fifteen.

Martin Hartigan, at the time, was private trainer to the financier Jimmy White and the stable jockey was the champion jockey of the era, Steve Donoghue. White had great wealth, the stable was run as if money showered down from heaven, and it was not long before Richards began to make his mark. Steve Donoghue noticed his promise and gave him encouragement whenever he came down to ride work and to stay as Jimmy White's guest. In return Gordon watched everything that Steve did, and tried to copy his style in the saddle. In only his second year as an apprentice Gordon rode his first winner, *Gay Lord*, for Martin Hartigan in a humble race at Leicester. He had climbed the first rung of the ladder which sometimes, but very rarely, leads to fame and fortune. Many boys join training stables as young apprentices. Only one in a thousand makes an outstanding success as a jockey.

Gordon Richards was not to stay at Foxhill for long. After he had been two seasons there Martin Hartigan's brother Paddy was killed in an accident and Martin went to take his brother's place as a public trainer at Ogbourne, near Marlborough. Martin Hartigan was very considerate to his apprentices and gave them every chance to shine, and he took great trouble to help the budding jockey.

In 1923, at the age of nineteen, Richards rode his fiftieth winner and thus lost the right to claim the five pounds apprentice allowance. The following season, in the final year of his apprenticeship, he rode over sixty winners and his great promise had been noted by many. His guv'nor had stored away for him the money he had earned in riding winners, and when Gordon heard from his parents that they were desperately hard up during a miners' strike, he was able to send £200 home to help

them out of a crisis. They had made sacrifices for him during his childhood and he now had the satisfaction of helping them when they needed it.

Gordon was a fully-fledged jockey for the first time at the age of twenty in 1925. He accepted a retainer that year from Captain Tommy Hogg who had a large public stable at Russley Park, between Marlborough and Lambourn. Gordon continued to live at Ogbourne and rode when available for Martin Hartigan. That season he was champion jockey for the first time, although he still weighed less than seven stone. All looked set fair, but life is unpredictable. In the spring of 1926, just after his twenty-first birthday, Gordon began to feel ill. An X-ray examination showed that he had tuberculosis, then one of the most dreaded of diseases.

He spent most of the year in a sanatorium in Norfolk, being nursed slowly back to health. At the sanatorium he made friends who gave him wise advice and, perhaps, helped to frame his character. There was the chance that he might never be able to ride again, but he was determined to get well, and the splendid staff of doctors and nurses was equally determined. By the beginning of 1927 he was fit again and then, with one exception, throughout the 1930s he was champion jockey.

From the time Gordon was a fully-fledged jockey out of his apprenticeship in 1925, until the time he retired from riding in 1954, he failed only once to be champion, except for years when illness or accident meant that he missed much of the racing season. In 1926 he was off through illness, in 1941 and 1954 through accident, and in 1930 he was beaten by his friend and rival Freddy Fox. There will never again be such a dramatic ending to the jockeys' championship. On the final day at Manchester, Freddy was one winner ahead of Gordon. Gordon rode the first winner of the afternoon, and the third winner, to go one up. Freddy retaliated by winning the fourth and fifth races to clinch the championship.

Freddy Fox was riding that year for Fred Darling of Beckhampton, who had one of the most successful stables in the country. Gordon Richards was still riding for Captain Hogg, who had moved to Newmarket to train for Lord Glanely, an immensely wealthy Welsh shipping magnate. Lord Glanely, known as 'Guts and Gaiters', was believed to have a very mean streak in his character, and, although Gordon Richards rode brilliantly for him, in 1931 he cut the size of his retainer, apparently without good cause. Gordon gave him the chance to restore it, which was not taken; so Gordon transferred his allegiance to Fred Darling, who invited him to ride as his first jockey in 1932. He was associated with Darling, and then with his successor Noel Murless, for the rest of his riding career.

Gordon Richards was to have a marvellous run at Beckhampton, winning on such brilliant horses as *Myrobella*, *Fair Trial*, *Pasch*, *Sun Chariot*, and the Two Thousand Guineas' winners *Big Game* and *Tudor Minstrel*. In 1933 he broke all

records by winning twelve races off the reel – the last race one day at Nottingham, all six races the next day at Chepstow and the first five races the following day on the same course.

He was in the public eye throughout that autumn for not only did he reach the 200 mark in September, but there seemed a distinct possibility that he might break the great Fred Archer's record of 246 winners, set forty-eight years previously. Wherever he went he faced fierce publicity and his winners became front-page news as he steadily closed the gap. He broke the record on a November day at Aintree, when he led from start to finish on Frank Hartigan's *Golden King*. On his return to his Liverpool hotel he was besieged by supporters and inundated with congratulatory telegrams, including one sent on behalf of King George V. He ended the season by riding 259 winners. It was a staggering performance – and there were no evening racing fixtures to help him.

The Second World War came and after it, throughout the remainder of the 1940s, Gordon Richards was still supreme. In 1953 came his greatest month. In the middle of May he heard from the Prime Minister, Sir Winston Churchill, that the Queen was to bestow the honour of knighthood upon him for his great services to Racing. No jockey had ever been so honoured before. In the same week he realised that, with ordinary fortune, he had a great chance of winning the Derby for Sir Victor Sassoon on *Pinza*, a colt Sir Victor had bought from Gordon's old guv'nor, Fred Darling. He had won every big race in the year except the Derby, in which his luck had been abysmal. It was probably his last chance. Happily, Sir Gordon won the 1953 Derby on *Pinza* from *Aureole*, owned by Her Majesty the Queen.

It was in fact the final Derby in which Gordon Richards rode, for a month before the following year's race he had the accident at Sandown which ended his riding career.

It is doubtful if Gordon Richards' number of races won will ever be beaten in the history of English racing. He won 4,870 races out of 21,834 mounts, his best season being 1947 when he won 269 races. He was champion jockey twenty-six times.

Amongst his many attributes was a great will to win. He never knew when he was beaten, and often pulled a race out of the fire when all looked lost. Admittedly he rode in the days before starting stalls and he was marvellously quick at the gate.

He never had to waste, as does Lester Piggott. In the late 1930s he rode regularly at about 7st 12lbs, so he had many more mounts than those who could not do less than about 8st 4lbs.

Horses ran for him in a marvellous way. He seemed to imbue them with his will to win, and throughout his career he was always approachable, always friendly, and a wonderful friend to punters. With Gordon Richards up they knew they were going to get a fair crack of the whip, and the cry 'come on Gordon', heard on every racecourse in the kingdom, was the racegoer's accolade to the most popular and most respected jockey in Turf history.

The Melbourne Cup

THE GREATEST and richest handicap in Australia is the Melbourne Cup at Flemington, and Cup day, virtually a national bank holiday, is part of Australia's heritage. With justification has the Cup been described as:

the most democratic, the most egalitarian race in the world, which is the kernel of its continuing appeal . . . the stringent handicap conditions and the gruelling 3,200 metre course are the perfect leveller of all thoroughbred racehorses . . .

The inaugural race was run on 7 November 1861 and was won by *Archer* who was bred in 1856 by Mr Charles Roberts of the Exeter Stud Farm, Braidwood, New South Wales. A bay horse of 16.2 hands, unusually large for the era, *Archer* had powerful hindquarters and the curious habit of letting his tongue loll from his mouth when galloping. Because of his powerful appearance he was known as 'The Bull'. Mr Etienne de Mestre, whose son was to become a successful trainer in England, was in charge of *Archer* whom he leased for his racing career. In de Mestre's all-black racing silks *Archer* won the Melbourne Cup in 1861 carrying 9st 7lbs. The following year he carried 10st 2lbs and for the 1863 race was allocated the welter burden of 11st 4lbs when the weights were published. He was being trained especially for the race when he broke down and had to be scratched. On 12 October 1960 a postage stamp in sepia was issued by Australia to commemorate the Centenary of the Melbourne Cup and the achievements of *Archer*. No other horse won the Cup in successive years until *Rain Lover* in 1968 and 1969.

During the past hundred years many great handicappers have won the Melbourne Cup but few of them have received as great acclaim as *Carbine* who won in 1890 carrying the colossal weight of 10st 5lbs. It was the twenty-seventh victory of the famous five-year-old New Zealand bred horse, and was worth £10,080 to the winner, as compared to the £5,940 of the Epsom Derby. Years later *Carbine* was bought by the Duke of Portland who wrote in his autobiography:

The weather on Melbourne Cup day was fine, with a breeze. It was the largest field, thirty-nine, that had ever started . . . it was an occasion worthy of a champion and *Carbine* proved himself one. Before the race *Carbine* was sleepy and lazy which was looked upon as a favourable sign by those who understood him best. The immense field was stretched right across the course at the starting point, and soon 100,000 voices yelled 'OFF' . . . at the Sheds *Carbine*

was now seen to be making a forward move, and he passed horse after horse, and before the distance was reached, he had shot out and taken the lead. *Eruc* now followed by *Highborn*, *Melos* and *Correze* were each making gallant efforts to get up, but Ramage was taking no risks, for he sat down and drove *Carbine* along with hands and knees, and the old champion responded most wonderfully and, as he approached the winning post, he drew away and won at full speed by two lengths and a half . . .

The achievements of *Carbine* made him immortal in Australian Turf history and he remained the supreme idol of racegoers until the advent of *Phar Lap* who won the 1930 Melbourne Cup. Comparing the two Turf giants a contemporary wrote: 'Most Australians are reluctant to believe that there could ever be a horse worthy to be compared to "Old Jack" as *Carbine* was affectionately recalled. They are, however, bound to admit that *Phar Lap* is a formidable challenger. This ordinary-looking horse is a phenomenal racing machine who makes opponents of high repute look mere platers.' When *Phar Lap* left Sydney for the Melbourne Cup he was thought to be a certainty provided that he could give the

On Melbourne Cup day 1939 the thoughts of the majority were turned to the events in Europe and the outbreak of the Second World War, but such thoughts did not prevent deserved acclaim being given to *Rivette* who completed the double of winning the Caulfield Cup and the Melbourne Cup in the same season. Only two other horses had achieved this unique double, *Poseidon* in 1906, and *The Trump* in 1937. *Rivette* was the first mare to do so, and a popular idol on account of her consistency and gameness.

In the next two decades the most outstanding Melbourne Cup winner was *Rising Fast* who won the 1954 race carrying top weight, and thus became the fourth top weight to win in five years. Bill Williamson, a jockey as well known in Europe as in Australia, should have ridden *Rising Fast* but a serious race accident at Caulfield prevented him from accepting the mount which was given to J. Purtell. *Rising Fast* had the vital ability needed by all brilliant stayers of being able to lie up alongside the leaders, despite the fast pace they set, without expending his reserves of energy and his powers of acceleration.

The following year *Rising Fast* was concerned in a sensational Melbourne Cup. Carrying 10st and ridden by

best of his three-year-old rivals 15lbs more than weight-for-age, for this was the task set him. When he passed the winning post three lengths ahead of his nearest rival the cheering was tumultuous. For the record book he was carrying 9lbs more than any other four-year-old winner in the history of the race – and as a four-year-old *Carbine* had failed! Such was the brilliance of *Phar Lap* who had cost only 160 guineas as a yearling!

Above: An Australian postage stamp to commemorate the centenary of the Melbourne Cup.

W. Williamson, *Rising Fast* could not find his usual acceleration on the rain-soaked turf and under his huge weight failed to peg back the light-weight *Toparoa* ridden by Neville Sellwood. There was little doubt that *Rising Fast* was an unlucky loser for he had met with interference and ought to have been hailed as the first dual Melbourne Cup winner since *Archer*. The following day it was announced that the Stewards had found Sellwood guilty of allowing *Toparoa* to veer out and hamper *Rising Fast*. Consequently they suspended him for two months. Such a suspension caused an outcry, especially in Sydney where it was suggested that New South Wales jockeys were too often singled out for punishment for alleged riding misdemeanours when they rode in Melbourne. Sellwood appealed but *Toparoa* kept the Cup despite the suspension, thus depriving *Rising Fast* of a unique achievement – that of winning both the Melbourne Cup and the Caulfield Cup in 1954 and 1955.

Since the era of *Rising Fast* the Melbourne Cup has been won in consecutive years by *Rain Lover* who was victorious in 1968 and 1969 and *Think Big* in 1974 and 1975. *Rain Lover*, a grandson of the mighty *Ribot*, bred by Federico Tessio, won easily in 1968 but his second victory was gained only by a head after an epic final furlong struggle with *Alsop*. *Think Big*, a tough gelding sired by *Summertime*'s most successful stallion son *Sobig*, defeated the heroine *Leilani* to win the 1974 Melbourne Cup. Twelve months later *Think Big* won again to credit trainer Bart Cummings with the distinction of having trained five Melbourne Cup winners. On three of these occasions he had also trained the runner-up. The only other trainer to have achieved five Cup triumphs was Etienne de Mestre who sent out four winners between 1861 and 1878 including the celebrated *Archer*.

Winners of the Melbourne Cup

1861—Archer, 9.7
1862—Archer, 10.2
1863—Banker, 5.4
1864—Lantern, 6.3
1865—Toryboy, 7.0
1866—The Barb, 6.9
1867—Tim Whiffler, 8.11
1868—Glencoe, 9.1
1869—Warrior, 8.10
1870—Nimblefoot, 6.0
1871—The Pearl, 7.3
1872—The Quack, 7.10
1873—Don Juan, 6.12
1874—Haricot, 6.7
1875—Wollomai, 7.8
1876—Briseis, 6.4
1877—Chester, 6.12
1878—Calamia, 8.2
1879—Darriwell, 7.4
1880—Grand Flaneur, 6.10
1881—Zulu, 5.10
1882—The Assyrian, 7.13
1883—Martini-Henri, 7.5
1884—Malua, 9.9
1885—Sheet Anchor, 7.11
1886—Arsenal, 7.5
1887—Dunlop, 8.3
1888—Mentor, 8.3
1889—Bravo, 8.7
1890—Carbine, 10.5
1891—Malvolio, 8.4
1892—Glenloth, 7.13
1893—Tarcoola, 8.4
1894—Patron, 9.3
1895—Auraria, 7.4
1896—Newhaven, 7.13
1897—Gaulus, 7.8
1898—The Grafter, 9.2
1899—Merriwee, 7.6

1900—Clean Sweep, 7.0
1901—Revenue, 7.10
1902—The Victory, 8.12
1903—Lord Cardigan, 6.8
1904—Acrasia, 7.6
1905—Blue Spec, 8.0
1906—Poseidon, 7.6
1907—Apologue, 7.9
1908—Lord Nolan, 6.10
1909—Prince Foote, 7.8
1910—Comedy King, 7.11
1911—The Parisian, 8.9
1912—Piastre, 7.9
1913—Posinatus, 7.10
1914—Kingsburgh, 6.12
1915—Patrobas, 7.6
1916—Sasanof, 6.12
1917—Westcourt, 8.5
1918—Night Watch, 6.9
1919—Artilleryman, 7.6
1920—Poitrel, 10.0
1921—Sister Olive, 6.9
1922—King Ingoda, 7.1
1923—Bitalli, 7.0
1924—Backwood, 8.2
1925—Windbag, 9.2
1926—Spearfelt, 9.3
1927—Trivalve, 7.6
1928—Statesman, 8.0
1929—Nightmarch, 9.2
1930—Phar Lap, 9.12
1931—White Nose, 6.12
1932—Peter Pan, 7.6
1933—Hall Mark, 7.8
1934—Peter Pan, 9.10
1935—Marabou, 7.11
1936—Wotan, 7.11
1937—The Trump, 8.5
1938—Catalogue, 8.4
1939—Rivette, 7.9
1940—Old Rowley, 7.12
1941—Skipton, 7.7
1942—Colonus, 7.2
1943—Dark Felt, 8.4
1944—Sirius, 8.5
1945—Rainbird, 7.7
1946—Russia, 9.0
1947—Hiraji, 7.11
1948—Rimfire, 7.2
1949—Foxzami, 8.8
1950—Comic Court, 9.5
1951—Delta, 9.5
1952—Dalray, 9.8
1953—Wodalla, 8.4
1954—Rising Fast, 9.5
1955—Toparoa, 7.8
1956—Evening Peal, 8.0
1957—Straight Draw, 8.5
1958—Baystone, 8.9
1959—Macdougal, 8.11
1960—Hi Jinx, 7.10
1961—Lord Fury, 7.8
1962—Even Stevens, 8.5
1963—Gatum Gatum, 7.12
1964—Polo Prince, 8.3
1965—Light Fingers, 8.4
1966—Galilee, 8.13
1967—Red Handed, 8.9
1968—Rain Lover, 8.2
1969—Rain Lover, 9.7
1970—Baghdad Note, 8.7
1971—Silver Knight, 8.9
1972—Piping Lane, 48 (kg)
1973—Gala Supreme, 49
1974—Think Big, 53
1975—Think Big, 58½
1976—Van Der Hum, 53

Above: 'Carbine' carried 10st 5lbs when he proved himself a worthy champion in winning the 1890 Melbourne Cup in a field of thirty-nine. An idol of Australian racegoers, 'Carbine' had already won twenty-six races before the Melbourne Cup brought another £10,080 to his owner. 'Old Jack', as 'Carbine' was affectionately called, was later bought by the Duke of Portland and featured by the Duke in his autobiography. AUSTRALIAN JOCKEY CLUB

Tattersalls

RICHARD TATTERSALL, founder of the most famous firm of bloodstock dealers in the world, was born in Lancashire in 1724. His affluent father was a wool stapler who fondly imagined that Richard would eventually follow in his footsteps and manage the family business. Richard had other ideas, and at the age of twenty-one left home to seek his fortune in London.

He was ambitious, honest and able, and had the added advantage of the indefinable attribute of charm. As a boy he had been taught to ride and to fish, whilst his classical education had included the study of Ovid, Horace and Cicero. His father had given him letters of introduction to some of his London friends who welcomed Richard, gave him hospitality and introduced him to a wide circle of noblemen, country squires and merchants.

To such men horses were of paramount importance, and bloodstock was a constant topic of conversation. Sales of Thoroughbreds, carriage horses and hacks took place in the courtyards of inns and taverns, whilst catalogues giving details of the lots to be sold were delivered free to such exclusive meeting places as White's Chocolate House in St James's.

Richard Tattersall saw his future career in such a world, and as a preliminary step took a job working in Mr Beevor's Repository in St Martin's Lane. Little is known of his life at this time, although it seems evident that he worked as a groom and ostler and occasionally accompanied Mr Beevor on trips into the country to inspect horses.

His first opportunity of advancement came when the Duke of Kingston invited him to manage his horses and stud. The Duke was a member of the newly established Jockey Club, lived at Thoresby in Sherwood Forest and frequently raced his horses at Newmarket. With the grandiose title of 'Master of the Duke's Horse', Richard Tattersall began to fraternise with those to whom horseracing was the spice of life, rubbing shoulders with the affluent and the influential. In 1756 he married Catherine Somerville, a granddaughter of the twelfth Earl of Somerville. Two years later their son, whom they christened Edmund, was born.

In 1766 Richard Tattersall took the decision which was to bring him fame and fortune. The decision was to request the Earl of Grosvenor to lease him land on the south side of Hyde Park Corner where he planned to establish his own bloodstock sales. The Earl approved of 'young Tattersall', and had little interest in the marshy, highwayman-infested land upon which Belgrave Square and Eaton Place were later to be built. With a casual indifference as to the outcome he told Richard to see his agents, who would be ordered to give the necessary assistance. A ninety-nine year lease was secured, and Richard began to turn his dreams into reality.

Gradually over the years Tattersall prospered. He made his headquarters at the Turf Tavern near Grosvenor Place, rented some stables and built others, and exercised his horses in neighbouring fields. Sometimes he made forays into the country to look for new business and to see existing clients, and on a few occasions to conduct sales. He was not without rivals, but his reputation for integrity and fair dealing, allied to his attractive personality, brought him a lucrative business.

Such was his reputation that he was known and respected even by the highwaymen. On one occasion a pikeman near Grantham said to him 'Don't go on, Sir. I have had several through tonight and they have all been robbed.'

Tattersall did not heed his warning. Two miles further on he was met by a masked horseman who rode silently by his side for half a mile. 'I think your name is Tattersall,' said the highwayman. 'Yes, it is,' replied the unperturbed Richard. With a courteous rejoinder of 'I thought so, and I beg your pardon,' the highway robber departed.

By 1785 Tattersall's sale paddocks covered almost eleven acres, with accommodation and stabling for more than one hundred horses. Over the years racing men had become accustomed to congregate at Tattersalls to watch the horses being sold, and found it convenient to use his headquarters as a meeting place where they could settle their wagers. Richard Tattersall made a Subscription Room available to them for the striking and settling of bets, and also put a room at the disposal of the Jockey Club where matters of policy were discussed. Every Monday he gave a dinner to which invitations were eagerly sought, for his hospitality was on a lavish scale.

Richard Tattersall was genuinely interested in horseracing, and in 1779 paid £800 for a colt named *Highflyer* which had been bred by Sir Charles Bunbury. *Highflyer*, so called because he had been foaled in a field where some highflyer walnut trees grew, proved the greatest horse of his generation.

With the blood of the Byerly Turk, the Godolphin Arabian and the Darley Arabian in his veins, it was no wonder that *Highflyer* became a brilliantly successful stallion, especially when mated with mares sired by *Eclipse*. Richard Tattersall realised

the potential of such matings, and whenever an *Eclipse* mare came up for sale he bought her. He sent the mares to *Highflyer* and sold the progeny as foals or yearlings rather than race them himself. *Highflyer* brought him a fortune, which enabled him to build a mansion near Ely which he named Highflyer Hall and where he entertained the Prince Regent.

As a mark of his gratitude, Tattersall composed the following epitaph, which was engraved on *Highflyer*'s memorial stone after the horse died in 1794:

Here lieth the perfect and beautiful symmetry of the much lamented *Highflyer* by whom and his wonderful offspring the celebrated Tattersall acquired a noble fortune, but was not ashamed to acknowledge it.

Richard Tattersall died in 1795, and the business was carried on by his only child, Edmund.

During the nineteenth century the firm continued to prosper. In 1838 they started holding sales outside the Salutation Inn at Doncaster, in addition to dispersal sales of bloodstock all over the country. At Newmarket, sales were held outside the Jockey Club Rooms, but in the early 1860s these were moved to paddocks near Queensbury House. In 1870 a further move was made and the sales transferred to Park Paddocks, where they remain to the present day.

Meanwhile, in London the end of an era

Below: A scene at Tattersalls from a wood engraving by M. J. Linton (1812-98).
ILLUSTRATED LONDON NEWS, 11 OCTOBER 1856

was approaching. The lease on the Hyde Park Corner land expired, and the Marquess of Westminster was not willing to grant a new one. A new site was found at Albert Gate, Knightsbridge, and the final sales session was held at The Corner on 8 April 1865.

As workmen began to pull down the buildings, racing men reminisced over the historic site. Years later Lord Brampton, the distinguished judge, wrote:

Tattersalls in my time was one of the pleasantest Sunday afternoon lounges in London. There was a spirit of freedom and social equality pervading the place which only belongs to assemblies where sport is the principal object and pleasure of all ... the institution has perhaps known more great men than Parliament itself – not so many bishops perhaps as the Church, but more statesmen than could get into the House of Lords ... here the great and small mingled on terms of friendly intimacy and equality. The wit met the fool in joyous rivalry and the rich met the poor in the same spirit of friendly emulation. Country squire and Cockney sportsman talked of the merits of *The Flying Dutchman* or *Voltigeur* ... the names of all the great and mediocre people who visited the famous rendezvous would fill a respectable Court guide, and the money transactions that have taken place would pay off the National Debt ... there used to be in the centre of the yard or court at Tattersalls a significant representation of an old fox, and I often wondered if it was set up as a warning, or merely by way of ornamentation, or the symbol of sport. It might have been to tell you to be wary and on the alert ...

The move to the new premises was celebrated by a banquet given at Willis's Rooms on 11 April 1865. Admiral Rous proposed the toast of the evening, 'Prosperity to the House of Tattersall', and in his reply Richard Tattersall, a great-grandson of the founder of the firm, made comment on the rise of bookmaking. He stated:

Although large sums of money depend upon horseracing, yet the occupation of the bookmaker was a few years since a very small business. It was confined to but a few persons. Like the electric telegraph and the railways it has sprung into importance only of late years, and has now passed from noblemen and gentlemen of high standing and means to persons of lower rank, who, years since, would as soon have thought of keeping a tame elephant as a book. The art of bookmaking has, however, increased with the number of trainers and horses. In 1818 my father opened a small room, then used as a laundry, in his house for a subscription room. The number of members gradually increased, until in 1842, the room not being big enough, a more spacious one for this class of patrons of the establishment was opened on the lawn. That was the room where we have seen so many ups and downs in horses and races and where such

large sums of money have changed hands.

No one incident in Tattersall's history was more dramatic than the dispersal sale of the Duke of Westminster's bloodstock in 1900.

The preparation of the catalogues and the auctioning of the horses were carried out by Somerville Tattersall, one of the greatest members of the family. Born in 1863, Somerville Tattersall had been closely associated with the annual sales of the royal yearlings from the Hampton Court stud, and had horses in training with Richard Marsh who trained for the Prince of Wales.

Tattersall agreed to sell some of the Duke's horses at Kingsclere, and on 8 March nineteen lots were disposed of, including the Triple Crown winner *Flying Fox* who was purchased by M Edmond Blanc for 37,500 guineas. It was the highest price ever paid for a Thoroughbred, and the final bid was greeted with a burst of applause from the spectators who thronged the ringside.

Four months later the Duke's remaining brood mares and yearlings were sold by Somerville Tattersall at Newmarket. On the eve of the sale Robert Standish Sievier, known as an actor, journalist, professional punter and adventurer, walked into the Rutland Arms Hotel at Newmarket and asked to speak to Mr Somerville Tattersall. Sievier informed the renowned auctioneer that he intended to buy the filly by *Persimmon* out of *Ornament* and that as he did not have a credit account with Tattersalls he wished to give a cash deposit. Before the surprised Somerville Tattersall could make any comment Sievier thrust £20,000 in Bank of England notes into his hands.

Sievier departed, leaving Somerville Tattersall in a quandary as to how to guard so immense a sum of money until the banks opened in the morning. Eventually he decided to hide the banknotes on the top of his bedroom wardrobe, where they remained safely while he hardly slept a wink.

On the morrow the ringside was packed with owners, trainers and spectators, all curious to see how high the bidding might be. Once Sievier started bidding for the filly which he had told Somerville Tattersall he was determined to buy, only the agent for the new Duke of Westminster bid against him. At 9,500 guineas the agent's nerve failed, and with a flamboyant bid of 10,000 guineas Sievier acquired the incomparable filly to whom he gave the name of *Sceptre*.

During the first half of the twentieth century many yearlings who were destined to make Turf history were sold by Tattersalls. In 1912 a grey colt was sold to Mr D. McCalmont for 1,300 guineas. Named *The Tetrarch* and popularly acclaimed as 'the spotted wonder', the grey became one of the fastest horses ever seen on a racecourse. Four years later the first draft of yearlings from the National Stud at Tully were sold for an average of 506 guineas.

The following year the eighteen-year-old *Sceptre* passed through Tattersalls sale ring for the fifth time in her career. She was bought by Sir William Tatem (later Lord

Above: 'The Man Who Bid Half a Guinea at Tattersalls' by H. M. Bateman.
BY KIND PERMISSION OF TATTERSALLS

Glanely) for 2,500 guineas, with the promise that she would never enter the sales ring again. Her purchase price was donated to the Red Cross.

After the end of the First World War prices began to soar, and in 1920 Lord Glanely paid a new record price of 14,500 guineas for a yearling bred by the Sledmere stud at Tattersall's Doncaster sales on the eve of the St Leger. Twelve months later the subsequent Derby winner *Papyrus* was sold at the same sales, whilst another future Derby winner, *Manna*, fell to the 6,300 guinea bid of Fred Darling in 1923. Between the wars the prices fetched by bloodstock steadily increased and Tattersalls acquired a world-wide reputation. Bloodstock breeders from every corner of the globe attended their sales at Doncaster, Newmarket and Knightsbridge Green. The final sale at the London branch was held in 1939, and the site sold in 1946.

The Second World War over, Tattersalls, who had valiantly struggled on in an effort to maintain bloodstock sales during the years between 1939 and 1944, began to pick up the threads, and in 1945 at the

Doncaster September sales they sold the brother to *Dante*, *Sayajirao*, for a record price of 28,000 guineas.

Since then many Classic winners have passed through their sale rings as yearlings. *Nimbus*, *Musidora*, *Nearula*, *Pinza*, *Ballymoss*, *Aurelius* and *Zabara* had this distinction prior to 1960. Every year new record prices were achieved, and the names of Classic winners added to the list. Statistics showed that in the years from 1921 to 1966 eight-four per cent of the English Classic winners bought at public auction had been sold by Tattersalls.

The abandonment of the Doncaster Yearling Sales made the partners of Tattersalls decide in the early 1960s that they should build a new Sales Ring at Newmarket. The building, one of the last major undertakings of Professor Sir Albert Richardson, was in use at the end of 1965 and marked the bicentenary of the great firm. The famous fox under his rotunda was re-erected in the sales paddock.

Two years later another milestone in Tattersall's history occurred when *Vaguely Noble* was sold at the December sales. The colt had won the Observer Gold Cup two months before and was being sold as a result of the death of his owner, Major

Lionel Holliday. The bidding started at 80,000 guineas and within seconds had reached the colossal total of 136,000 guineas. At this price he was knocked down to an American agency bidding on behalf of Dr Robert Franklyn, a Hollywood plastic surgeon. For a colt with no Classic engagements the price seemed stupendous, but the wisdom of the purchase was proved when *Vaguely Noble* won the Prix de l'Arc de Triomphe before being syndicated for five million dollars.

For today's partners in Tattersalls, Kenneth Watt, Michael Watt, A. Bruce Dean and Richard Mildmay-White, a nephew of the great 'Corinthian', Lord Mildmay, such sales are highlights which offset the disappointment felt when they remember the many expensive yearlings which have passed through their hands, and which have not repaid their owners a fraction of their original costs. Most recent of their highlights has been the sale of Classic winner *Grundy*, bought on behalf of Dr Carlo Vittadini for 11,000 guineas at the 1973 Yearling Sales. How proud Richard Tattersall would be to know of these highlights and the great esteem shown today for the firm he established more than two hundred years ago.

Running a Racing Stable

WE OFTEN HEAR it said that the racehorses of today are not as tough and hardy as those of fifty years ago. It is pointed out that the modern horse cannot race as often or do as much work at home and that it suffers more ailments of every sort. However, folk who make these criticisms do not know, or perhaps have forgotten, just how pampered racehorses were in the old days. In fact the modern horse must be every bit as tough to put up with the lack of the detailed attention that was lavished on his forebears and yet still put up better times on the racecourse.

Many of our racing stables are over a hundred years old and those loose boxes originally designed to provide warmth and prevent draughts become colder and draughtier each year. The old walls crack, the doors and window-frames warp, the floors wear and there is often a hole in the ceiling and the odd tile off the roof. The long, clean wheat straw which made such cosy and inviting bedding has been replaced by sawdust, shavings, or short and often mouldy modern wheat straw. The meticulous mucking-out twice a day, with the litter 'picked up' to dry the floor before a sprinkling of disinfectant powder was applied, is now just a memory.

The thirty minutes' careful grooming after morning exercise and the forty-five minutes of hard strapping at evening stables has also been discontinued. Many horses today receive less attention from their grooms than children's ponies get from their fanatical young owners. Even such vital daily jobs as washing-out feet and sponging the nose and dock are often neglected. A well-known trainer said recently that when in exasperation he ordered a lad to wash-out the horse's feet when he came in from exercise the lad said 'If you want that done you had better get someone else' and with that walked out of the yard!

Fifty years ago if a hot spell of weather occurred the trainer would order his first lot to pull out at 6 a.m. to avoid his horses working in the heat and being teased by flies after their work. One rather suspects that if a trainer issued such a sensible order today he would find himself the only man on parade!

Not only has labour become less experienced, but most small trainers find themselves under-staffed. This is often due to the trainer being unable to pay the increased wages demanded unless he increases his fees considerably and if he does that he is likely to lose his owners.

A visitor to any of the smaller racing stables today during the morning is most likely to find the trainer either 'doing up' the horse that he has just ridden or making ready the next horse which he is about to exercise. One quite naturally admires a hard-working man of this sort but actually he would be better employed supervising the care of *all* his horses.

From these rather depressing facts one must gather that the running of a racing stable today is no picnic. The bigger and more prosperous establishments have fewer problems because they are in a better position to afford a full staff, but even so their cares are enough for most people.

To run any business there must be method, and provided everything remains *status quo* the same method handed down

Below: On the way to the gallops.
BARRY DUFFIELD, AEROMARINE PHOTOGRAPHIC LIMITED

from father to son is usually the best. But when, as has happened in racing, many changes take place the method has to be changed to suit the case, although it is often still possible to keep to the main part.

For example, the routine in a racing stable remains very much the same. Six a.m. should see the head man on his rounds with the breakfast feed. At 7 a.m. the lads start work and prepare the first lot for exercise. The period from 7.45 to 8.45 is taken up by exercise. Breakfast is from 9 to 9.30. The second lot are prepared from 9.30 to 10, and exercised from 10.30 to 11.30. From 11.30 to 12 noon the lads feed horses, sweep yards and clean tack. Evening stables and feed occupy from 4 p.m. to 6 p.m.

This is approximately the weekday routine, which means that thirty-six hours and four hours on Sunday (two in the morning and two at night) complete (on paper anyway) forty hours' work in a seven-day week. It is customary in most yards for lads to have at least one in three short weekends off duty.

These hours are of course entirely dependent on circumstances. The horse may be running at an evening meeting and possibly he and his lad will not return until midnight, and yet the lad may be asked to start again next day at 7 a.m. This is the sort of point which, as more lads become trades union members, will need a lot of sorting out. The lad has sat in comfort in a horsebox being driven to the races. He has been involved with his horse for one and a half hours at the most. He has enjoyed watching four races and has been paid £3 for his night out. In fact, if his trainer had not allowed him to take his horse to the meeting he would have been very upset. However, add his hours on this occasion to possibly a repeat performance with his other horse, and during that one week he would have worked very much above the normal forty to forty-two working hours.

Likewise, when it is too wet or cold to take any horse out of its box for exercise, which is not an infrequent occurrence during an English winter, the lads are let off duty in some stables as early as 10.30 a.m. This sort of give and take has been going on for years between trainers and their staff and as they are the only people who understand the workings of a racing stable it would be tragic if outsiders did anything to spoil the spirit of loyalty and understanding which has existed for so long.

The feeding of his horses is undoubtedly one of the vital concerns that a trainer has on his mind. He cannot forget or ignore the old slogan that 'races are won in the manger'.

To revert once again to the distant past, when racehorse cubes were not invented, a feed-house in a well-run stable was a sight to be seen. The head man or the trainer would have arranged beside him a series of ingredients rather in the form of a well-produced hors d'oeuvre trolley! He would scoop from his bin of crushed oats a care-

Right: A Thoroughbred in his stable yard.
ANNE SCHWABE

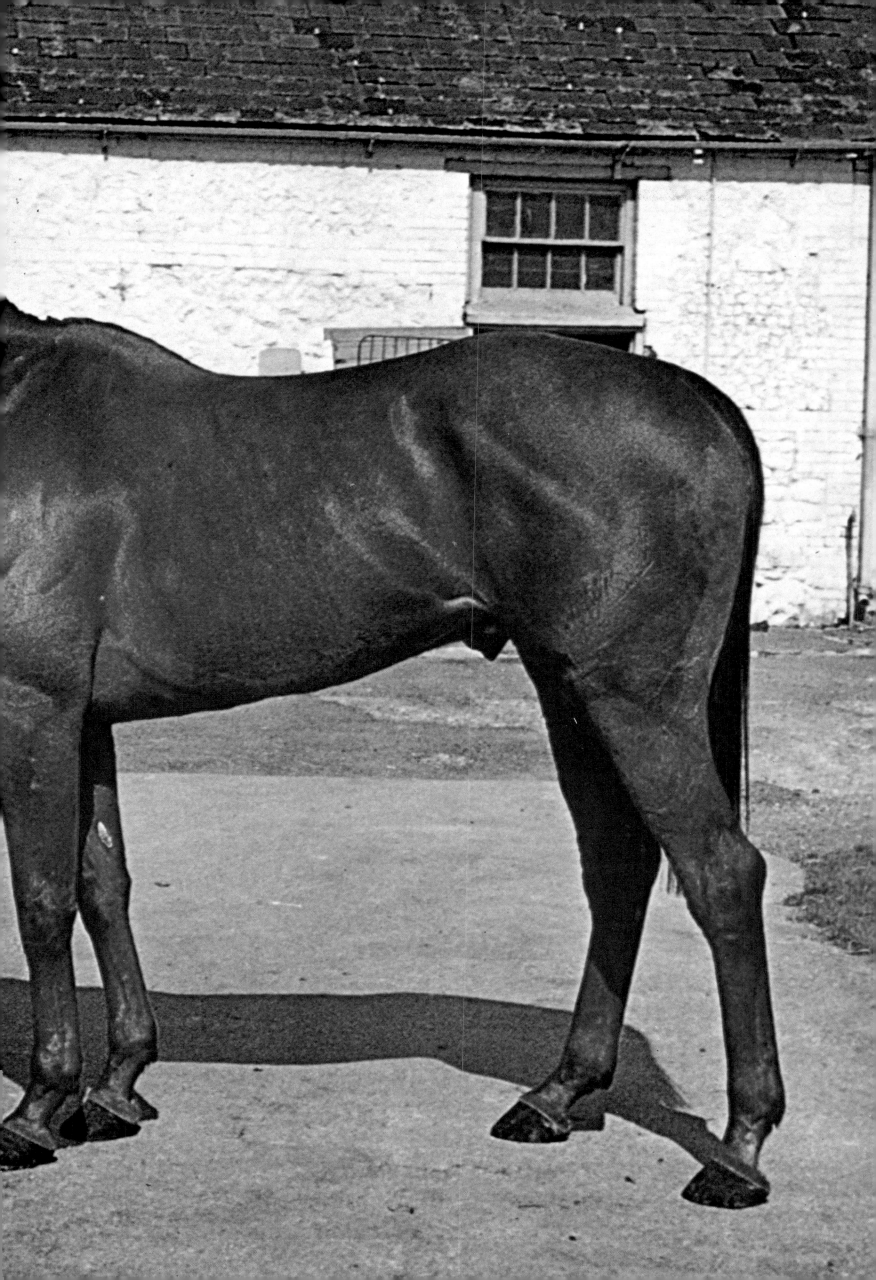

fully measured bowl, place it in his sieve and, according to the horse's appetite and whether the feed was a mid-day or a night one, he would add a further half-bowl, one bowl, or two bowls. He then would add bran (often damped), then two handfuls of chaff and then, again according to the likes and dislikes of the horse about to be fed, in would go fresh grass, dandelions, carrots, apples, cod-liver oil, tonic powders and other dainties. The sieve would now be vigorously shaken to get rid of the dust and the contents poured into a clean stable rubber held by a lad with two corners pinioned to his hips by his elbows. The feeder would then say 'that is for so-and-so' and God help the boy if he gave the specially prepared feed to the wrong horse!

With the ever-increasing cost of oats and bran (to say nothing of the difficulty of obtaining good oats and bran) most trainers now use cubes, which contain a balanced diet. Some rely entirely on them and others do a half-and-half mixture with oats, but it seems more than likely that racehorse cubes are here to stay. There is no doubt that they have many advantages such as no wastage, no need to add the bits and pieces from the 'hors d'oeuvre' trolley, no real need to use hay, no need for a linseed mash twice a week. But there is one more advantage which which may also be a disadvantage and that is that there is no need for an expert and intelligent feeder. The man who studied each horse's eating capacity down to the last oat finds it impossible to know if one and a half bowls of nuts equal one and a half bowls of oats and his additives. He also does not know whether adding a tablespoonful of cod-liver oil is necessary. In fact to feed racehorse cubes *only* reduces the job from being highly skilled to being relatively simple.

The time at exercise still varies considerably and anything from fifteen minutes to two hours takes place according to the circumstances. A horse who has just raced will be led out to pick grass for fifteen minutes and a gross horse who has suffered a long lay-off may be sent on a two-hour-long trotting and walking exercise in an attempt to get him fit. 'It is an ill wind which blows no good' and since racing stables have suffered severe staff shortages trainers have learned that their horses do just as well on forty-five minutes at exercise as they do on one and a half hours.

This is a fortunate discovery when some trainers are forced to take their charges out in three lots and sometimes even in four lots. A willing groom can look after three or four horses in the stable but he can ride only one at a time, and a yard containing thirty horses may have a staff of whom only ten are competent to ride out.

In America and other countries the problem of daily exercise and the trip to the gallops is taken care of by employing a body of men who never ride fast work at all. Their job is to groom and to lead or ride the horse to the track, where a work rider or jockey gets up to ride it.

Perhaps as the human race gets larger and heavier, and if the authorities in racing continue to keep the Flat race weights as low as they are today, Britain

will be forced to follow this example. It would work well enough because a man of 11st is better equipped to deal with a horse in every way apart from riding it in fast work. A would-be jockey must not weigh more than 6st when he becomes apprenticed if he is to be able to ride at 7st in a year or two, and this often means that he is not tall enough even to put the bridle on a horse unless he climbs into the manger. Yet he is expected to be able both to control a horse in the stable and to lead it around the paddock at a racecourse.

The racing secretary has become almost an essential, and yet as things are today the small trainers cannot afford a permanent one.

Keeping accounts, stamping the NHI cards, coping with VAT returns, paying the staff and sending out the monthly bills to owners are one side of the job. In a racing area there is often a person to be found who will call in for an hour once a week to deal with them. The other side of the office work, which comprises the day-to-day decisions such as four-day forfeits, withdrawals, engaging jockeys, telephoning owners, making entries, booking up entries, arranging transport for horses, lads' catering, apprentices' clothing, and endless other chores, needs to be done by someone on the spot. In the stables of the small man it is either himself, his wife, or his daughter who does it. In many cases the wife or daughter cooks for and looks after half a dozen apprentices as well!

One reads so much of the top twenty trainers and their success that one is apt to overlook the fact that despite Henry Cecil winning £261,041 and Peter Walwyn amassing £260,347 in stakes for their owners in 1976, the majority of the two hundred English trainers earned less than £2,500 for their owners. That means that their own reward has been less than £250, so it is unlikely that a winter holiday in the sun will come their way. They are more likely to be found mucking-out whilst their staff are on holiday for Christmas or the New Year.

It is only during the last year or so that the owners' long-standing plea for an increase of stake money in *all* races has had any support. Hitherto the attitude has seemed to be 'owners are rich men and they are not forced to own – so why help them?' It is only now that at last folk realise the obvious – that, if owners cannot afford to keep a horse in training, racing will grind to an abrupt halt. It is not that owners are more grasping today than of old or that they ask for an *overall* increase in stake money. In fact their grandfathers would have felt the same way if confronted with the necessity of winning no less than nine races (each valued at £307) in order to equal the £2,700 plus which it costs to keep a horse in training today.

The small trainer is the man who suffers most because his bread and butter depends on his ten per cent of winning stakes given to him by the owner. It is an unfortunate fact that small stables, as a rule, have to rely on the small stakes, whereas the large and more prosperous establishments regularly mop up the high stakes.

Although statistics can be boring, the

following information is still as true as it was forty years ago:

Only one in five horses wins a race;
If a trainer wins with one out of every two horses in his yard he has not done badly; i.e. ten wins from twenty horses;
If a trainer doubles the cost of a lad's wage and charges the result as a weekly fee per horse to his owner, he should make £1 per horse profit.

These are very old principles but nevertheless they will need a lot of disproving – even today!

The small trainer has to face the consequences if he is in no position to handle these problems. He may for instance have a stableful of the 'other four' who cannot win. He may win his ten races from his twenty horses, only to find that his ten per cent money equals a meagre £500. He will then certainly find that if he doubles his labour at £25 and asks it as a weekly training fee he won't have any owners left!

To return to the statistics, it is interesting to note that over the years the leading trainers do not always have to rely on the one horse in two theory. In 1976, Henry Cecil's total stake winnings were achieved by twenty-four horses, and Peter Walwyn's from sixty-eight horses. In 1977 these two 'ace' trainers had more than 220 horses in their yards at Newmarket and Lambourn.

One frequently sees a stable of eighty-plus horses top the list with thirty well-directed victories. This often means that the trainer has not run a third of his yard because they need time and will be all the better the following year. However, the small trainer, who is low down on the list, may have won twenty races from a stable of only twenty horses; but he has had to run every horse frequently to get this good result and will still be hard up in spite of achieving the near impossible.

All trainers are optimists because they have got to be – so, for that matter, are stable-lads, jockeys and owners – therefore the answer to 'How is it going?' will be 'Fine!' but that answer will not be confirmed by their bank managers!

Racing needs more money to survive and has done for the last decade but, from whatever source it comes, one must hope that this time the cash goes fairly and squarely across the table and is not diverted to many other worthy enterprises that can well wait their turn.

It is by no means easy to run a racing stable even with unlimited private means, but to try, as over seventy-five per cent of our trainers are doing, to run it on a shoestring must end in disaster.

If the rulers of racing would give priority to that ever-important item, 'putting the owners up in front of the column', as they march into the future, the 'other ranks' would find themselves well enough paid to carry on their jobs in the way which put English training standards far ahead of the rest of the world in past decades.

Right: Applying a travelling bandage before setting off for the races.
BARRY DUFFIELD, AEROMARINE PHOTOGRAPHIC LIMITED

lead, however, he had edged to his right and there were several nail-biting moments before the result of the Stewards' enquiry gave him the all-clear.

York's newly instituted Benson and Hedges Gold Cup was then reckoned to be a mere formality for him, but in one of the most amazing results of all time he was beaten by three lengths by *Roberto*, the far-from-popular winner of the Derby and later unplaced in the Irish Sweeps Derby. *Roberto*, who was ridden by the New York based Panamanian jockey Braulio Baeza, set a track record and never showed form within stones of this run either before or afterwards. It was not a case of *Brigadier Gerard* running far below his best, for he showed much the usual superiority over his other rivals, but simply of *Roberto* excelling himself in a manner which has many people utterly and permanently baffled.

So the *Brigadier*'s unbeaten record was finally broken in his sixteenth race. Happily he was soon back in winning vein, setting a second Ascot track record in the Queen Elizabeth II Stakes, and ending his racing career in the way all his many admirers desired, by a second victory in the Champion Stakes. The scenes in the unsaddling enclosure after his courageous triumph left John and Jean Hislop in no doubt as to the stupendous hero-worship given by the racing public to their idol.

During the summer *Brigadier Gerard* had been syndicated by the Hislops who reserved the right – as they were fully entitled to do – to select those breeders who could take a share. The twenty-four shares which were sold went for £25,000 each, which gave the *Brigadier* a value of one million pounds when he retired to the Egerton Stud on the outskirts of Newmarket, only a stone's throw from his old rival *Mill Reef* at the National Stud.

Training a Racehorse

THERE ARE NO two racehorse trainers who carry out their job on identical lines, and furthermore there are no two racehorses who require identical treatment. However, certain basic principles are generally accepted.

For the purpose of an example we will take the hypothetical case of a yearling bought at one of the important autumn sales for 15,000 guineas. The colt, a good-looking individual of average size, has been sent up by a renowned stud whose policy is to keep their fillies and sell their colts. Before he enters the sale ring many bloodstock dealers have inspected him on behalf of potential clients, for he is fashionably bred, his dam was a winner, and it is expected that he will be good enough to be trained for the Classics as a three-year-old.

After the sale his new trainer arranges for him to be transported to his stables. Once safely installed the first important task facing both the trainer and his horse is that of 'breaking in'. One still talks about 'breaking' to describe the period spent in accustoming the horse to being lunged both ways on a long rein, and then to wearing a roller and being driven for a week or more before being ridden. It may be because this word 'break' has always been used that one clings to the rather rough and ready procedure handed down over the centuries.

Strangely, a yearling seldom takes a serious dislike to being ridden for the first time. It is the stages prior to this which cause all the anxiety – it is when the crupper is placed under the horse's tail and fastened and the girth of the roller slowly tightened under its belly, and during the following stage of tying a rope or short rein around

Above: Leaving the yard for exercise.
SALLY ANNE THOMPSON

Below: Early morning training.
IAIN MACMILLAN

the quarters just above the hocks, that trouble breaks out. On each of these occasions most high-spirited horses will complete every sort of contortion in their efforts to get rid of these restrictions.

The trainer can only watch and pray that his new treasure is still in one piece at the end of its antics because there is no way of stopping them once started. Perhaps the day will come when all breeders will fit a miniature roller and tail string on their foals when they are still only a few days old. If this were done one would have none of the injury risks now run eighteen months later.

Provided the weather has been favourable and the horse has met with no minor injury or suffered a cough, he should be ready to be ridden with others of his age in fourteen days. It is more from necessity

than desire that a racehorse's breaking period is so short. The successful trainer has thirty other yearlings to break and ours is by no means the only Classic hope. He knows that it is essential to have them all ridden away before the hard weather sets in and, whereas he has plenty of good lightweight riders to ride them, he has only three or four men to tack them and drive them in long reins. Hence what may seem (to non-racing tolk) to be rather a rushed job.

By the end of October our yearling has not only been ridden for about forty-five minutes each day but will have learned to hack canter both in single file and upsides. He is continually asked to go upsides his contemporaries even when walking and trotting and it is in this way that he first learns not to object to being bunched amongst other horses. In addition he is asked on occasions to leave the others for a few yards or to go in front for a while.

The next important decision to be made on behalf of the yearling is which lad is going to look after him and possibly be his sole companion for the next two years. The trainer and his head man have to decide this point, if it is not to become a free fight amongst the lads!

If our yearling colt is rather high-spirited and a little on the cheeky side he will most likely be handed over to one of the experienced lads (who may be any age from twenty to sixty) because this man has dealt with countless others of the same sort and will be capable of taking the horse to the races, riding him at exercise, and grooming him without nagging at him when he makes a few childish bites and nibbles. The

girl grooms and young apprentices will be found horses to suit them in just the same way and there is no guarantee at this stage that ours will turn up trumps anyway. The trainer has now made sure that his charge is not going to be spoilt in the stable, which is by no means a rare occurrence.

Although it is a long time before the horse will experience starting-stalls on the racecourse it is a very sound plan to practise walking through, and standing in, a set of mock stalls kept conveniently near the yard. Even when the frost has made the ground too hard to trot on there is nothing to prevent this practice, and it will make it all so much easier when an introduction to the real practice stalls takes place in March or April.

Throughout the winter months our horse will continue with his ordinary exercise, sometimes trotting on the roads and sometimes cantering, either upsides another or in single file, but never allowed to join in the fast work which some of his companions will be doing in January, February and March with an early race in view. The trainer has decided to give him his first race in June and realises that he can afford to wait until the cold March winds have finished before he starts allowing him to work at half-speed.

Those horses who *have* to be got ready to win a race in the middle of March have to endure gallops in January and February, which often means being stripped of their exercise sheets in order to gallop. There is then sometimes an unavoidable delay in getting the sheet from the start to the finish in time to cover the horse whilst he is still sweating. A cold north-east wind can do a lot of harm to a horse who has just galloped, especially in the early spring when he is beginning to change his coat.

The trainer in this case has decided to start giving faster work towards the end of April. This will consist of half-speed work about twice a week and whenever possible the stable jockey will ride the horse from now on. The first fortnight of May will see

our horse have his first gallop and that is a red-letter day. The result will tell the trainer whether to go ahead with his plan to run early in June. The other horses in the gallop consist of a useful three-year-old (carrying nearly two stone more weight) and three other two-year-olds, one of whom has recently won a minor event.

The atmosphere is tense as the owner and trainer peer through race-glasses from their position at the end of the five-furlong gallop. It is difficult for them to tell which is going best of the small group of horses galloping straight towards them but as they approach the final furlong the owner is thrilled to see that his horse and the older horse have drawn well clear and finish locked together some eight lengths ahead of the winning two-year-old.

The stable jockey is also delighted and tells them how much better the colt will go next time and how well he stayed on at the end. That is just what the trainer hoped for because one of his reasons for wishing to delay running him until after 1 June is to be able to run him in a six-furlong race with increased prize-money, neither of which is

Below: Starting-stalls practice.
SALLY ANNE THOMPSON

permitted for two-year-olds before that date. He feels that in this way he will avoid the risk of meeting one of the very fast early types who might take our horse off his legs in a five-furlong race.

Another gallop is arranged for ten days later and this time the colt, who has now learned what is expected of him, slams the opposition in the most impressive style.

In the same way that the first trial gallop is an anxious moment, so is the first time out on a racecourse. Some horses can 'catch pigeons' on the gallops but show nothing like their ability on the racecourse. As this is a success story our horse has no qualms about all the strange sights encountered and wins a six-furlong maiden race impressively on 2 June.

The trainer now knows for certain that his hopes have been confirmed and that, provided he plays his cards right, the colt will stand a good chance in the Classics next year. He therefore advises the owner to run him twice more over six furlongs during the next six weeks, then to wait until September when a seven-furlong race can be tackled and finally, if the horse is still fit and well, to run him over one mile in October – making five races in all.

Gallops and fast work will probably not take place during June and July provided that the going has not been too hard for the horse to run as planned, but no doubt after his rest in August he will need a gallop over six furlongs a week before his seven-furlong race in September.

The colt, throughout his career to date, has caused his trainer little worry. He has not suffered from sore shins or other injuries, he has not been a shy feeder, nor has he been the victim of any virus infection. Despite ever-mounting costs his owner has paid his bills promptly. All is set fair for the future, and the trainer breathes a sigh of relief, for he knows that training a good Classic horse is far easier than the task of persuading a reluctant four-year-old maiden to put its heart and soul into fighting out a finish.

Newmarket

THE TOWN of Newmarket lies like the body of a butterfly between the two wings of the world-famous Heath. On the west are the racecourses and on the east such splendid working grounds as The Limekilns, Warren Hill and Waterhall.

Each of those gallops is tended with the same care a farmer gives to his richest pastures, and is made available to trainers in rotation according to the time of year or the dictates of the weather. Warren Hill, negotiation of whose slopes is so well calculated to tone up horses' muscles, is used for early spring work prior to the opening of the Flat season, while The Limekilns, where the going is never firm even at the height of summer, are always closed after heavy rain to prevent them from being cut to pieces.

Around the Heath and the other environs of the town are a large number of important breeding establishments including the National Stud, Egerton Stud, Chevely Park Stud, Dunchurch Lodge Stud and Hamilton Stud, which stands at the end of Hamilton Road. A few years ago a line of paddocks divided this road from the Heath, on which some two thousand horses work at the height of the season. Today a succession of new, ultra-modern, training stables stand on the ground that used to be grazed by mares and foals.

At the top of Hamilton Road are the Loder stables, where former champion jockey Doug Smith started training in 1968. Next comes Henry Cecil in the Marriott stables and further down is the yard that Lester Piggott has had built against the time of his retirement from the saddle.

The position of these new stables reflects a trend that has been only too discernible in Newmarket during the last ten years. They are built on the perimeter because today there is no room for them in the centre of a town that has been built up by generations of racing people over a period of time that stretches back to the reign of King Charles II.

It was Charles II's grandfather, James I, who discovered the sporting potential of the Heath around Newmarket; which is so called simply because the traders of the more ancient village of Exning, two miles to the north, had set up a new market there during time of plague in AD 1227.

Soon after his restoration in 1660 Charles began taking his court on frequent and prolonged visits to the town to escape from the weariness of politics. For his own accommodation he had a palace on or near the site of the Rutland Arms, behind which Nell Gwyn's House still stands. An

underground tunnel is said to have linked it to the palace. But little of Stuart Newmarket remained even before the recent development of the centre of the town, as much of it was destroyed by a fire started by a lad smoking in Lord Sunderland's stable in 1683.

Following the death of Charles II in 1685 Newmarket receded into the background of national life. There it remained throughout most of the reigns of the first two Georges from 1714 until 1760. The town began to regain its popularity when the founding members of the Jockey Club made it their headquarters in 1752.

Thence forward it became increasingly fashionable amongst the great magnates of the Whig oligarchy, such as the Dukes of Bedford and Grafton, and their relatives, such as Lord Holland's younger son Charles James Fox, the great radical parliamentarian.

In the middle of the nineteenth century the fortunes of Newmarket began to decline. Owners became obsessed with the idea that the going on the Heath became too firm for the proper training of horses in the summer. Long strings were transferred to the downlands of Berkshire and Wiltshire and many a yard stood empty

Right: Leaving the paddock before a race on the Rowley Mile. MILES BROS

and neglected in what was almost a ghost town.

Matters began to take a turn for the better in 1863 when florid Jem Godding, who had the Palace House stable, declared that if he could not train *Macaroni* to win the Derby on The Limekilns he could not train him anywhere. As soon as the news that *Macaroni* had won at Epsom reached Newmarket the bells of All Saints' Church rang out to proclaim the town's salvation as a training centre. Soon afterwards the horses started to return, thanks to the faith Jem Godding had in the Heath.

Three years after *Macaroni* had won the Derby taciturn and secretive Tom Jennings sent out *Gladiateur* from Phantom House to become the first French-bred winner of the race. Other trainers besides Jem Godding and Tom Jennings who played important parts in the redemption of Newmarket during the second half of Queen Victoria's reign were the Scottish brothers, Mat, Joe and John Dawson,

their compatriots Jimmy Waugh and Jimmy Ryan, Godding's son-in-law Bill Jarvis, Charlie Archer, Richard Marsh and Billy Walters.

Mat Dawson, to whom Fred Archer, the greatest of the Victorian jockeys, was apprenticed, trained *St Simon* and the Derby winners *Kingcraft* (1870), *Silvio* (1877) and *Melton* (1885) at Heath House opposite The Severals. At the western end of that stretch of open ground Dawson's fellow-trainer Charlie Blanton built the Clock Tower at the top of the High Street to commemorate Queen Victoria's Golden Jubilee in 1887.

In those latter years of Queen Victoria's reign Joe Dawson was at Bedford Lodge, which he built after purchasing the Newmarket property of the seventh Duke of Bedford in about 1860, while the third brother, John Dawson, was in Bill Chifney's old quarters at Warren House, where he trained *Galopin* to win the Derby in 1875.

Almost exactly a century after the Prince Regent left Newmarket as a result of the *Escape* affair, the horses of another Prince of Wales, his great-nephew, the future King Edward VII, arrived at Richard Marsh's Egerton House stable on the first day of 1893. That event marked the beginning of the period of the greatest prosperity that Newmarket has probably ever known. Until the outbreak of the First World War twenty-one years later the town was the playground of some of the richest men on earth. These included King Edward's financier friends Leopold de Rothschild and Sir Ernest Cassell. Mr de Rothschild lived in princely style at Palace House, where he often entertained the King, and had his horses trained by Alf Hayhoe in the stable opposite it.

In 1895 Mr de Rothschild won the Two Thousand Guineas with *St Frusquin*, who was then beaten by *Persimmon*, the best horse Richard Marsh trained for King Edward, in the Derby. Nine years later Mr de Rothschild had his compensation when *St Amant*, a son of *St Frusquin*, won the Derby. No such good fortune attended Sir Ernest Cassell on the Turf, for he lavished a fortune on the Moulton Paddocks establishment without seeing much return for his money.

During those last years of the nineteenth century and the early part of the present one, new stables were built along the Bury Road at something like the rate that they are being built along Hamilton Road today. Shrewd but illiterate Martin Gurry built Harry Wragg's present stable with the money a court awarded him for wrongful termination of contract as private trainer to the dissolute young Scottish millionaire George Alexander Baird, who raced under the 'nom de course' of Mr Abington. With an apt sense of humour Gurry called his new yard Abington Place.

On the opposite side of the Bury Road Stanley House, Freemason Lodge, Carlburg and Clarehaven appeared. Stanley House was built by the sixteenth Earl of Derby shortly after he decided to renew his family's racing interests when he inherited the title in 1893. Freemason Lodge was built by a Mr Steadall, as famous for the amount of port he drank as for his freemasonry. Carlburg was the creation of Jimmy Waugh's son Charles, who gave it a name indicative of his family's strong ties with Continental racing; while Clarehaven was built by Peter Purcell Gilpin after he had brought off a big gamble with a filly of that name in the Cesarewitch of 1900.

As important as the increase of stabling in the Edwardian era was the significance of the appointment of the Hon George Lambton, brother of the Earl of Durham, to be private trainer to Lord Derby at Stanley House in 1893. Hitherto most trainers had come from the ranks of the ex-jockeys, or from families with long traditions in racing like the Arnulls, who flourished at Newmarket for almost a hundred years after Sam Arnull rode the first Derby winner in 1780, or the Jarvises, one of whom trained *Gustavus*, the first grey to win the Derby, in 1821.

By becoming a professional trainer the Hon George Lambton started a small

social revolution. Before long other men from the nobility, gentry or professional classes had followed his example. Captain R.H. Dewhurst took over the Bedford Lodge stable, where old Etonian Mr Cecil Boyd-Rochfort was his assistant. Next door, at Bedford Cottage, Captain Percy Bewicke had his string and P.P. Gilpin, another former soldier, was in the newly constructed Clarehaven stable further up the Bury Road. After the First World War Major Vandy Beatty, brother of Admiral of the Fleet Earl Beatty, took control of Phantom House on the retirement of Tom Jennings junior, and Lord George Dundas trained for his father the Marquis of Zetland at Beaufort House.

Between the wars Newmarket was dominated by these men who, for want of a better term, may be designated as gentlemen trainers and those from the town's racing families, who included the three sons of Bill Jarvis, the four of Jimmy Waugh and the four of Tom Leader, who had come to the town from Wroughton in 1887. William Jarvis was training for King George V at Egerton House, Jack Jarvis was at Park Lodge, while Basil Jarvis was at Green Lodge, formerly the quarters of their uncle Jimmy Ryan.

At this period the Jockey Club, whose influence had been sufficient to ensure that the railway line ran under the bottom of Warren Hill instead of across the working grounds, was reluctant to permit former jockeys to train at Newmarket. Even more unwelcome on the Heath were horses belonging to bookmakers.

Since the end of the Second World War Captain Sir Cecil Boyd-Rochfort at Freemason Lodge and Noel Murless, who came to Warren Place from Beckhampton in 1952, have made outstanding contributions to maintaining the prestige of Newmarket as a training centre.

Sir Cecil Boyd-Rochfort, the tall, handsome ex-guardsman with impeccable manners, took over the royal horses in the middle of the war. He also trained for Mr William Woodward and other wealthy American owners, and in 1959 won the only Derby of his career with *Parthia*, owned by Sir Humphrey de Trafford. Sir Cecil received his knighthood in 1968, at the end of which season he retired. Since his retirement Freemason Lodge has been pulled down. Noel Murless became Sir Noel when he was knighted in the Queen's Jubilee – Birthday Honours of 1977.

Noel Murless became the first trainer to win six figures' worth of prize money in a season when his horses were successful in forty-eight races worth £116,898 in 1957. The principal contributors to that aggregate were Sir Victor Sassoon's *Crepello*, who completed the double in the Two Thousand Guineas and the Derby, the Oaks winner *Carrozza*, whom the Queen leased from the National Stud, and Colonel Giles Loder's *Arctic Explorer*, who won the Eclipse Stakes at Sandown. Ten years later Noel Murless made another important piece of Turf history by becoming the first trainer to amass £200,000 for his owners in a season. An immensely dedicated and essentially kind and modest man, Sir Noel is happier on the gallops or in the stable-yard than in the public eye on the racecourse.

When Sir Cecil Boyd-Rochfort retired and Sir Jack Jarvis died shortly after receiving his own knighthood in 1968, Newmarket was very different from the town that they had known as young men in the years before the First World War. Soon after the end of the Second World War light industry, notably the manufacture of caravans, increased significantly. In 1955 the Newmarket Urban District Council let it be known that the racing industry would be encouraged only to the extent that it was compatible with the requirements of an expanding modern town. In practice this meant that racing stables were to be driven from the centre of the town to make way for supermarkets and car parks.

Historic buildings were to be unnecessarily sacrificed on the altar of progress and Falmouth House, to which Fred Archer brought his tragic bride and which was the scene of his suicide, was demolished and a crescent of bungalows rose upon its site. Proposals that it might be called Fred Archer Close were rejected.

Another sign of the times has been seen in the decline in the number of private stables in the last couple of decades, though as recently as 1972 Mr David

Robinson had no fewer than three such establishments with Michael Jarvis at Carlburg, Paul Davey at Clarehaven and John Powney in a third yard.

Fifteen years ago Jack Watts, grandson and namesake of *Persimmon*'s jockey, was private trainer to Lord Derby at Stanley House, Ted Leader to Mr H.J. Joel at Sefton Lodge and Major Dick Hern to Major L.B. Holliday at Lagrange. In 1963 Lord Derby turned Stanley House into a public stable by leasing it to his friend Bernard van Cutsem, who trained for him until his death in 1976. Mr Joel closed his stable at the end of 1967, dividing his horses amongst Noel Murless and various other trainers, while the Lagrange stable, occupied by Atty Corbett, who was tragically killed in an accident early in 1977, was dispersed following the death of Major Holliday in December 1965. Mr Robinson retains his private stable, though he has reduced his racing commitments to the extent of having the one string under the control of Michael Jarvis at Clarehaven.

The conditions and identity of the racing population at Newmarket, the trainers, the jockeys, the head lads, the travelling head lads, lads, girls, stud workers, farriers and so on have changed almost as much as the stables over the past ten years. Labour has been a recurring problem, inevitably aggravated by the shortage of money circulating in the racing industry due to inadequate prize money, but trainers are fully aware of the problems involved in trying to achieve satisfactory payment and conditions for the staff of their stables in these days when lads ride out three, if not four, lots, as opposed to the two they did before the war.

There are reasons however for supposing that Newmarket has assumed a shape and character that it will, with modifications, retain for a long time in the future. Much of its history and tradition has been destroyed and no longer does the visitor exploring the centre of the town follow little alleyways that led to some quaint, half-forgotten stable, where the brass gas fittings remained after the installation of electricity. Those little yards exuded the romance of racing and brought back memories of the days of King Charles II and the Chifneys, but even their destruction cannot take away Newmarket's reputation as the Headquarters of Racing.

Below: The grandstand weather vane.
TRANSWORLD FEATURES

The National Stud

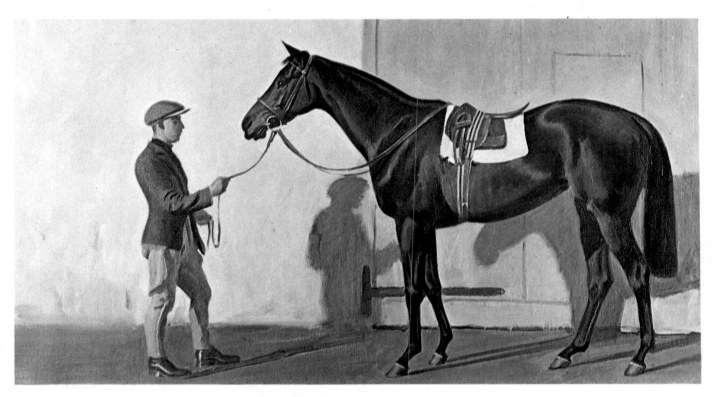

Above: 'Sun Chariot', sired by 'Hyperion', bred at the National Stud, and winner of the 1942 One Thousand Guineas, the Oaks and St Leger, painted by Sir Alfred Munnings.
THE JOCKEY CLUB

Left: A foal at the National Stud.
J. A. BROOKS

T HE NATIONAL STUD was established in 1916 as a result of a gift of land and bloodstock presented to the British Government by Colonel 'Willie' Hall Walker. Hall Walker, born on Christmas Day 1856, entered his family brewery business after leaving Harrow, and from 1900 to 1919 was Member of Parliament for the Widnes division of Lancashire. As a young man he raced ponies and Galloways before registering his racing colours under Jockey Club rules in 1895. The following year he won the Grand National with *The Soarer*. At the beginning of the twentieth century he created a stud farm at Tully on the Curragh. During the next decade his success was phenomenal for Tully-bred horses won five Classics. The highlight of these triumphs was the 1909 Derby victory of *Minoru* leased to King Edward VII.

In the autumn of 1915 Hall Walker offered to give all his bloodstock to the Government provided that they would buy his stud farm at Tully and his racing stables at Russley near Lambourn for a total sum to be assessed by Government valuers. It was a munificent gesture, although the reasons for it were shrouded in obscurity. It has been suggested that the Colonel was perturbed by the political situation in Ireland, and that he had decided on an impulse to abandon Racing in consequence of disagreements with his trainers and jockeys. The latter reason would seem more in character with the eccentric nature of the Colonel who frequently mapped out the racing careers of Tully-bred yearlings by studying their horoscopes.

With typical ineptitude the Government, having referred details of the proposed gift to the Army Council and the Board of

Agriculture, took no action. It was generally accepted that the idea behind the gift was to enable the Government to breed stallions who could be used to increase the supply of Army horses. The Army Council was in favour of acceptance, the Board of Agriculture less certain. Time marched on, until Hall Walker felt compelled to state:

the comprehensive scheme of a National Stud suggested by my offer to the Government has met with some difficulties in departmental etiquette, and the long delay in deliberating upon it has caused me to assume that it was impossible to

carry it through in time. The offer is therefore withdrawn.

Hall Walker entered his bloodstock in the December Sales at Newmarket, and received enquiries from bloodstock agents and dealers from free countries throughout the world. On the eve of the sale he received a brief telegram from the President of the Board of Agriculture: 'Gladly accept your generous offer, and buy your properties at Tully and Russley.' The telegram reached him at the Jockey Club rooms in Newmarket at 7.45 p.m.! An embarrassed Mr Somerville Tattersall was compelled to announce the withdrawal of the Hall Walker horses to frustrated prospective purchasers the following morning. Once details of Hall Walker's bequest were agreed, the Government paid £65,625 for the 1,000 acres of Tully and the racing stables at Russley, and were presented with six stallions, forty-three brood mares, ten two-year-olds, nineteen yearlings and more than three hundred head of pure and half-bred short-horn cattle. The Ministry of Agriculture appointed Henry Greer, a member of the Irish Turf Club and a Steward of the Jockey Club, as Director of the newly-named National Stud. In 1889 Greer had bought the Brownstown Stud on the edge of the Curragh where he stood *Gallinule* who sired *Pretty Polly*, *White Eagle*, *Slieve Gallion* and *Wildfowler*.

A man renowned for his appreciation of the intricacies of the bloodstock industry, his appointment was acclaimed throughout the racing world. He hoped to establish at Russley a depot for stallions who would serve farmers' mares in country districts, but his idea did not materialise owing to the Government's decision to sell Russley. Shortly after his appointment to the National Stud, Henry Greer sold Brownstown so that he might devote his energies to the organising of the National Stud. Not until he was satisfied, years later, that the Stud was operating efficiently did he

agree to advise HH Aga Khan on the management of his stud at Sheshoon. Greer resigned in 1933, by which time *Blandford*, the outstanding horse bred at the National Stud between the wars, had sired two Epsom Derby winners *Trigo* (1929) and *Blenheim* (1930). The following summer *Blandford* sired his third Derby winner, *Windsor Lad*, and achieved a fourth Derby triumph when *Bahram* was successful at Epsom in 1935.

Greer was succeeded as Director by Mr Noble Johnson, who at one time had owned several horses in partnership with

him. Before accepting the invitation to manage the National Stud, Noble Johnson had been manager of Major Eustace Loder's Eyrefield Stud which was also situated near the Curragh. Johnson died in 1937 and Peter Burrell, who had assisted him for the past year and who had previously worked at Mr J.P. Horning's West Grinstead stud which adjoined the Burrells' family estate at Knepp Castle, was appointed in his stead. For the next thirty-three years Peter Burrell was to be the driving force in the history of the Stud.

The outbreak of the Second World War

stud where additional stallions could be stood, food stuffs grown and cattle bred, leased 600 acres of the West Grinstead stud in Sussex where Mr J.P. Horning had stood the 1923 Derby winner *Papyrus*.

By the end of the 1950s criticism was growing throughout the British bloodstock industry that too many top-class mares and potential stallions were being exported, to the detriment of the industry. When the Horserace Betting Levy Board was created in 1961 under the chairmanship of Field-Marshal Lord Harding, it was suggested that the Board should acquire control of the National Stud and that the policy of the stud should change. The suggestion was acted upon, and in 1963 the responsibility for the operation and control of the stud was transferred to the Horserace Betting Levy Board under an agreement made between Lord Harding and the Minister for Agriculture, Mr Christopher Soames. The most significant financial alteration of the agreement was that the Government no longer contributed to the annual expenditure of the stud which became a separate entity. A more vital alteration was the decision to concentrate the future policy of the stud on maintaining stallions, and to discontinue the previous policy of keeping about fifteen high-class brood mares. Fundamentally the reasoned thought behind the alterations in policy was to assist the British bloodstock industry by standing stallions for breeders, possibly in competition with commercial breeders, thus preventing the drain upon the industry through the export of its best stock.

These radical changes brought a further problem. It became apparent that if they were to be implemented then a new home for the National Stud would have to be

brought problems to the National Stud which reached a climax in 1943 when the Irish Government bought Tully in order to establish their own stud and the bloodstock was transferred to England. The decision to vacate Tully at short notice necessitated an alternative stud farm being found during the months when the fortunes of war were beginning to turn in favour of the Allies. Despite the sense of optimism that prevailed, it was no easy task for Peter Burrell to decide upon future policy or to find a suitable stud for the bloodstock in his care. After due consideration, the

400-acre Sandley Stud at Gillingham in Dorset was purchased from the executors of Lord Furness, and the National Stud moved to its new home. Despite the war news which dominated events of lesser importance, the victories of *Big Game* and *Sun Chariot*, both bred at Tully, in the 1942 Classics brought credit to the stud at the time of the move to England.

The next decade was comparatively uneventful for the National Stud as Britain slowly recovered from the stress and strain of the war. In 1949 Peter Burrell, believing that it was essential to acquire an overflow

found. Since 1946 eight stallions – *Jock Scot, Tenerani, Elopement, Pindari, Sammy Davis, Acropolis, Never Say Die* and *Alcide* – had stood at the two studs at various times, but it was now considered essential to establish a stud capable of maintaining at least six stallions at once. At this moment the Horserace Betting Levy Board acquired, on behalf of the National Stud, a 999-year lease of the Jockey Club's Bunbury Farm and Heath Stud at Newmarket, comprising a total of some 500 acres. The farm, bearing the name of the owner of the first Epsom Derby winner, was situated near the July course, and had the advantage that it was arable land which had never carried horses. A far greater advantage to be gained from accepting the Jockey Club's offer was that Newmarket, being the headquarters of the British Turf, was surrounded by many other stud farms. In addition the practical advantage of the Equine Research Station at Balaton Lodge being less than three miles away was a bonus too great to be discarded. The Rubicon was crossed, the Gillingham stud closed down and subsequently sold to Mr Simon Wingfield Digby, and plans drawn up to create from scratch the finest stud in the world.

In the autumn of 1964 the mares, fillies and foals from the Gillingham stud were sold, and work commenced on the Bunbury Farm. The ground was ploughed, paddocks laid out and seeded, roads constructed, and trees, including Canadian maples, planted to give shelter to the paddocks. It was estimated that the total cost of the new stud would be £400,000 of which the buildings would cost £290,000. Eighteen miles of post-and-rail fencing would be erected, water piped to the paddocks, and a hostel built for the unmarried stud hands and students in addition to the houses for the married stud hands and their families. Six months later Her Majesty the Queen, accompanied by Princess Anne, visited the stud to see the intended positions for the stud buildings. In April 1967 Her Majesty officially opened the stud when she planted a copper beech tree outside the stallion unit. At the time of the official opening two stallions, *Never Say Die* and *Tudor Melody*, were already installed. Later in the year the American colt *Stupendous* joined them, whilst *Hopeful Venture*, bred by the National Stud, arrived in 1969. The 1971 Derby winner *Blakeney* was the next stallion to be brought there. In November 1972 *Stupendous* was sold to Japan and three months later *Mill Reef* completed the team of stallions. *Hopeful Venture* and *Never Say Die* (who was put down in 1975) were the property of the National Stud whilst *Mill Reef*, *Blakeney* and *Tudor Melody* are the property of syndicates. *Hopeful Venture* was leased to Australia early in 1975 to stand at the Balcrest stud near Adelaide, and subsequently sold by the National Stud. The syndication of a stallion is based upon the theoretical division of the total value of the horse into forty equal shares. These shares can be bought and sold either privately or by auction and fluctuate in price according to the merit of the stallion as a sire, his age and the racecourse performances of his progeny. Fashions change, and so too can the popularity of a stallion whose fee can vary from year to year. The ownership of a share in a stallion entitles the holder to send one mare annually to the stallion. If the holder does not possess a suitable mare, or wish to use the stallion, he may sell this right which is known as a nomination. Nominations to the stallions at the National Stud in which the stud has an interest are governed by rules laid down by the Levy Board. A public ballot is held every September, but if an application for a nomination is received from the owner of a mare of proven outstanding ability, or from the Queen, a nomination may be granted without recourse to the ballot. In principle, the prime objective of the National Stud is to retain top-class stallions for the benefit of United Kingdom-based breeders, who must reside in Great Britain or Northern Ireland and own Thoroughbred mares permanently accommodated at breeders' studs in the United Kingdom. These restrictions do not preclude the acceptance of a mare who has been sent abroad to be covered by a foreign stallion. Understandably, the demands for the services of the National Stud stallions are great, for their achievements are outstanding:

MILL REEF (Bay 1968) by *Never Bend* out of *Milan Mill*.
Winner of twelve races from fourteen starts earning £309,225 and already the sire of winners.
Fee £15,000 (£7,500 non-returnable plus £7,500 live foal).
His first crop of yearlings sold in 1975 for an average of 89,500 gns.

BLAKENEY (Bay 1966) by *Hethersett* out of *Windmill Girl*.
Winner of the Derby and £83,665. Fee £3,000.

Sire of *Juliette Marny*, winner of the English Oaks and the Irish Oaks, from his first crop.

TUDOR MELODY (Brown 1956) by *Tudor Minstrel* out of *Matelda*.
Sire of winners of more than £1,000,000. Fee £1,500, nfnf.
In 1977 he serves only approximately eleven mares a season.

GRUNDY (Chestnut 1972) by *Great Nephew* out of *Word from Lundy*.
Winner of the Derby and leading British money winner with £324,847.
Fee £7,000 (£3,500 non-returnable plus £3,500 live foal).

STAR APPEAL (Bay 1970) by *Appiani II* out of *Sterna*.
Winner of eleven races including the 1975 Prix de l'Arc de Triomphe, Eclipse Stakes and Gran Premio di Milano. Fee £3,000 nfnf.

HABAT (Grey 1972) by *Habitat* out of *Atrevida*.
Top English two-year-old of 1973. Fee £1,500; standing for three years in a period which expired in July 1977.

It was announced in October 1974 that a new committee had been set up by the Levy Board to advise on the purchase of suitable stallions for the National Stud. The Chairman of the Board, Sir Desmond Plummer, made it clear, however, that the Stallion Advisory Committee would not be responsible for the purchase of stallions but would keep a continuous and broadly-based watch for suitable animals and make recommendations.

The administration of the National Stud was the responsibility until 1975 of Lieutenant-Colonel Douglas Gray who succeeded Peter Burrell in 1971. As a Second-Lieutenant of Skinner's Horse, the famous Bengal Lancer regiment, he had won the coveted Kadir Cup. At the end of the Second World War he left the Army and was appointed manager of the Hadrian Stud and later leased the Stetchworth from the Duke of Sutherland before taking over the National Stud. On his retirement in 1975 his assistant Mr Michael Bramwell was appointed to succeed him as Director of the Stud. Mr Bramwell had formerly been racing and stud manager for the Cliveden stud which had been founded by Lord Astor and is now owned by Mr Louis Freedman. During the time that Mr Bramwell was at Cliveden the stud produced the 1974 Oaks heroine *Polygamy*. His National Stud assistant is Robert Acton, previously assistant manager at the Gestut Erlenhof owned by Countess Batthyany. At the National Stud are a staff of approximately thirty, including grooms, maintenance men, gardeners, a hostel housekeeper and secretaries. With such a team it is understandable that the National Stud has a world-wide reputation.

38
Lady Jockeys

IN THE AUTUMN of 1971 Mrs Judy Goodhew, wife of a Kent permit holder, wrote to the Jockey Club and asked for a licence to ride in hurdle races. She was probably not unduly surprised when her application was turned down.

But the Jockey Club had already been considering allowing girls to race on the Flat under Rules, at least for an experimental period, for they were already allowed to do so in many other countries. Before the end of the year the Jockey Club announced that during 1972 six races for lady riders would be permitted. The response from would-be lady riders was so great that the number of races was doubled.

Turf history was being made by the Jockey Club's decision, for previously the four-mile Newmarket Town Plate, run each October 'for ever' on the Round Course, had been the only race on a racecourse open to women, although it has never been run under Jockey Club rules. Initiated in 1665 by King Charles II, who twice rode the winner, the Town Plate has conditions which do not specifically exclude girl riders, and they have more or less dominated the race in recent years.

Until they achieved this virtual monopoly of the Town Plate, the only lady rider whose racing career was recorded in Turf annals was Mrs Alicia Thornton, who rode two matches on York racecourse in 1804 and 1805. The dashing Mrs Thornton, who rode side-saddle, lost the first race when her horse went lame, and won the second against no less an opponent than the famous jockey, F. Buckle.

The first modern ladies' race was allocated to Kempton Park, and was sponsored by Goya cosmetics whose managing director, Chris Collins, is a former Amateur National Hunt Champion and a member of the Jockey Club. Racing people were inclined to regard the race as rather a joke, with innumerable facetious puns about 'looking over form in the paddock'. The press insisted that the race was a blow for Women's Lib, while the girls themselves, far too skilful as horsewomen, and far too aware of their deficiencies, to set themselves up as 'jockeys', just wanted to get on with it and ride their races.

The Goya Stakes was run in pouring rain on Saturday 6 May 1972. There were twenty-one runners after balloting. An incredible swarm of photographers and reporters besieged the guarded caravan in which the girls changed. There was a last-minute drama when Brooke Sanders, who had been riding out, was delayed in traffic: her place was taken by Katharine Freeman, who had been balloted out, but brought her riding kit 'just in case'.

A few of those taking part had raced on the Continent, including point-to-point champion Sue Aston, Norwegian trainer Mrs Ruth Hegard and Yorkshire trainer

Above: Meriel Tufnell who, with a shoulder strapped up after a fall, won the Goya Stakes on 'Scorched Earth' in pouring rain at Kempton Park in May 1972.

Below: 'Fire Fairy', ridden by Diana Thorne, being led in after a victory at Sandown. DAVID HASTINGS

Sally Hall. Mary Gordon-Watson was an Olympic Gold Medallist in eventing. All were good riders, but most were completely inexperienced in race riding.

Though the race was safe and successful, those who took part now look wryly at the photographs that show their somewhat untidy bend-taking and finish-riding! The winner was Meriel Tufnell, her shoulder strapped up after a fall. Her mount, *Scorched Earth*, started at 50 to 1. Second was former point-to-point star Mrs Jenny Barons, wife of West Country trainer David Barons. The racing world was impressed when they finished in the same order in the second ladies' race at Folkestone. Perhaps results in ladies' races would not be as random as had been feared? And so they have proved.

The Jockey Club allowed any woman rider to take part in a race provided she was capable as a rider, and had not ridden for hire in a race. This was a tremendous encouragement to the great and increasing number of girls in stables, who have slogged away in the background getting their horses ready for the great day, but used to be unable to partner them on the course. But the Sex Discrimination Act requires stable-girls to ride on equal terms with stablemen, who are not allowed to ride as amateurs and the privilege was withdrawn, in 1977. From 1976 girls rode on the same terms as men over fences, and in 1977 one – Charlotte Brew – safely completed twenty-six fences in the Grand

National before her horse refused.

By the end of the season ninety girls had ridden 229 runners in the twelve races. The Jockey Club considered the experiment a success, and increased the number of permitted races to twenty in 1973. Lady riders were allowed to take part in mixed races with the amateur men in 1974, and the number of races in which they could take part was increased to fifty, about the same number as in 1975. The girls are delighted to be allowed to ride in the mixed races, although there will always be a problem about weights – at least one girl, faced with four stone of deadweight, had to have help to carry her saddle back to weigh in.

In 1975 girls reaching a sufficiently high standard were permitted to turn professional and ride on equal terms against men jockeys. Girls are also allowed to sign indentures as apprentices on the same terms as boys. Apprentice girls are not allowed to ride in ladies' races or point-to-points. Professional girls may not ride in mixed races.

By the summer of 1975 two senior girls had turned professional: Linda Goodwill, assistant trainer to her father, 'Fiddler' Goodwill, and Mrs Mavis Yeoman, wife of the York trainer. A few girls have been apprenticed, but so far they have had few opportunities and have done little. A Welsh girl, Joanna Morgan, apprenticed in Ireland, has, however, made the grade. Their opportunities have so far been rather limited, but some day someone's chance will come.

Women trainers had to fight for their licences, but the lady riders have blossomed in a climate of tolerance and helpfulness. The Jockey Club and their secretariat, Weatherbys, have gone to great lengths to introduce ladies' races in the safest way possible. The jockeys, led by Peter Smith, Secretary of their Association, have given help and guidance – even if the lady riders have sometimes added to their fund of funny stories! There was the girl, for instance, who weighed in with her number-cloth wrapped round her. The man whose job it is to collect number-cloths made a grab for it. She snatched it back – her breeches had split.

Officials in the weighing room and executives of the racecourse have also looked after the girls well, and the 'posh' permanent accommodation for lady riders now installed on some racecourses indicates that the courses know they are here to stay.

Ladies' races have certain special conditions attached to them. They must be a seventh race (although they may be placed where the executive prefers), to avoid reducing the number of rides available to the jockeys. They cannot be divided, but runners above the safety limit must be balloted out, to avoid an eight-race card. At present only ten ladies' races a year can be staged – every Flat racecourse apart from Epsom and Windsor now runs ladies' races.

The enthusiasm of the lady riders has been sustained. By the end of 1976 over 2,000 horses had been ridden by girls in Flat races. They have starved, and run the

pounds off, forsworn late nights, made awkward, uncomfortable cross-country journeys, all to ride in a race. Around 250 lady riders have taken part in the races, ranging from grandmothers Mrs Mary Alexander and Mrs Jocelyn Reavey to seventeen-year-old, seven-stone Jayne Fisher, and Carolyn Mercer, daughter of Manny Mercer and granddaughter of Harry Wragg. The minimum age has now been reduced to sixteen to bring it in line with that for male apprentices.

The Ladies' Championship is stoutly fought. It was won in 1972 by Meriel Tufnell with three wins, by Linda Goodwill in 1973 with four wins on the game Pee Mai (the same horse on which she won the first mixed race, the Ladbroke Lads and Lassies Stakes, on 1 April 1974 at Nottingham), by Brooke Sanders, a strong and powerful finisher, with six wins in 1974, Elain Mellor, wife of a former jump jockey, and Diana Bissill, daughter of a former jump jockey.

The championship is not judged on the number of winners, but on a points system to spread the interest. Originally this was five for first, three for second, two for third and one for fourth, but is now on a ten, five, three, two basis. The prize is a specially designed challenge Trophy presented by the Daily Mirror, and the winner's weight in Laurent Perrier champagne.

This is not the only championship. Brooke Bond Oxo have been tremendous supporters of the ladies' races in recent seasons, putting on four races in 1973, eight in both 1974 and 1975, and nine in 1977. For the last few seasons they have given a car to the lady rider doing best in their races, on a five, three, two, one basis. They were delighted when their splendid prize of a scarlet Ford Escort car was won by Joy Penn, a girl who has worked for years for Bob Turnell and schools his big chasers over fences. But perhaps their managing director had second thoughts when Joy, asked by the press to show the car's paces, inadvertently put her new acquisition into reverse and nearly mowed him down!

A fine ladies' race is put on at Ascot on Diamond Day, when the King George VI and Queen Elizabeth Diamond Stakes is run. This is sponsored, like the big race, by De Beers Consolidated Mines Ltd. Each year the race is named after a different world-famous diamond, and the memento given to the lady rider is a diamond ring. Indeed, the ladies' races have been very fortunate in their sponsors, many of them new to racing and all much valued.

The occupations of the lady riders are varied. Many work with horses. Sally Hall and Rosemary Lomax are trainers, Marie Tinkler is a veterinary surgeon, while Diana Bissill, Sarah Hollinshead, Margaret Bell, and Diana Weeden are among those working as assistant trainers to their fathers. Elain Mellor, runner-up for the championship last year, is the wife of former jockey Stan Mellor, who is now a successful trainer. Joan Calvert is the wife of Yorkshire trainer Jack Calvert. There are 'head lads' like Carol Leah and former stable-girls like Joy Gibson, who won the first three races at Great Yarmouth, Joy

Penn and Joanne Eade, as well as stud owners, work riders, a hunt whip, horse-breakers, trainers' secretaries and a pedigree consultant, Jane Leggat. Among those who ride purely as a hobby are an investment analyst, a photographer, an hotel proprietor, a receptionist; secretaries, farmers' wives, a social worker and schoolteachers. They have distinguished themselves in every branch of equitation, and are specially strong in point-to-point riders.

On the initiative of Meriel Tufnell, the lady riders of Britain have formed themselves into an incorporated association, the Lady Jockeys Association of Great Britain Ltd. All lady riders who intend riding in races under Jockey Club rules are eligible to become full members, and all well-wishers, of either sex and any age, may be elected associate members.

The LJA liaises with the Jockey Club and other bodies on points arising from women riders in racing. They have compiled a list of Do's and Don'ts for new riders, circulate a news letter, and organise dances, talks and various get-togethers. The Chairman is now Miss Diana Bissill of Enville Hall, Stourbridge, Worcestershire, the Hon Secretary is Mrs Vivien Kay and the Hon Treasurer is Mrs Joy Gibson – all are race-riding members. Full membership costs £3 a year, and associate membership £2. It is the first such association in the world.

With the races have come opportunities to ride abroad. Meriel Tufnell was European champion lady rider in 1974. Lavinia Aykroyd, Brooke Sanders, Susan Hogan and others have ridden in Brazil. Mrs Joy Gibson, together with Mrs Jacqueline Ward from Eire, competed in international ladies' races in Queensland, Australia. A party of eight riders and two reserves flew out to Malta for the first-ever ladies' races on the island, where they broke the course record in both distances over which they rode. Joy Gibson was the first lady champion of Malta, and Elain Mellor and Carolyn Mercer have ridden in New Zealand.

The first International Ladies' Race in Britain was the Goya International Stakes at Kempton Park in 1974. Lady riders from Germany, Holland, Norway, Sweden, Ireland, Italy, Spain, Switzerland and Czechoslovakia took part. Unfortunately, the horse to be ridden by a Danish lady went lame. Although a considerable logistic task, the race was a great success. It was won by Rosemary Rooney, daughter of the North of Ireland trainer and assistant to Paddy Prendergast – incidentally her cousin Joan, who lives in England, won another ladies' race, the Haywards Military Pickles Stakes, at Bath in 1975.

The girls still lack race experience. Even those who have had most chances have ridden in less than fifty races under Jockey Club rules, little enough against Willie Carson (908 races in 1974) or Pat Eddery (749 in 1974) or even Shawn Salmon's 338 and A. Bond's 327 rides as apprentices in that season. But the standard of riding in the ladies' races has risen out of all recognition in the short period since the races were permitted, and they are now a welcome and accepted part of the racing scene.